THE STRUGGLE
TO STAY

THE STRUGGLE
TO STAY

WHY SINGLE EVANGELICAL
WOMEN ARE LEAVING
THE CHURCH

KATIE GADDINI

Columbia University Press   *New York*

Columbia University Press
Publishers Since 1893
New York   Chichester, West Sussex
cup.columbia.edu
Copyright © 2022 Columbia University Press
All rights reserved

Library of Congress Cataloging-in-Publication Data
Names: Gaddini, Katie, author.
Title: The struggle to stay : why single evangelical women are
leaving the church / Katie Gaddini.
Description: New York : Columbia University Press, [2022] |
Includes bibliographical references and index.
Identifiers: LCCN 2021039853 | ISBN 9780231196741 (hardback) |
ISBN 9780231551809 (ebook)
Subjects: LCSH: Single women—Religious life. | Church membership. |
Church attendance. | Evangelicalism.
Classification: LCC BV4596.S5 G33 2022 | DDC 248.8/432—dc23
LC record available at https://lccn.loc.gov/2021039853

Columbia University Press books are printed on permanent
and durable acid-free paper.
Printed in the United States of America

Cover design: Milenda Nan Ok Lee
Cover art: Lily Bungay

For Addy

CONTENTS

PREFACE

A few years ago, on a gray afternoon in New York, I attended a feminist arts festival with my friend Carys. We met in midtown Manhattan and, running late, hurried up to a talk called "Faith and Feminism," which featured a panel of women from different religious backgrounds. As an earnest young academic, I was hoping to meet the editor of *Magnify*, a magazine for evangelical women, who was due to speak about Christian feminism. The panelists—Muslim, Orthodox Jewish, and Christian women—each shared how their faith supported their feminism. The women referred to their own personal stories, at times drawing on scriptures. When, halfway through the event, the chair of the panel turned to the audience and solicited questions, a middle-aged woman timidly raised her hand. The chair of the event gestured for the microphone to be passed to the woman, and members of the audience shifted in their seats as they waited.

The woman brought the microphone close to her mouth, sat up a bit straighter, and then started to speak. "I'm so tired of fighting Christian church leaders to be treated equally. But at the same time, I don't want to leave the church. So, what do I do?" She paused before reformulating her question: "How do I stay?"

Her inquiry was met with silence, as uncomfortable fidgeting moved through the audience. Out of the corner of my eye I glanced over at Carys, knowing full well her similar frustrations with the church. Carys gazed straight ahead, implacable. Her body remained unmoved except for the gentle play of her fingers crisscrossing each other again and again.

That audience member's question stayed with me long after the event. It ended up catalyzing four years of in-depth research with single evangelical women, and it now drives this book. Through the intimate stories of four women, this book grapples with the complex question Why do women stay in a religion that they consider oppressive?

Carys was in her thirties and was working as a pediatric oncology nurse when we met. We bonded instantly at a service at Wellspring Community Church, a large and influential evangelical church in New York City.[1] I had attended the service that wintry evening on the invitation of Liv, a cheerful woman with a heart-shaped face who worked at the church as director of communications and led a feminist group called Women Rise. Among the women profiled here, Liv faced the longest and most painful battle with the church—right up until the end.

The same night I met Carys, I also met Jo, a no-nonsense Midwesterner who wanted to make the church more inclusive for women. Jo grew up in the suburbs of Chicago, where her parents—both pastors—encouraged her to read feminist classics while also learning the biblical justification for feminism. In time, however, she too would question her devotion to the church. Carys, Jo, and Liv all ended up working for Wellspring at some point during my research, and their struggles with the majority male leadership intensified as the church served as both a workplace and a place of worship.

Maddie, the other single evangelical woman whose narrative I trace closely, attended Thames Gathering Place, a popular evangelical church in London. A reserved and stylish artist, Maddie also wanted to be valued as a single woman in Christianity, though she never aspired to church leadership. These four women's desires and ambitions within Christianity vary, as do their opinions on feminism, politics, and theology. Yet through the events that unfolded over four years, their lives collided, and their stories spun together in unpredictable, intimate ways.

I chronicle these women's experiences alongside prolonged, in-depth research I conducted with other single evangelical women in the United Kingdom and the United States over six years. To answer the question of why women stay in the church, I lived among, observed, and interviewed evangelical women—a research method known to anthropologists and sociologists as ethnography. On a practical level, this meant I regularly met with the women casually. We "hung out" a lot. I read the books and magazines they read, participated in group texts, went on coffee dates and for walks in the park. I attended their birthday parties and met their other friends, and sometimes their families, too. Many believers' experience of evangelicalism is all-encompassing, so ethnography allowed me to examine which areas of women's lives their faith touched and which areas it did not. Focusing in on quotidian social exchanges, practices, and ways of being inside and outside of the church revealed the subtle burdens that single evangelical women bear by remaining in the church.

I have conducted more than fifty interviews with evangelical women, the majority in New York, London, and California. These women come from different countries and Christian denominations, and while they all desire to be accepted and validated in their church communities, they did not all aspire to church leadership. Zibby, for example, yearned for a Christian marriage, children, and a career. A stylish advertising executive in Austin, Texas, Zibby would never call herself a feminist. She hated public speaking and had no interest in pastoring. Another woman, Olivia declared, "My heart's cry is to be married." At the age of just twenty-three when we spoke, Olivia already worried that she might end up like her single Christian friends in their thirties who were still single and experiencing the pain of an unmet desire.

I returned to these women again and again over the years to ask follow-up questions and clarify certain points, especially as I wrote this book. I chose to focus on a community of evangelical women, who are not bound to a church and who carry their faith with them across various locations, rather than to study one particular church. Even though most of the women featured here attended Wellspring or Thames Gathering Place, many migrated elsewhere. As this book makes clear at various junctures, this is not the story of one single church. It's the story of what it means to be single and female in evangelical Christianity.

In New York, I joined a Bible study group led by Liv, with other single women in their twenties and thirties. We met once a month in someone's home and combined brunch with prayer, Bible study, and conversation. I also attended women's-only events and Sunday services at different churches. My fieldwork journal contains thoughts, observations, and quotes from these interactions, which I have transposed onto these pages. Over the past four years, I have remained embedded in the social circles of several women I met, and as is often the case in ethnographic research, I have become very close to these women. Our ongoing relationships inform the detail and depth of this book.

In what follows, I puzzle out why four intelligent, aware, modern women continue to invest in evangelical Christianity, a movement that, by their own admission, is often unfair to women. The women in my research were aware of the constraints they faced in the church, and I show how their growing resentment toward these limitations hovered like a viscous smoke across all the spheres of their lives, weightless yet ubiquitous. What they were less aware of, according to my evaluation, is just how high a price they paid as evangelical women. The sacrifices and compromises made by these women form the main objective of this book: to expose the costs of being an evangelical woman.

The account I give here is also told through the prism of my own personal story. In my midtwenties I made a slow and deliberate walk out the door of evangelicalism and toward a life that promised more freedom. I lost my religion gradually, piece by piece, as disillusionment unspooled a tightly wound coil of belief. Until I was gone. The years I spent exiting evangelicalism were painful and riddled with family strife, broken friendships, and all-consuming fear. Simultaneously, I felt exhilarated with the thrill of my newfound liberty. During this process an unsettling question persisted: Who am I if not an evangelical Christian? After all, my evangelical qualifications ran deep. I grew up a pastor's daughter in a conservative and patriarchal Baptist church in the United States and was often referred to as a PK (Pastor's Kid), an identity that I despised for its connotations of selflessness and perfection. I attended Christian schools all the way through college, and I remained close to my evangelical family, which included three other evangelical pastors.

Fast-forward seven years and I am living in London, embarking on a PhD, and no longer attending church. In this recreated version of my life, I thought the past was well behind me. And when I began my doctoral research at the University of

Cambridge, I set out to investigate what it meant to be a single evangelical woman today. Since I still had many Christian connections, it was easy to recruit participants for my research, and I soon had interviews lined up. Every single Christian woman I contacted wanted to talk about her experience in the church.

I jumped into my fieldwork, but soon my former selves appeared. They sat there in the figures of the women I met: the one who struggled to unite her faith and feminism, the one earnestly devoted to God, and the one engulfed in shame from a sexual transgression. I was confronted with the realization that when leaving a religion, you don't really leave. Psychic traces remain, whether in the form of memory, nostalgia for the past, or haunting iterations of the self. In her essay "On Keeping a Notebook," Joan Didion warns, "I think we are well advised to keep on nodding terms with the people we used to be, whether we find them attractive company or not. Otherwise they turn up unannounced and surprise us . . . We forget all too soon the things we thought we could never forget."[2] These were selves I did not want to remember. At times, I felt I was drowning in the experiences of my participants and in my past. My research became driven by rage that I had spent so many years in a patriarchal religious environment where I had no voice.

In time, my anger settled into empathy and appreciation for women who are frustrated with their evangelical community but remain invested in it. Instead of pitying or mocking them, I have grown to respect them, and the choices they make. The evangelical women I have met over the years have reminded me of past versions of myself, but they also differ from me in many ways. Uncovering these points of similarity and difference sheds light on the variable nature of religious identity. As I will explore in the chapters that follow, religion is so much more than theology, beliefs, or ritual. It is precisely because of its plenitude that religion takes on a Janus-faced character: it is the instrument that injures and the balm that heals. From this position, I make sympathetic but critical claims about the many dimensions of religion and its inseparability from social life. By extension, I bring into sharp relief the complex and often difficult process of deciding to leave or to stay in a religious community.

Writing this book, I have reached into the past in order to remember what it was like to be an evangelical woman, and in the process I have mourned the loss of that identity. Paradoxically, it is only by examining my own loss and leaving that I have been able to understand what it means to be religious in the first place. Even now, nine years after I left the church, I continue to slip in and out of the category "evangelical" as easily as I would a lightweight cardigan. When I return home to California and have dinner with my relatives, I am an evangelical once again; over lunch with friends in London, I am not. On a few occasions, the women I interviewed asked me if I was a Christian or what church I attended. In my fumbling responses, I unearthed complicated questions such as who decides what it means to be a Christian, and what practices must one follow in order to lay claim to this identification?

Christians, and evangelicals in particular, carry quite a lot of baggage these days, especially after the majority of them voted to elect Donald Trump as president in 2016 and 2020.[3] Who evangelicals are, and what exactly they believe, however, remains largely misunderstood. It still bewilders me when I meet a stranger at a party in London and start speaking about my research on single evangelical women and their eyebrows lift in surprise as they tell me they didn't know that there were evangelicals in the United Kingdom. In the United States, I encounter a similar reaction; people often say they didn't think any evangelicals live in California or New York City, as if they are barred entrance to these famously liberal regions of the country.

The truth is, compared to some Muslim or Orthodox Jewish women, evangelicals are not always outwardly identifiable. While many observe modest dress, it isn't recognizable as religious apparel. The women in this book are doctors, social workers, consultants, personal assistants, lawyers, students, and artists. Often, they blend in at their workplaces, without anyone knowing how deep their piety runs. As I tell astonished friends in America and Britain, these evangelical women are "normal." They consume culture in similar ways to most twentysomething Londoners and Californians do; they are attentive to politics, art, and social issues. What distinguishes these women is their devotion to God and their religious community, which sometimes, though not always, includes their church.

In addition to surprise, the other common reaction I receive from nonreligious people is contempt.[4] Sometimes when I tell a stranger about my research topic, they express their pity for the women in my study, who are, to their mind, so trapped. A colleague of mine, a brilliant feminist academic, once told me she wished she could rescue them. She went on to compare evangelical women to domestic violence victims. I wince when I hear these reactions, not only because that was me not so long ago but also because of the way these responses flatten the complexity and evacuate the agency of the women I've come to care about.[5] Within such exchanges, I find myself defending Christianity—much to my surprise. Temporarily relocated from critiquing evangelicalism to defending it is dizzying. Such movements, however, instigate an additional bundle of questions, including: Who is the single evangelical woman? Is she brainwashed and victimized, as many believe, or is she free?

Orthodox Jewish and Muslim women also have been subject to ongoing criticism and attempts to "rescue."[6] Muslim woman, especially, remain the target of ongoing fascination, pity, and censure in an increasingly Islamophobic Western context. Every day, newspapers in Britain and America are littered with images and stories depicting Muslim women as oppressed. This negativity also falls on evangelical women, though, to be sure, it lacks the racialization and political motivation behind the critique of Muslim women.

Interestingly, if you ask single Christian women about their experiences in the church, they feel far from trapped. This is not a case of false consciousness or willful ignorance; these women are aware of the limitations they face and also the benefits they gain. Released from the world of one-night stands, drug-fueled parties, and relentless careerism, one woman told me, "Coming to Christianity, I've never been freer." As I navigated these two opposing perspectives, and two worlds—as she who left but still remains—I found the paradox between freedom and constraint unsettling. How could it be that the same pursuit of freedom driving my departure from Christianity pulled women *into* Christianity? Answering this question first requires a thorough understanding of evangelicalism, and of how it is positioned in mainstream society.

Evangelicalism is a conservative form of Christianity that promotes conversion, full life transformation, and a biblically based lifestyle. Like all religions, it takes on a different form in each social and political location where it lands.[7] In both American and British evangelicalism, there are significant differences along racial and ethnic lines. For example, Black evangelicals in the United States are most likely to identify with the National Baptist Convention, a Baptist denomination, whereas Latinx evangelicals predominately attend Assemblies of God churches.[8] And there are significant differences in political affiliation. The majority of Black evangelicals tend to vote Democrat, while an overwhelming majority of white and Latinx evangelicals vote Republican.[9] In the UK, many white evangelical churches are Anglican, whereas Black evangelical churches tend to be Pentecostal and to feature a more fervent adherence to proselytizing, fasting, and conservative moral beliefs.[10] For my research, I intentionally interviewed an ethnically and racially diverse group of women in order to have a sense of how different axes of marginality impacted women who attended white-majority evangelical churches.

White evangelicals still constitute the single largest religious group in the United States, with over a quarter of the American population identifying as evangelical Protestant, even though their numbers are now declining.[11] And they are often known for their unwavering alignment with right-wing politics. The religious right, a marriage between conservative politics and Christianity, first developed in the late 1970s in opposition to the desegregation of private schools.[12] As they consolidated their political power, the religious right focused on other issues, such as abortion and abstinence-only education, under Ronald Reagan's presidency in the 1980s. Today, white evangelical Christians remain politically powerful within the Republican Party. Their influence on American politics extends from domestic to foreign policies, to individual voting behavior, to the federal funding of faith-based organizations and the formation of special lobbying groups.[13]

In the UK, on the other hand, the religious–political relationship differs significantly. Scholars refute the presence of a religious right, due in part to the institutional role of the Church of England.[14] As is true across most of Western Europe,

Christianity has suffered a slow and steady death in Britain over the past sixty years, and church attendance is at an all-time low.[15] As of 2019, only 1.5 percent of the English population attended an Anglican church on a given Sunday.[16] Despite an overall decline in Christianity, however, evangelicalism is on the rise in Great Britain, as it is in other parts of the world, though here it's largely due to African and Caribbean immigrant churches.

Evangelicals burst onto the religion scene in the UK in the 1960s, primarily through American evangelical leaders who imported this charismatic, supernatural form of Christianity from the United States.[17] The close relationship between white evangelicals on both sides of the Atlantic continues today. British and American evangelicals read the same books and listen to the same music, and well-known evangelical pastors move often and freely between the two countries. Stepping into a Sunday service at Thames Gathering Place in London for the first time, I could have mistaken the service for one of the many I had attended in California over the years. Apart from the British accents, everything was exactly as it was five thousand miles away at Bethel Church in Redding, California—the same smiling, friendly faces, the same worship songs, and the same passionate sermons from male preachers dressed casually in jeans and plaid button-down shirts. It turns out that fervent believers, hoping for a reenergization of their faith, regularly move between evangelical churches around the globe in a pilgrimage-like voyage. The women I met spoke offhandedly of their Christian brothers and sisters internationally, indicating a shared social identity that connected them to other Christians around the globe.[18]

This imagined global community of evangelical believers stretches well beyond the United States and the UK. For example, British churches have started sister branches in Malaysia and

Kenya and have advised the Chinese government on marriage preparation courses. Bethel Church, which I also visited, has developed similar transcontinental connections, including an international leaders' network. A quick glance at many churches' websites reveals the emphasis they place on global links and a widespread reach.

One of the most significant links is Roots International, a pseudonym for a global evangelizing program sponsored by churches, which claims to have reached 24 million people. Many of the women in this book either came to evangelical Christianity or deepened their faith via Roots, and many went on to lead Roots courses at Wellspring and Thames Gathering, sometimes for years. One of the central tenets of the eleven-week Roots course is the incorporation of the supernatural; the course ends with a Holy Spirit weekend, where participants are encouraged to encounter the "gifts of the spirit." Carys reminisced about the Holy Spirit weekend with the warm glow that comes when recalling a first date. "It just radically changed my life," she told me. "It set me on fire."

As most of the women in this book make clear, their evangelicalism is charismatic and supernaturally inflected. They speak in tongues, an incomprehensible language used to communicate with God; they believe in miracles and healing; they practice intercessory prayer, an intense form of prayer for self and others; and they relate to God on a personal, intimate level. A few women even referred to God as "Papa" or "Daddy."[19] Their relationship with God guides every aspect of their lives. One woman I spoke to in London even told me she considers intercessory prayer to be her part-time job. She spends her days walking around central London, praying—for people who are suffering, for unbelievers to come to Christ, for her dreams and hopes to come to fruition.

Another similarity between British and American evangelicals concerns the treatment of women. In both countries, women outstrip men in terms of church attendance, at an almost two-to-one ratio.[20] Emphasizing gender differences is a key organizing principle of evangelical Christianity, and perhaps is instrumental to its success as a cohesive religious group.[21] Interestingly, Wellspring, Thames Gathering, and Bethel theologically support women in leadership roles, which many other evangelical churches do not. As I will show, though, such a theological stance frustrates women even more when they are unable to access these positions, since in theory leadership remains within their grasp.

Like many contemporary evangelical and Pentecostal churches in England and America, most of the churches where I conducted research espouse the model of husband and wife "co-pastors." However, even in the case of co-pastoring, it's nearly always the male counterpart who leads the public-facing roles in the church, including preaching, administration, and church leadership.[22] As such, it's the male pastor who is most visible. He makes big decisions for the church; he holds the power.

In both countries, women are reaching a boiling point. There are many reasons for this, as the stories in this book make clear, but one of the biggest is that women feel invisible in their churches. More specifically, they feel invisible for being *single* women.[23] In a context where heterosexual marriage is highly valued, women who do not fit the traditional roles of wives and mothers face a difficult choice: stay and face marginalization or leave.

Many are opting for the latter option. Sociologists of religion propose that evangelical women in Britain are leaving churches in large numbers, and the gender imbalance in evangelicalism has been narrowing, pro rata, more than in any other religious group.[24] Similar studies are emerging in the United States, where the gender gap has been declining since the mid-1980s, as less evangelical women are attending church services every week.[25] Since the advent of industrialization, women have increasingly worked outside the home, leaving them less time for church duties, a phenomenon that skyrocketed with the women's liberation movement in the 1960s and 1970s. This raises an interesting question: If women's participation in Christian churches has kept the religious movement afloat, what will it mean for Christianity as a religion, now that many are leaving?[26]

Beyond numbers monitoring church attendance, the reality of what it means to leave or stay in a religious community is murky and often very difficult to capture. Not only is exit an excruciating choice for women who stand to lose their social communities, their familial ties, and their religious identity, but also many women are deeply committed to utilizing their anger to change their Christian communities from the inside. In what follows, I carefully examine these tensions and explore why single women stay in evangelical Christianity despite the limitations and strictures it imposes. My aim is to show the benefits that women gain from their evangelical religious community, and the costs. "Are there always costs to be paid for the adoption of a collective identity?" asks Denise Riley. "Each collectivity necessitates its own answers."[27]

At the feminist art festival, a female pastor named Lynn Davis responded to the audience member's question "How do I stay?" Pastor Davis, a pastor who has weathered decades of discrimination in evangelical churches, directly and unapologetically stated that not everyone is meant to stay. Some are called to leave the church, some are meant to stay, and we need each other to survive.

This absolution from a pastor, a *female* pastor, at once leveled the guilt I had accumulated for years since leaving evangelicalism. What is more, Davis's words support the many single evangelical women I met who feel passionately convicted to stay and change the church from the inside. After decades of growing up inside an oppressive form of evangelical Christianity, in which I was silenced and sidelined because of my gender, I have found a semblance of healing in writing this book. In *The Hour of the Star*, Clarice Lispector's self-reflective narrator admits, "I write and that way rid myself of me and then at last I can rest."[28]

This book is my pursuit of rest.

THE STRUGGLE
TO STAY

1

HOMECOMING

The goblet mouth on the table speaks
To your thirst, saying, Longing, your longing, is infinite.
—Mary Jo Bang

She can't remember exactly when it started, this shapeless presence, this bland emptiness. It could have been last January, when the sky decomposed to a dull gray and her younger sister stopped swallowing. Cancer of the esophagus, the doctors pronounced. Nine months of treatment and a close brush with death, but she's stabilized now, and the sun has returned. Yet Carys still feels *off.*

Early in the morning, she wakes to silence. The harrowing stories that she has yet to hear, that will trickle into her throughout the day like the intravenous fluid she threads into small veins, line up in preparation. She covers her face with a pillow, dreading what is to come: reading reports from the night nurse, an evaluation of all the patients who have worsened, improved, or stabilized. Then a visit to the three-year-old with stage 4 leukemia who most certainly won't make it. It's just a matter of time, Carys will think upon reviewing her file, even though the parents won't hear it. She'll plead with them once again to take their weakening baby girl off treatment, to give her a peaceful ending. *It's always the same*, she'll think to herself as they refuse.

Carys regards the person in the mirror, wondering what she's missing. What it would take to make her feel better—less empty, more alive? *There has to be more than this*, she muses, as she brushes her teeth. *Please tell me there's more than this.*

Out on the street, she joins 4 million other commuters, all of them marching in formation like mindless ants as they disperse into the city. Head down, gaze down, a vacancy in their eyes.

Is this what loneliness feels like? she wonders. But she has so many friends, a meaningful job, a loving family, more than enough money. The abundance feels too much and not enough at the same time.

The day passes quickly. Some time ago Carys realized that if she moved fast enough, she could outpace this hollowness. Except at night. Nights are the worst: darkness spreads in all directions like steam rising from an iron that's been left on too long, steam filling the room, filling her lungs, leaving her breathless, suffocating her. On this particular night, she manages to avoid the darkness by stacking after-work drinks with a friend's birthday party, where impersonal sex and a joint do more than distract her. They plunge her into another stratum, one where the ache cannot reach.

But the next morning it's back tenfold. She lies in bed and stares at the white ceiling, noticing that the paint has started to flake. She is longing for something, but she isn't even sure what it is. *Is this depression?* Carys asks herself. *Maybe I need to see a doctor. Or a therapist. Or change jobs.* She crawls to the bathroom, passing her crumpled clothes on the way.

I can't keep living like this.

By now emptiness has somatized into physical discomfort. It feels like a hole somewhere deep in her belly, a hole corroded by every one-night stand, every party, every beer she guzzles in between superficial laughs. She sits on the bathroom floor and places her hands on her abdomen, gripping the flesh, as if to keep the hole from expanding further, or maybe to keep it from being seen.

The next weekend, Carys travels out of New York to attend her friend Emma's wedding. Emma is a friend from Carys's past life, back when she was a fervent evangelical Christian who prayed and read the Bible every day. She rides the train in trepidation, knowing that the current version of herself will be compared to the past one and that the contrast always leaves Emma disappointed.

Drifting through a large banquet hall crowded with pink peonies, Carys snatches a flute of champagne from the waiter. "Carys!" a high-pitched voice calls out. She spins around and finds Emma's aunt standing there, beaming. "I knew it was you, once I saw that curly mop!" The older woman rushes over and they embrace. As they catch up on the decade since they've last seen each other, the aunt admits that she no longer goes to church, is not even a Christian anymore. Carys sighs in relief. She sets her drink down on the table but doesn't let go of it. Then the aunt drops her voice and leans in closer.

"But you know what?" she says. "Even after all this time, I still miss it. Even after ten years away, I can't extinguish that spark and that longing."

Carys stiffens.

"Do you know what I mean?"

"I don't, actually. Because I'm happier now that I left Christianity. Much happier. In fact, I don't think I've ever been so happy in my life!" Her words gush out like blood from a fresh cut. She mutters an excuse about needing to find Emma and hurries off.

A few weeks later, as Carys trudges along the street on her way to work, worried thoughts of the day to come swirl in her head. She passes a stooped-over, white-haired man and he smiles at her. It's only a half-smile, the corners of his mouth quivering as they rise. But something about that half-smile loosens a knot inside of her. The little ants continue to swarm around her as she stands motionless, head bowed low, hands covering her face, hot tears streaming down. She's weeping openly now, and she doesn't care if anyone sees; she's got to let it out. It's finally being expelled, this longing, this ache that has been cannibalizing her from the inside for so long. And it's a relief to have physical proof of what she's been feeling, the outsides finally matching the insides.

Before going to sleep that night, Carys sends a message to Emma and asks about church. Emma responds right away and suggests that Carys join Roots, an eight-week course that her church runs for people interested in learning more about Christianity. It brands itself as a course for people "wanting to explore the deeper questions of life."

And that's how Carys finds herself standing at a wrought iron gate, watching people stream into church, the next Sunday afternoon. Smiling, wholesome-looking people. People with faces, the realness of their bodies coming through in a 3-D quality that feels almost otherworldly. She remembers, somewhat nostalgically, attending church almost a decade ago. That time seems so far away, the memory of it like expired milk that leaves you no choice but to throw it away and start fresh.

I have to do this. I have to draw a line under it. If nothing else, then to be able to say, once and for all, that religion is not for me.

She glances at her phone: five o'clock. Time to go in. Emma will be waiting in the lobby. Carys strolls cautiously toward the entrance, skeptical, yet desperate for relief. She pulls in a deep breath, letting her lungs inflate, and releases it slowly. Then she steps inside.

Carys told me this story, her story, soon after we met at a Wellspring church service in January 2016. From across the room, I spotted her standing alone in a corner: leather cowboy boots, black nail polish, and a canvas bag with the words "This is what a feminist looks like" dangling from her shoulder. I slowly approached and introduced myself, admiring her bag.

"Oh, thanks. Seemed like the right kind of bag to bring to a church event, you know?" she said, and winked.

I liked Carys instantly. She embodied that attractive combination of masculinity and femininity in perfect measure. She appeared so sturdy, so comfortable in her own skin—that decisive way of stating opinion as fact; her dry witticisms. And yet, every so often, indications of vulnerability surfaced—arms folded protectively across her chest, nervous glances around the room, the fluctuations of her voice, which occasionally dipped to a whisper, so that I had to ask her to repeat herself.

On our way out of Wellspring that night, I asked how long she'd been a Christian.

"I just came back to Christianity a few months ago, actually," she answered, her Boston accent causing her vowels to rise, fall, flatten. The cold winter air rushed at us and Carys quickened her pace to keep warm. "I was out of the church for eight years. I envisioned going along to Roots and arguing with the people there and proving all my points. But instead I had the opposite experience. Everyone there was so loving, really intelligent, really kind . . . And intellectually it all started to make more sense."

We paused at a red light and Carys turned to face me, the gold glitter on her eyelids twinkling in the darkness. "But also,

I had an encounter with the Holy Spirit, and I understood more about the person of Jesus. I started to feel much happier and secure and stable in myself."

Happy, secure, stable. This is the version of Carys I first came to know. When I look back now, four years later, I remember how observing her back then felt like watching someone fall in love. The falling: that period marked by a complicated interplay of surrender and resistance, of cool intoxication and a restraining fear. Back then, I didn't think that anything could break the spell she was under.

The next week, Carys and I sit across from each other in a university café populated with students hunched over laptops and disheveled academics nursing mugs of coffee. As Carys bites into a pastry, I ask her, as I do all evangelical women, to tell me the story of how she became a Christian. In evangelical lingo, this narrative is known as a "testimony," as it testifies to the magical transformation that takes place when a person commits their life to God.[1] I am eight months into my research, and so far nearly every testimony I've heard has an identical narrative pattern. The more I hear these stories, the more I begin to doubt their randomness.[2] It seems as if there's a script that women have to learn in order to be inscribed in the evangelical community. It goes like this: a woman grows up in a nominally Christian family, she wanders away at some point (usually as a teen or in her early twenties), experiences a profound emptiness about five years later, and then rejoins Christianity, usually after being invited by a friend, or after doing Roots.[3] From there, she transforms into a new (Christian) person; she is spiritually and emotionally reborn. I begin calling this narrative a "traditional trajectory," because of how commonplace it is in evangelical Christianity.[4]

"I think it was a bit of a sense of longing as much as anything else," Carys says. "I didn't want to admit it, but I really missed church. And there was something about that relationship with God that was missing from my life. I think once you have that, there is a bit of a pull."

She tells me that when she decided to try church again her sister had just been diagnosed with cancer, and that she was feeling overwhelmed with the suffering she saw every day, working as a pediatric oncology nurse.

Then, just as in the week before, Carys qualifies her narrative of longing with deep skepticism: "But to be perfectly honest, I never really liked church all that much. I've never been someone who had, you know, *church buddies*. I was never actively involved. My close friends have always been from outside the church."

By confessing her cynicism and hesitation, Carys signals that she hasn't fully committed to Christianity yet. She's got one foot on either side of the doorway of evangelicalism, and she's stepping across the threshold carefully.

I ask her what made her leave Christianity eight years ago and she tells me that she was engaged to be married. She and her evangelical fiancé were living outside of Boston and attending a local church, and although they weren't supposed to, they were having sex.

"Part of what drove me away from Christianity was that relationship and the way his Christian friends responded to me. I never felt our relationship was just between the two of us. The community was always involved, and it was not particularly helpful. I can see now that the church leaders were involved in an emotionally abusive way, and eventually neither of us ended up in church and neither of us called ourselves Christians."

After Carys discovered her fiancé was cheating on her and ended their relationship, she stayed away from Christianity. "Because I'm politically on the left, feminist, working class, and very pro LGBTQ. All of that felt unacceptable in a Christian context, so it drove me away."

And then she mentions the longing—an irrepressible longing for more. "I just reached a point where I needed to draw a line under it. I had a nagging faith thing in the back in my mind, that little tug, and I wanted to extinguish it."

We finish our tea, and then Carys rushes off to a Roots meeting. I watch her leave, this woman so full of contrasts, who supports gay rights and left-wing politics and also loves an institution that often preaches the opposite. Who spends her days reading feminist theory and immerses herself in a church in which few women hold leadership roles. Who simultaneously remains wary of Christianity yet so desirous of it.

I want to understand why these testimonies are all identical, when and how evangelicals are trained in the same rhetorical movements. But even more, I want to understand why women convert in the first place. I want to understand the longing. So far, I'd focused my investigation into the faith lives of single evangelical women around one question: Why do they stay in a religion that they consider oppressive? Sitting in the café that afternoon, I realized that in order to figure out why they stay in evangelicalism, I first had to understand why they came. What would make someone wipe clean the slate of their life—the friends they see, the hobbies they enjoy, the job they love—and begin again?

People convert to religion for myriad reasons. Some convert out of devotion to a beloved, or as a requirement bound up with marriage. For others, conversion is a solitary endeavor, born of a deep intellectual interest, a rational mind that concludes that a particular tradition just makes sense. The theologian Sallie McFague writes, "I would like to suggest that the great conversions bring not comfort (in any superficial sense) but demand courage, a willingness to risk and suffer, to live lives of dis-ease and spiritual adventure that is unsettling if not terrifying to contemplate."[5] Certainly, the conversions I witnessed during my research testify to this suffering. One woman explained that when she converted to evangelicalism she broke up with her boyfriend, deleted all social media, quit her job, sold her car, and moved. She told me, "It was really difficult. Probably for the first year and a bit, being a Christian was absolute hell." She stated that her transformation from party girl to devout evangelical was "worse than coming off drugs."

But for other women, conversion brought tremendous comfort. And for most, it wasn't even a conversion, in the true sense of the word. It was a *re*conversion. In fact, *conversion* is not even a word that is used in the evangelical context. If you speak to an evangelical woman in London or California or somewhere in between, she will likely say that she "came back to God" or "found God" after a period of emptiness. But make no mistake: even if a Christian past precedes this experience, it still features all the same elements of a traditional trajectory, including a radical stripping back of one's life with the aim to rebuild it afresh.[6]

It's not a coincidence that evangelical Christian testimonies all feature a similar narrative patterning; after all, the theme of rupture and rebirth is woven throughout the Bible and Christian history.[7] Take, for example, the story of Paul, an early apostle of the gospel of Jesus Christ. Originally named Saul, he experienced a conversion moment on the road to Damascus, as he was traveling to persecute Jesus's apostles. His conversion involved a supernatural experience of being struck blind and given a vision of the resurrected Christ, as detailed in Galatians. The experience was so dramatic that he changed his name to Paul, became an apostle himself, and began telling others about Christ.

Carys's conversion story—"I had a spiritual encounter with the Holy Spirit"—follows in this rhetorical vein.

Returning to God after wandering away is another biblical theme. "There was something about that relationship with God that was missing," Carys told me. The most famous example of this is the story of the prodigal son in Luke, chapter 15.[8] The younger son leaves his father's estate with his portion of his inheritance only to spend it all on "wild living." Then a famine breaks out and the son finds himself without food and without work—"in need," according to Luke 15:14. Similarly, Carys found herself in need, after her sister was diagnosed with cancer, and her job as a pediatric nurse meant she witnessed unbearable pain. In her words: "When you see that level of despair on a daily basis, you start to wonder about larger meanings and faith issues a lot more." In the prodigal son story, the younger son makes his way back to his father, who welcomes him back with open arms.

Thus, evangelical testimonies follow a biblical narrative patterning that corresponds with a religious tradition of longing and fulfillment, rupture and rebirth, of being lost and then found. Of homecoming. Indeed, many American evangelicals describe themselves as "born again Christians," which emphasizes the regenerative aspect of conversion. In her examination of fundamentalist Christian language in the 1990s, the anthropologist Susan Harding understood conversion to be "a process of acquiring a specific religious language."[9] In other words, by adopting the evangelical script and arranging their memories and histories according to this schema, the believer announces their Christian identity, like a Masonic handshake or a secret password. Their recitation of the story conveys that they have successfully learned a new language and are able to speak it fluently.

But the uniformity of testimonies is also a way of displaying a commitment to the faith. In telling a conversion narrative that features the pageantry of a transformation, the believer indicates that they have gone through a sort of initiation process and come out the other side. The drama of testimonies attests to just how much the believer has changed and the value of the Christian faith. After all, the higher the price paid, the more valuable the membership.[10] Repeating these stories reminds the believer, and others, of God's all-encompassing power and ability to save. In these ways, testimonies may be more of a signaling mechanism for fellow Christians than a tool for saving unbelievers.

But understanding conversion stories didn't help me understand why these women converted in the first place. The academic literature on conversion reports that a key reason for conversion is community—an antidote to the swelling angst involved with late modernity, the spirit of our times, which is marked by turbulence, isolation, and ruthless individualism. And churches are one institution that counteracts this uncertainty.[11] George Orwell wrote about the intimacy and support provided by religion in the mid-1940s in an essay called "Inside the Whale."

For the fact is that being inside a whale is a very comfortable, cozy, homelike thought. The historical Jonah, if he can be so called, was glad enough to escape, but in imagination, in daydream, countless people have envied him. It is, of course, quite obvious why. The whale's belly is simply a womb big enough for an adult. There you are, in the dark, cushioned space that exactly fits you, with yards of blubber between yourself and reality, able to keep up an attitude of the completest indifference, no matter *what* happens. A storm that would sink all the battleships in the world would hardly reach you as an echo.[12]

It makes sense that people tired with anonymity and isolation climb into the belly of the Leviathan. Religion offers reprieve from the chaos plaguing modern life; it offers intimate social connections and a sense of meaning, which are otherwise fraying in our globalized and transient world. And perhaps this need is heightened if you are single in a city of 8 million. Conversion allows you to close down the life you are currently inhabiting—the one that leaves you lonely and unhappy—and enter a more promising one.[13]

Psychological research on conversion supports this theory by finding that people in the midst of a crisis or a major life transition are especially open to religious conversion.[14] But, certainly, not all conversions are premised on unhappiness. A few women I interviewed said that when they converted, everything had been going well in their lives, raising the important point that conversion also needs to be understood outside of deficiency and lack. One woman at Wellspring told me, "I had a good job, a great apartment, everything was fine, and then I woke up one day and I felt like there was a hole in my heart." The hole, she went on to say, was a God-shaped hole that could only be filled by returning to God and reentering evangelicalism. In her case, the drive to convert was supernaturally inspired and separate from any material qualities of her life. The "God-shaped hole," evangelicals believe, is created by God when you are born; it is a void that exists above and beyond circumstances. This concept was described in a sermon by a pastor at Wellspring as "a spiritual hunger and thirst" that cannot be filled by anything other than God.[15]

If God calls believers back to him via a gentle pull, a "tug" as Carys said, then he also requests a lot in return. Evangelical Christianity is a demanding religion that requires its followers to go all-in, to commit completely and be transformed. Like the woman who quit her job, her relationship, and moved away when she converted, Carys would soon submerge herself in the evangelical community, and in so doing would submit herself to a profound shift in terms of her ways of being and her very identity.

For me, leaving was a slow extraction. It started more than a decade ago, when I moved to the East Coast for graduate school. This was my first foray outside Christianity. I was born into a Christian family, which includes an extended family of pastors, and spent my childhood at church. From middle school onward, I went to Christian schools, where I memorized Bible verses and attended weekly chapel services. College: evangelical. Friends: all evangelical. Roommates: evangelical. Even the therapist I had seen was an evangelical.

And then I left my familiar enclave. I moved into a ramshackle house with two non-Christian housemates. One of them had just discovered that she liked women; the other regularly brought both men and women over for sleepovers. Up until that point, everyone I knew was straight—so straight that heterosexuality didn't even need to be mentioned; it was assumed and compulsory.[16] I started a master's program, which was filled with unbelievers, and an internship at a secular social work center. I felt as though I had been dropped into a foreign country where I didn't speak the language and had never learned the customs. The experience terrified me more than living in a village in rural Peru the year before. At least there I was surrounded by Christians. By comparison, this world felt stranger.

To add to my distress, I had been taught my whole life to be wary of non-Christians. I was told that I could be friends with them but only in order to convert them to Christ. By living apart from God, they were lost and shrouded in darkness; they were going to hell. And now I was surrounded by these hell-bound heathens who not only didn't understand me or my world but actually despised my world. They hated everything associated with right-wing evangelicals, which, at this point, I still was. I joined a church and a women's Bible study group that met weekly. I clung to my evangelical boyfriend, who had moved across the country with me, and to my religious certitude.

One dark November evening, I reach a breaking point. I sit in a class on diversity, glancing at the clock on the wall, noticing that class is almost over. A talkative student with a strong jaw and lots of tattoos speaks up. "I think evangelical Christians are destroying our country," she states plainly. "And we need get rid of all public displays of Christianity. Like the president putting his hand on the Bible when he is inaugurated. And saying 'One nation under God' in the Pledge of Allegiance. It's unbelievable this still happens, and we still support these rabid fundamentalists."

I look toward our professor, waiting for her to intervene as she has done so many times in the past. But she remains quiet. Soon, others join in, their voices coalescing into a collective outcry, like an angry group of villagers shouting and lifting their torches in the air. I slide down the back of my chair, wishing I could hide. But there I am, in plain sight, the person they are coming for. I voted for Bush in the last election; I thought our country needed saving. I am the evangelical, the "rabid fundamentalist."

Class ends and I'm the first one out, racing down the corridor and out into the university courtyard, where my boyfriend, Ryan, waits for me.

"Drive," I order, as I get into the car, slamming the door closed. I recount what just happened in class. "I don't understand how it's completely okay to say that about Christians," I fume. "I mean, did they even consider that there might be an evangelical in the classroom with them?"

We brake at a red light and soft drops of rain begin to fall. Ryan turns on the windshield wipers. He remains silent. I look out my window to the car waiting next to us. A couple inside is arguing. The man takes his hands off the steering wheel and gesticulates wildly. The woman looks back at him, nonplussed.

The light turns green and we lurch forward.

"I just felt so out of place. So uncomfortable . . . and—just awful. I wanted to run out crying." At the sound of the word, tears begin to roll down my cheeks.

Ryan pulls the car over and places his hand on my shoulder. The windshield wipers are frantic now, the rain coming down faster than they can clear it away. "You're just not used to it," he says. "It's normal for me because I have spent a lot of time around non-Christians. But you will get used to it. Just give it some time. I'm sure it feels really foreign right now."

In this moment, he is the only reminder I have of the world I've come from. But that will soon come to an end. A month later he will confess that he's been saving for an engagement ring. In response, I will admit that I want to move abroad after graduate school. "Just for a year," I'll say, bargaining for time. Wounded, he'll ask if I will ever be ready to settle down, to be a wife, to have the Christian marriage we've been told to pursue. Told to want. But I don't want it—it's been two and a half years and I still don't want it. I'm too young, I will argue. Just give me more time. But secretly I'll begin to wonder what's wrong with me, and if I'll ever want it. We will leave the topic for another month, a relational armistice on account of the holidays.

"I can't," I say simply, when the time finally comes.

Ryan looks away when I say this, accepting my truth, swallowing it whole. I dig my fingernails into the palm of my hand, knowing what the truth has cost me.

But instead of being sad, I'm angry. Furious, because we did everything right: we remained virgins, remained pure; we prayed together and attended church every Sunday; we even did premarital counseling with an older Christian couple back in California, who gave us the seal of approval. I was promised a rich and fulfilling marriage if I did all these things—or at least the *desire* for a rich and fulfilling marriage—and neither came. We did everything right, and these evangelical guarantees failed us.

Once Ryan moves back to California, I am on my own in this foreign world. I take the subway to and from class every day, staring out the window at the sullied snow that piles up on curbs, reading about Ernest Shackleton's Antarctic expedition and wondering if I too will freeze to death. I can't eat, so I lose a bunch of weight. The doctor prescribes me antidepressants to help me sleep. I take up smoking. I begin to lean on my two housemates and a friend from graduate school, and they comfort me and care for me. Slowly, I realize that they aren't the dangerous people I've been warned about. I see a therapist again, and this one isn't a Christian. Then I fall in love again, and he isn't a Christian either. I become fed up with my Bible study group—they keep referring to my social work job as "missionary work," when it clearly has nothing to do with proselytizing.

Sitting on my front porch one rainy afternoon in spring, smoking and listening to music, I realize that the balance has tipped: there are now more non-Christians in my life than Christians. And I'm okay. I've cracked open the door of Christianity and, as I peer out, I can see a whole other life ahead of me. Untethered from the circumscribed ways of being a woman, I can stretch out and expand in directions never before accessible. I can have an opinion. I can have not just a job but a *career*. I can choose to not get married (and to not have children). I can choose. Even still, I can't fully let go. I still attend church every Sunday and pray regularly, because I don't know who I would be without Christianity or what map would guide me through this life. And so I linger at that doorway, unwilling to make a definitive move either way.

I was speaking to a fellow "deconvert" recently and she remarked, "It's a strange feeling, like I was holding something and suddenly it's gone so quickly." She looked down at her lap after she said this, drawing attention to her empty hands, which were tucked neatly inside each other, cradling nothing. For a long time after, I pondered her choice of words: *holding* her faith, like a parcel or a porcelain vase. Was it taken, I wondered, or did it slip from her hands, breaking into irretrievable pieces?

McFague writes, "Conversion will be a process, usually a painful and lifelong process, fraught with doubt, with ambiguity, with great discomfort, with risk; and certainly, it will demand courage to a high degree."[17] Having researched evangelicals and their conversions in depth, I know this description to be true. But I know that these also are the hallmarks of *de*conversion. It, too, is a process, a disorienting, agonizing, and maddening one, which you must endure patiently. It, too, demands courage. And it can start without you being conscious that it's even happening.

Before I met Carys—before I met any of the evangelical women whose stories populate this book—there was Maddie. Maddie, my research subject. Maddie, my friend. She was there when I first started my research, when I was stumbling through misshapen questions, unarticulated hunches. There's Maddie, perched on a high stool at the pub in East London, dressed head to toe in black, her short pixie cut and bright red lips, a snake tattoo slithering up her forearm, and that lilting voice that makes her speaking sound like singing. Those pointy elfin ears. There she is swiveling her head in my direction and saying hello, laughing softly at my brassy American humor, saying that she's an artist, but saying little else; withholding, always withholding, in words and emotions and physicality, so that you are always left wanting more.

We met in spring 2015, after an evening service at Thames Gathering Place in London, introduced by an evangelical friend from the United States. We exchanged phone numbers that night, and soon after, she invited me over to her house.

When I arrive at a warehouse conversion in East London, Maddie answers the door, barefoot and wearing the same black dress as the first time I met her. She leads me through the open-plan living room and into her bedroom. I take in all the objects in her room: an unframed black-and-white picture of Twiggy propped up against the wall; a stack of photography books; mismatched postcards taped to the wall: a sepia-colored picture of an U-Bahn train, a lone bird flying in a cloudy sky, a Mark Rothko painting shrunk down to four-by-six size.

"How long have you been at Thames Gathering?" I ask, as I look around.

"Only a year. I came back to Christianity only a year ago. I grew up in a Christian home, but then I went off to college and lived a bit of a crazy life. You know, drugs, alcohol, sleeping around . . . And I had no connection to Christianity. I probably only went to church at Easter and Christmas—so, the big celebrations."

A knock at the front door and Maddie excuses herself to answer it. Even though I don't hear more of Maddie's testimony until later, I never hear it in full. Instead, it comes out in bits and pieces, and I tape these fragments together like the postcards taped to her wall, so that, eventually, they make up a coherent narrative. And while I'm piecing together the story, I observe Maddie, just like Carys, transform before my eyes, from a tentative convert into a devoted evangelical woman.

The next Sunday, after a service at Thames Gathering, she says, "I'm so much happier now, more peaceful, calmer. I don't know what I'd do if I didn't have my faith." Then she trails off, signaling that this is all she's willing to say on the subject for now. In the silence that swells between us, I wonder if I'm being found out, if my position as she-who-left announces itself.

Another time, while having an early dinner at a restaurant near her house, she says, "I know a lot of people come into their faith when they're clutching at straws . . . and for me it was a very large straw. I suppose I was probably looking for something to pep me up a bit." She changes the subject after saying this, refusing me entry.

Late one night, lounging on the couch, having just finished a film, she confides, "I used to be dancer, and had an eating disorder. Did I tell you that already? So, during the 'crazy phase' from teenage to midtwenties, my self-esteem kind of rollercoastered. I suffered from depression and stuff like that as well."

"What brought you back to Christianity?" I ask this time.

A pause, a thoughtful consideration, and then: "Well, I was new to the city. I found that my social circle wasn't as welcoming . . . Well, everyone is doing their own thing, and it's very hard to find your own identity when you are a newcomer in London. So I'd say it was the community that brought me back. It's what tethers me; it holds me steady amidst all the chaos and the uncertainty. And I missed God, my connection with him."

Several months later, when Maddie was fully immersed in the evangelical community, I had heard most of her story. And

I noticed that it followed the template of the other evangelical testimonies: growing up in a vaguely Christian family, wandering away, experiencing a period of darkness, and then the longing. It drew Maddie back, beckoning her from afar until she returned, like a prodigal daughter, and experienced redemption.

Evangelical women like Maddie organize their memories in such a way as to dramatically define who they were before becoming a Christian—and, crucially, who they are now. One woman I interviewed flippantly referred to her conversion story as "textbook." Her admission indicates an awareness of just how formulaic testimonies are, even as she herself repeats the formula. Further, it reveals that women learn to order their histories according to a common narrative template—a "textbook."[18]

I agree with anthropologist Susan Harding, who notes that evangelicals' identical testimonies reveal a desire to suture themselves to a biblical narrative tradition that is valorized in evangelicalism. But I also think there is something else going on. When women narrate their conversion stories, they are sharing something with one another. They are sharing not only the story itself but also the experience it symbolizes.[19] These stories provide a shared language and a shared history, and they enable intimacy—with God and with each other.[20] Learning and adopting this narrative is only the beginning of the Christian journey and of the intimacy that evangelicalism fosters. The real transformation occurs when the convert immerses herself in the community, when she learns and performs religious practices, when she surrenders to a tightly regulated network of norms—norms that create impermeable boundaries from the outside, promising relief from meaninglessness and isolation, promising stability and intimacy.

Not long after we met, I join Maddie at another Sunday evening service at Thames Gathering. I'm supposed to meet her out front before it starts, but my sister has just called to tell me she's pregnant and I'm excitedly pacing around the church garden. Maddie arrives and waves me over.

Worship has already started by the time we enter the foyer, and the lights are dimmed low. An usher comes over to guide us through the dark auditorium and help us find empty seats.

All around us men and women are worshipping. Their arms are lifted upward, eyes shut, voices loud, bodies responding to the rhythm of the music. A team of ten musicians fills the stage. A guitarist with torn black jeans and a beard stamps his foot on the floor to keep the beat of the music, or maybe to emphasize his passion for God. The woman next to him sways from side to side as if marching in place. She cups her hands around the microphone, her voice rising higher and higher.

The lyrics flash across multiple screens: "God in my living / There in my breathing / God in my waking / God in my sleeping."

As we slide into our seats, a blond woman relocates to the aisle, giving her more room to worship unencumbered. The singers on stage repeat the refrain "God in my resting / There in my working / God in my thinking / God in my speaking."

Maddie stretches both arms out toward the heavens. She tosses her head back and squeezes her eyes closed, her snake tattoo illuminated by the flashing lights. This restrained woman suddenly explodes, spreading out her limbs, taking up space. The chorus breaks out, a spotlight sweeps the audience, and hands reach even higher into the darkness. "Be my everything / Be my everything / Be my everything / Be my everything." Maddie's fingers are electrified now; they go rigid and spread out wide, and she rolls her head from side to side, her short hairs trembling with the movement.

I notice my impulse to join in. Why is it, I wonder, that even after all this time my instinct is to reach my hands out in space when I hear these worship songs? As if to touch the transcendence that once bathed me during Sunday worship services. Just to touch it once more. In these moments my body acts of its own volition; it betrays me, commits treason, until my mind can come stumbling after it and say, "We don't do that anymore." What does it mean that the body still retains traces of a religion, long after the mind has let it go?[21]

The middle-aged man in front of me falls to his knees. His head is bowed and he rocks forward and back as if in a trance. He presses his hands together and his index fingers brush up against his lips. Tears squeeze out of the corners of his eyes.

The chorus again: "Be my everything / Be my everything / Be my everything."

2

WITHOUT YOU, I AM NOTHING

The Other concerns me despite myself.
—Emmanuel Levinas

February 2016. The air was stale and cold in New York City. Christmas and New Years had passed, along with the spirit of festivity that lit up the city. I had spent the past eight months interviewing women, one after the next, each interview serving as a bread crumb that led me to the next, never quite sure where I was going. I continued to meet up with Carys in New York and Maddie in London, observing the deepening of their faith, but I wasn't finding the answers I wanted. "You have to infiltrate their world," my friend, a fellow researcher, told me one afternoon as we waited at the counter of a busy café for our to-go coffees. "Find out why they love the church so much. What is the draw?"

I mulled over my friend's question the next day on my way to meet a woman named Liv, who I'd heard about for months. "You *have* to meet Liv," evangelical women at Wellspring would urge during our interviews. "Have you asked Liv about that?" others would ask, in response to my questions. They'd tell me about

Women Rise, the feminist group Liv had helped start at Wellspring and her prominent role as director of communications at the church. This system of gender discrimination within the church spawned its own female-led hierarchy, and Liv was right at the top. She was the champion for single Christian women. The queen bee.

When I arrive at the crowded deli near Wellspring, Liv is already there, squinting into the screen of her phone and typing furiously. I pause, taken aback at this larger-than-life maverick who barely fills the chair with her petite frame. I look closer, the contrast of myth and reality colliding in front of my eyes. As I do, Liv glances up and meets my eyes. She begins to enthusiastically wave me over. Her hair has been piled haphazardly on top of her head, held in place by a giant claw clip. Down on the floor, her bright red coat lies bunched around the chair legs, having slipped off the coat hanger, or perhaps simply discarded hastily. Fire truck red, as my grandpa used to call it.

As I walk over, I pick up the coat and introduce myself.

"Oh, thank you! I don't know how that happened! Anyway, I'm Liv," she says brightly. She stands and wraps her arms around me, pulling me close so that we are in one of those tight hugs that feels just a shade too intimate for a first encounter.

After we sit down, I tell her a bit about my research and ask about her faith background.

"Well, I grew up in Washington State, outside of Seattle, in a Christian family," Liv begins. "I am one of those rare evangelicals who has never really strayed. But of course, like everyone, I have had moments of doubt and struggle in my Christian journey. I would say I'm in a really good place with my faith now, probably a more mature place."

"Tell me about Women Rise," I say, knowing our time is limited.

"Well, I think it's biblical to have women in prominent positions, and yet the church is one of the only contexts where sexism seems to be fine. I don't know if you know this, but Wellspring has recently cut all their funding for women's ministries."

"No, I don't know anything about this. What happened?"

Liv looks around and then leans in close.

"They said it was necessary. I have been told that we have enough women in the church, so why would we want to encourage more?" She reclines back in her chair and raises her eyebrows. "I completely disagree with that. If sixty-five percent of your congregation is female, you should be looking to support them, not trying to stop other women from coming!"

Liv shakes her head and changes the topic. She tells me about her plans for Women Rise—bringing in notable female business leaders to speak, three-course dinners organized around different themes, networking nights. Then she invites me to come along to their event the following Tuesday. "I mean, a big part of Women Rise is to encourage people in their calling. And if researching evangelical women is your calling, I want to help you in some way. So, come along on Tuesday! Maybe it will be a good way to meet some other people."

She lets me know our time is up by setting down her glass of water and standing up, somewhat abruptly, and wrapping herself in the red coat.

"There are really amazing women there," Liv adds.

I'm still seated, so although though Liv is small, she towers over me, her eyes lit up like the paper-bag lanterns that used to line our driveway at Christmas. Even now, years later, after so much has happened, this is how I always picture Liv, the image imprinted on me like an outdated photograph. Though the surface has deteriorated with time, the likeness remains intact, still captivating.

A few days later, as I prepare to go to Women Rise, apprehension that borders on dread flutters in my belly. I perform the act of getting ready ritualistically: I bathe and dress myself, selecting clothing that will leave me inconspicuous. I smooth the duvet on my bed and sit there for a while, staring straight ahead.

I know what will be required of me as I conduct the first round of participant observation. I will seek the infiltration that my friend recommended. Interviews demand a lot of the researcher—restraint, collaboration, endurance—but they do not require much performance. Sometimes, a successful interview depends on silence. Participant observation, on the other hand, is a technique used by ethnographers to blend in with the field site while observing it. As the researcher *participates*, she sheds her natural skin and slips into a slightly altered version of herself. She performs the role of the Other in order to learn about the Other. It is an exercise in theater, which will disorient me as I move from who I am now to who I used to be and who I never want to be again.

At eight o'clock, I slowly approach the darkened church. The fluttering in my belly escalates to thrashing and I concentrate on scrubbing clean the judgments I have toward evangelicalism. A single porch light glows outside and it's deadly quiet. But when I open the door I enter a world of merriment. The basement is small and crowded and packed with young women; it erupts with the sounds of laugher and folk music. Fairy lights stretch across the exposed brick walls and flowers bloom from simple glass vases adorning the tables. Waiters circulate with glasses of bubbly atop silver trays. Liv sits at the welcome desk and greets me as I enter.

"Katie! You're here!" she exclaims, jumping up and enfolding me in another of her close-fitting hugs.

She introduces me to the woman sitting next to her. "This is Jo; she helps out with Women Rise."

"Hey, how's it going?" Jo reaches out her hand.

"Katie is doing research on single evangelical women, looking at the barriers they face and so on," Liv says. "And Jo is a social worker who manages a group home for teens. And you're both pastors' daughters, so you have that in common!"

Jo smiles. "Well, we should meet up sometime and chat more." Then she turns her attention toward a group of three who have just come in. "Welcome, ladies!"

I look out across the sea of women organized into little clusters. A friendly-looking woman with bright red lips walks past and offers me Prosecco. I thank her and take the drink with me. Live acoustic guitar plays in the adjoining room, and the deep, raspy voice of a soloist travels over to me.

Across the room, I see Carys emerge from the bathroom and I rush over to her. Just then, Liv gets on the microphone, encouraging us all to sit down. Carys and I search for seats together, and a woman we don't know smiles, moving her bag out of the way so we have space. *Thank you*, I mouth as we sit down.

Hours later, tipsy on Prosecco, my new friends and I loiter around the church basement.

"How do you all find balance living in such a big city? I'm really struggling with it," admits Carys. "Like, how do you have time to develop hobbies or try new things?"

I share with the group that I, too, am buried under the demands of work, friends, and activities. They all nod reassuringly in response.

Then Liv offers a suggestion. "So, this is what I do. I drew a big map of New York City and hung it up in my bedroom. Every month I place a sticker in a new neighborhood and then I go visit, no matter how far it is. That way, I don't feel too over-whelmed thinking about all I want to do."

"Yeah, but that's because you have a surplus of energy, Liv," says Jo. "I do fuck-all on the weekend."

The entrance of the word *fuck* into a church building makes us laugh.

When it comes time to leave, we all hug good-bye and Jo and I exchange phone numbers, promising to meet soon.

I amble out of Wellspring and down a darkened side alley leading to a bustling avenue with designer shops and high-end patisseries. The streetlights radiate against the blackened sky, generating their own nighttime planetarium. I feel transported. Euphoric even. Glancing down at my phone, I see that my friend, a fellow researcher, has sent me a message: *So, how did it go?* I swipe away her text and continue walking, wanting to savor this feeling.

Being at that church event, I felt comfortable—maybe *too* comfortable. I reflect on the facility with which I transitioned back into an earnest evangelical woman and it begins to disturb me. I keep walking, quickening my stride, hoping to outpace the prickling sense of alarm. I turn the corner to a main road. Empty buses rush past and well-dressed couples drift in and out of cock-tail bars. I look around for the characteristic black sign of a subway station, but it's nowhere to be found. As I turn my head around, a drunk woman smashes into me and I can smell soured liquor on her warm breath. She laughs and stumbles back into her date's arm. I look at my phone and see a message from Carys: *Was so good to see you tonight!* I slide my phone into my bag. Pangs of uneasiness begin to grip me.

Later that night, I sit at my kitchen table, a warm mug of tea in my hands, and jot down a few notes. *It went well. Maybe a little too well. That sense of community and a space to discuss real life struggles is intoxicating. And the people were so warm.* I close my notebook, tucking it into my work bag, and retreat upstairs to bed. But I cannot sleep that night; my mind spins with conversations, questions, and the resurrection of a familiar feeling.

The next Saturday, Jo invites me to her apartment for coffee and cake.

"I couldn't remember, what church did you say you go to?" she asks me, as I take off my shoes in the entrance hallway.

"Actually, I don't go to church," I say, wondering what she'll think of my response. "I still identify as Christian, but I'm no longer practicing."

She flops down on the couch. "Fair enough, man. Church isn't for everyone."

"How about you?" I ask. "How long have you been a Christian?"

"Pretty much my whole life. I would say there was never some kind of 'road to Damascus' moment for me, but at some point my faith just became my own.

"When my depression came, I felt like I could never fully turn my back on God, because I had seen too much evidence and felt so much of his presence. But my depression at some point made me go, *Okay, well, I can't believe you don't exist, God, but I don't believe you love me. So fuck you. I'm going to do what I want.*"

Jo pauses, letting the weight of her words hang in the air.

"So, what did you do?"

"I bought a ticket to southern Africa to travel solo, and the Lord healed me while I was out there."

"How did God heal you?" I ask.

"I was staying with a friend from Youth With a Mission in Tanzania, and one morning I was hysterical.[1] I was weeping and I could not control myself, even though I was trying to be quiet, because I didn't want to interrupt the prayer session happening in the hallway. Then a woman, one of the teachers on the base, came through and she said, 'I just feel like I'm supposed to be here with you, so I'm going to use the bathroom and then I'm going to come out and pray for you.' When she came out, we spoke, and we prayed, and something just lifted, and I—I just felt *differently*.

"And when I think about it, I think community, community is the thing—particularly with my depression, when I was at my lowest—that saved my life. I genuinely believe that. I believe that this community saved my life." Tears pool in her wide-set brown eyes.

I'm reminded of my recent conversation with Liv, when I admitted to her that I am no longer a practicing Christian.

"But don't you miss it?" she had asked, concern riding on her voice. "Don't you miss the community?"

I replied that I had a great community of friends, that I did not need the sort of community that evangelicalism offered, and concluded with a simple no.

Listening to Jo and seeing how much the community means to her, I admit to myself that I actually *have* started to miss the Christian community. And over the past week, I have begun to suspect that my longing is more than the typical ethnographer's desire to access the research site more profoundly.[2] Something different is happening to me; a strong current is pulling me back, and I fear I may be dragged under.

March 2016. I'm in Liv's living room on a dreary Sunday afternoon, my hands clasped with the hands of two others, head bowed in prayer.[3] The woman next to me, Fiona, speaks in tongues, the indecipherable words spilling out of her mouth quickly and quietly. Snow falls peacefully on the street outside. *How did I end up back here?* I wonder to myself.

When Liv first invited me to join her Bible study group, I hesitated. My doctoral supervisor was pleased—this is research gold, she'd told me. But still, something held me back. Even now, years later, I still struggle to make sense of what it was. Could it have been a reencounter with the painful experience of leaving? Or the equally painful experience of having stayed for so long? Perhaps I feared I would reconvert. Maybe I was afraid of myself.

Ethnography is a prolonged, in-depth, and immersive research method. In fact, it's precisely because of these features that social scientists use it to understand the lifeworld of others. Several anthropological texts are devoted to helping the researcher achieve greater familiarity with their research environment. But given my evangelical background, my pursuit was toward estrangement, which is both harder to achieve and more crucial.[4] I worried that joining this Bible study group might bring me too close to a world I had fought hard to leave.

I'd arrived at Liv's apartment early that day, carrying two cartons of orange juice and flowers, hoping to make a good impression.

Liv swings open the door and welcomes me in, cheerful as always. Her third-floor apartment is large and inviting: the floors are covered with soft beige carpet, and an eclectic mix of secondhand antique furniture and Target purchases fills the rooms. The sizzle of bacon drifts out from the kitchen, along with the bready smell of pancakes and slowly percolating coffee. A woman with an oversize sweater and black leggings is resting her weight on the kitchen door jamb. She turns her head my direction, smiles, and waves.

Another woman, named Fiona, introduces herself from inside the kitchen as she flips pancakes over a steaming griddle. The bacon starts to burn, the scent instantly overriding all others, and

Liv drops my coat and bag on the floor as she rushes to the frying pan to rescue the blackened strips of meat.

After casual small talk in the kitchen, the food is ready, and Liv steers us toward the dining room. I sit down at the old wooden table with nicks and dents around the edges and fold my hands in my lap, bowing my head to pray, as I've done for many years, the gesture so deeply encoded in my body that I don't even realize I am doing it. Liv prays for us, her normally high-pitched voice dropping to solemnity as she addresses her God.

After we pray, we eat. I remain quiet and let the other women direct the conversation, determining to follow their lead.

"What did everyone do this weekend?" Liv asks, as she takes a big gulp of orange juice.

Fiona answers first: "I just got back from London yesterday, actually. I went for an event at Thames Gathering with a few friends. We had a really great week, but it was a lot of eating out and parties so now I'm feeling pretty rough." She laughs self-consciously.

"Oh, that's right." Liv spears three pancakes and drops them on her plate. "I was out with Sophie on Friday night and she mentioned you guys were in London. We had *quite* the night out!" She pauses, holding us in suspense.

All eyes turn toward Liv, our curiosity visibly raised.

"So, we went out to this new club, Bungalow—have you guys heard of it? It's in the East Village. Anyway, we ran into a group of guys from Wellspring—Josh and Stewart and . . . what's the really hot one called?"

"Steve?" offers Tina, the woman in the oversize sweatshirt.

"Yes, Steve! Good job remembering. Not Steve Gilcrest, though. Steve Fox. Appropriate last name, right? Can't believe I even forgot it." She giggles. "Anyway, by the end of the night, Sophie and I had had about three gin and tonics each and were pretty tipsy. Next thing I know, I'm making out with Josh outside the club, while we wait for our taxis to arrive. I didn't get home until like four a.m. So yeah, I'm feeling pretty rough too!"

I think over my weekend. All I've done is a bit of cleaning, a long run on Saturday, dinner at home with a friend. My weekend has been dull compared to these evangelical women's.

After a while, we transition to the study portion of our Bible study, moving into the living room to signal a change in tone and subject matter. Once again, Liv leads the conversation, reminding the group that the session topic for this month is "dark night of the soul." She has sent around a passage by Saint John of the Cross a few weeks before and now reads it aloud to us.

"*This light led the way / more clearly than the risen sun / to where he was waiting for me / —the one I knew so intimately— / in a place where no one could find us.*"[5]

By the time she finishes reading, everyone appears to be deep in thought. Liv closes her eyes. Fiona takes a deep breath and exhales slowly. Unsure what to say, I look down at my notepad. Tina breaks the silence. She tells us about the time, a few years ago, when her mother was deathly ill. In the midst of it all, even when she had lost hope that her mother would recover, God was there, a continual comforting presence. Her disclosure is both deeply personal and vulnerable, yet she's offered it easily, without any hesitation.

The rest of us take turns sharing our personal stories of darkness and light. We finish by clasping hands and praying for one another. Afterwards, Fiona complains about her new coworker and Tina commiserates—she has a difficult one too. Liv describes the agony of dating apps and tells us a story about a date gone awry. I hang back and watch these women as they transition from lighthearted banter to spiritual and emotional depths, only to resurface collectively, in unison, like a flight of swallows, their maneuvers faultless.

Liv turns to me and asks if I've seen a mutual friend. The mention of someone outside this enclosed little world startles me, and I realize disconcertedly that I have fallen into a deep sleep, lulled by the warmth of the women around me.

"I need to call him, actually . . ." Liv continues, but I don't hear her now, because I've been roused from my slumber, jolted back to life, back to myself.

I pull my legs out from under me and stand up. I'm restless and I need to get out of here.

Liv walks me to the door and thanks me for coming, placing her small hand on the knife edge of my shoulder blade. The gesture is so thoroughly sincere, it makes me want to run back and curl up on her couch again. "The caress," writes Levinas, "is made up of this increase of hunger, of ever richer promises, opening new perspectives onto the ungraspable. It feeds on countless hungers."[6] Hungers that, until that moment, I did not know I had.

Tumbling onto the street, I glance at my watch. Our gathering has taken up half the day, and I feel drained.

As I ride the subway in silence, the image of these women's smiling faces crashes in on me, and I can see how entrenched they are in their close-knit community. I feel myself so far away from them. The distance between them and me, then and now, is finally revealed to me, brought into the light of day; it hits me with force. I can still taste the sweetness of belonging, though now the flavor has turned rancid and I want to spit it out of my mouth.

Abruptly, I get off at the next station and decide to change course. I cancel my dinner plans and switch off my phone. What I need now is a yoga class—one of those fast-paced, hot ones—to exorcise this bad feeling out of my body through sweat and breath. But it doesn't work. Running out of options, I show up unannounced at my friend's apartment. Three rings and she buzzes me in. I walk straight to her bedroom, dropping my bag and coat on the floor on my way there. I collapse on the bed and she strokes my back, a warm hand tenderly painting circles on a stilled body.

"Can you remind me why I'm doing this, and who I am?"

I don't want to lose myself, this version of me, and I can feel it slipping away, the quicksand of the past swallowing me up. I've spent all day outside myself, playacting the person I used to be, the person I might have been, had I never left evangelicalism. This is a self I do not want to remember; her vulnerability saddens me at the same time as it enrages.[7]

But it's not a pure resistance. Although I oppose this Christian self, I also long for it. I find myself neither there nor here, and the liminality is unbearable. Resting against my friend's quilted bedding, I close my eyes while she recites my biography over me, like an incantation, like a prayer.

What is this community that has stirred in me a yearning to return, so long after I'd left? That intoxicates and seduces at the same time as it smothers? What kind of community has the power to save a life? As I learned myself, that winter in New York, the beauty of the evangelical experience lies in the close embrace of community—an embrace that can be felt long after it has let you go.

It wasn't until much later, when I listened back to my interviews, that I noticed how often evangelical women mentioned "community." The word itself was used nearly a hundred times—and that was just during formal interviews. In more casual encounters, women spoke about the Christian community as if esteeming a new lover or raving about a cure-all supplement. "It's the

place where you can be vulnerable, where you can really be yourself," they would say. "It's what tethers you." "It just feels like
home." "No matter how far you fall from your faith, the community will catch you." "It's a cushion." "It's like this beautiful
family." "We come together, and we worship together, and we
have fellowship and we eat together. It's beautiful. A little glimpse
of heaven." "The communal experience of worship is so important to me. It fills a need."

Liv once told me, "I make church a priority because, at the
end of the day, I *need* this community."

As Jo indicated in her story of receiving healing in Tanzania,
the Christian community has both local and global dimensions.[8]
During my years as an evangelical woman, I developed various
Christian communities through churches I attended in California, Boston, Madrid, and Johannesburg. My Christian colleagues
at a nongovernmental organization in Peru were part of my community, as were my friends from the Christian university I
attended in California. Even my sister and cousins counted as
part of my community. Each of these were self-contained communities, which, when stitched together, formed one large archi-
pelago of Christians. A woman who worked for Wellspring
said, "I keep in touch with a lot of friends all over the world. A
lot of people in New York relocate, and now that I have been
here eight years, that has happened a lot. When I hear all of the
cool stuff they're doing at their new churches, it's really encouraging for my faith." For evangelicals, belonging to a global community creates a sense of being part of something larger than
oneself. And it provides connections that transcend distance,
language, or circumstance.

The intense desire for community is a direct consequence of
the transitory, temporal society that accompanies late modernity

in the West. According to sociologist Zygmunt Bauman, inter-personal relationships have become "liquefied"—meaning weak and ephemeral—in modern times. The splintering of stable con-nections leads to the fragmentation of individual identities, which are otherwise developed within secure relationships. Bauman writes, "After all, the hard core of identity—the answer to the question 'Who am I?' and even more importantly the continu-ing credibility of whatever answer might have been given to that question—cannot be formed unless in reference to the bonds connecting the self to other people and the assumption that such bonds are reliable and stable over time."[9] Liquid identities, Bauman goes on, have replaced solid ones, and these transitory ones can be taken up and easily discarded. Instead of leaving us unencumbered, this shift produces profound anxiety and a long-ing for fixity.

The weakening of your sense of self, and the desire for coher-ence, is more pronounced during transitional periods. A study of university students in Britain reported that they joined Chris-tian groups on campus in order to renegotiate their identities within a highly uncertain event: leaving home for the first time.[10] Another study, conducted at Claremont University in Califor-nia, found that identifying with organized religion reduced indi-viduals' sense of uncertainty.[11] And a qualitative study of Ortho-dox Jews in the United States found that the more lost and troubled a woman felt before converting, the more likely she was to adopt the stricter practices of the faith, in order to shore up a strong sense of self.[12]

Identity fragmentation is even more pronounced in urban settings.[13] Urban sociologists have documented the isolation involved with city dwelling, reporting that living in a city is asso-ciated with unhappiness. And the bigger the city, the unhappier the residents.[14] According to this body of research, residents are unhappy due to poor interpersonal relationships, a lack of community networks and trust, and no social support.[15] These studies all indicate that the fluid self cries out for some sort of permanence.[16] And during transitional periods—arriving at university, moving to a new city—this cry intensifies.

Categorical identification also allows us to secure a place in the world by organizing politically. Identity-based social movements such as #MeToo (organized around gender), and Black Lives Matter (organized around race) rely on identity categories to seek justice. Building a political movement around an identity, regardless of whether the aim is recrimination, redistribution, or assertion, leads to "identity politics." Those on the left and the right both criticize identity politics, though for various reasons. Progressives claim that identity-based movements ignore social class and thus never sufficiently disrupt power imbalances, while conservatives argue that the exclusionary nature of an identity-based movement encourages divisiveness.[17]

But critiques of identity politics fail to recognize the importance of these categories to the people who inhabit them.[18] In this age of uncertainty—whether this is political, economic, or relational uncertainty—we seek refuge inside categories; it is the place where we come to be known, where we know ourselves. And religion is one institution that counters the disorder of late modernity by proffering a religious identity to liquefied subjects.[19] In evangelicalism, a Christian identity is prized above all others. You are a Christian before you are anything else. It's a strongly felt identity, and a hotly pursued one. In return, this identity gives women the fixity they crave. As I showed in chapter 1, single women migrate to the evangelical community because they are tired of the shallowness of modern life and are seeking meaningful relationships with God and others.

It is through the community that women have their identities as Christians consolidated, validated, and mirrored back to them. In other words, only through relationships with one another can evangelical women become evangelical women. Poststructuralist theorists posit that we develop our identities relationally, through our encounters with one another. "If *I am only in the address to you*, then the 'I' that I am is nothing without this 'you,'" the theorist Judith Butler writes. Such is our reliance on the Other for our sense of self that "I am mired, given over, and even the word *dependency* cannot do the job here."[20]

As happens in all religions, evangelicals support and guide one another's religious experiences.[21] These are the people who know them intimately and love them anyway.[22] "Christians are the people who have my heart," said Liv. Delving into the world of single evangelical women, I learned that it wasn't just *any* community that women longed for; it was the vulnerability and the intimacy of *this* community that they wanted. As I remember from my years inside the community and from the deep longing I experienced after leaving, the intimacy created within the evangelical community is singular. This intimacy provides believers with meaningful relationships and a resolute answer to the question "Who am I?"

When I left the church, I was unable to satisfactorily answer this question for a long time. Without the mirroring of the Other, I found my religious identity splintered, broken, lost. And then, coming back as a researcher, as I became closer to this group of women and reencountered the support of a closely bound community, this question began asserting itself again.

Torn between wanting to dive deeper into the world of evangelical women and wanting to back as far away from it as possible, I took some time off from the research. I thought about all the reasons why I should quit, justifying them to myself.

"I *definitely* couldn't do what you're doing," a coworker who grew up Mormon and later renounced it, told me once. Her words sparked something inside me; they challenged me to keep going.

So I took the plunge and gave myself over to intimacy with these four women. I reimmersed myself in the community, fully aware that it could pull me back.

May 2016. Spring brings an early rush of heat this year, but I don't even notice the warmer weather because I'm staggering through the ugly end of a relationship. On Sunday morning, I attend Bible study. We are back at Liv's apartment this month. I arrive late and in shambles, unsure how to act, how to be in this setting, given my current state.

As usual we start with brunch. We discuss our weekends, what films we have recently enjoyed, the people we have seen. I'm quiet throughout, lacking the energy to participate. Liv chatters animatedly about the Hinge dates she has been on recently. There is John, the older, charming writer, and Will, an Australian who kissed her on the first date. The front-runner is Sam, a former advertising guy who now works for a start-up and doesn't seem to mind her being a Christian or waiting for marriage to have sex. Rather than living in the despair about dating that plagued her a few months back, Liv is now enlivened, hopeful, with energy beating wildly in her birdlike body.

Hours later, when it comes time to pray, Fiona suggests we share our prayer requests with the group and then pray for the person on our left. She goes first.

"I would like prayer for direction. I've been offered a job at Wellspring, and I'm not sure if God's calling me to it or if I should stay at my current organization. So I just would ask for prayer that he would guide me and make it clear what I should do."

Tina sits to the left of Fiona, so she writes down the request on her pad of paper before speaking.

"So . . . my mom has been struggling lately with some health issues again. Nothing serious this time, we hope, but she's having a bunch of tests done, so if you could pray for a good outcome, and that she starts feeling better, that would be great."

It's my turn. I pause. And then I tell them the truth about what I'm going through.

Fiona's face crumples into a sympathetic expression, her mouth drawing downward. Tina purses her lips and Liv nods vigorously as I speak.

"Yeah, it's been really hard, to be honest. I feel completely broken." Liv reaches over and places her hand on top of mine, an act of compassion. We bow our heads and enter into prayer.

Later that night, sitting at my desk and writing up my field notes, I look out the window facing onto my backyard. Although it's late, it's still bright out, and the neighbors are wrapping up an outdoor dinner party. I can see the host getting up from the table and hustling plates inside, his guests languishing on plastic lawn chairs, soaking up the light, their compensation for months of darkness.

I felt less drained this time, I write. *I wanted to be part of this close-knit, enveloped community, where being single doesn't feel so isolating or lonely.* And then, in small, lower-case letters at the bottom: *That feeling of being held . . .*

I am no longer afraid of the pull of the community, I realize. I have yielded to its current, softened to it, less out of choice and more out of necessity. Suddenly, I've joined Liv, Carys, and Jo as a single woman in a lonely, metropolitan city. The commonality deepens our intimacy, and I feel closer to them because of it.

Carys calls me later to ask how I am coping with the breakup. We've only known each other a few months, but she is more attentive to my pain than some of my closest friends, whom I have known for years. She promises me she will continue to pray for me, and when I hear this, instead of repelling me, for some reason it comforts me.

A constant, intimate relationality is at the heart of the Christian community. The immersive religious experience that evangelicalism provides creates what I call an "encasement" for believers, which creates impermeable boundaries from the outside. This intimacy protects women from meaninglessness and isolation, and it provides them with a durable identity.

The intimate bond they forge with God extends from the intimate bonds they form with other believers in community. Intimacy is fostered through various practices: prayer, Bible study groups, worship—and accountability.

Accountability is a practice that allows, and in some cases requires, Christians to check up on each other and enforce evangelical norms. It demands that believers breach notions of privacy to touch the most intimate parts of each other's lives, including sex, relationships, and beliefs. It is an essential part of an evangelical's formation; after conversion and before fully immersing yourself into the community, you learn about accountability.

As a young Christian woman, I was trained in how to hold others accountable to their faith. This might require me to tell a woman that her shirt was too tight or too low cut and that she should prevent our Christian "brothers" from sinning sexually. Or that I ask a friend how her "quiet time" with God was going.[23] I should be grateful for accountability, I was taught. After all, words of critique or discipline were meant to train me to be a better Christian, to refine my faith. And in some cases, church leaders told me, I ought to seek out accountability for myself. Prayer partners, Bible study groups, and mentors provided the infrastructure for other believers to check up on me and to ask uncomfortable questions from time to time.

In order to succeed, accountability must occupy a horizontal plane, usually within same-sex relationships. Denise explains this to me. A thoughtful and serious woman, she agrees to be interviewed after Liv introduces us over e-mail. A quarter of the way through our interview, the topic of sex arises. We're in a stuffy room upstairs at Wellspring, where Denise works. The single window in the corner is shut, and the air between us is stifling. Denise fiddles with the pen in her hand, rubbing her thumb up and down the cap, and furrows her brows.

"Actually, my best friend from home . . . That's an interesting one . . ." She trails off. "So, she and her male roommate were kind of living apart on paper but actually living together. That was the only time I should have said something. I should have asked her, 'Okay, what is really happening here?'"

It's easier to talk about someone else's sex life than your own, I reason, so I permit Denise this foray into her friend's personal life.

"Did you talk to her about this?"

"No. We did chat about what they were doing, but I didn't challenge her on it. That's just what they did until they got married."

Her words bulge with opacity, forcing me to fill in every *this* and *it* with supposition. Denise swaps the pen to her other hand. She stares into space as she formulates her thoughts.

"If I could go back, I think I would try and get more courage. I think sometimes, when we challenge others, we think that we're going to come down like a ton of bricks on someone, and that they're going to react quite badly, so there is a kind of hesitancy to challenge someone. There is a real fear of judging them and damaging a friendship. But I think there is a way of gently challenging someone, and that can come out of a really strong bond—and out of love as well. A real sense of 'I'm not doing this because I'm correcting you, because I have my own mistakes and we're trying to just do this journey together.'" Denise drops the pen on the table. "But I'm not sure what that would look like."

Trying to just do this journey together.

The practice of accountability, at its best, creates intimacy. It fosters the close, interpersonal social system that women are seeking when they come to evangelicalism, by forcing them to engage with one another on a deeply private plane. And women allow it because they know that a form of intimacy that cannot be found anywhere else thrives on that plane. But at its worst, accountability amounts to a religiously acceptable form of surveillance or policing, which is what had caused Carys to leave Christianity more than a decade before.

But Carys returned. And she continued to immerse herself in evangelicalism, just as I had predicted, that day in the university café when I watched her vacillate between longing and resistance. Looking back now, I don't begrudge her this. In fact, I'm grateful she reentered a close-knit community, especially when I consider everything she would go through later: losing her job, a mysterious illness, her close friend suddenly dying. Throughout each of those events, the community sustained her. If I asked her now, she might even say that it saved her.

July 2016. It's a Saturday night and I'm in London, visiting Maddie at her new apartment. She has just moved to a rapidly gentrifying neighborhood in East London that hits all the markers of coolness: a rooftop yoga studio, overpriced coffee drinks served by prickly baristas, and a vegan pop-up café.

We're tearing through our second bottle of red wine, sprawled out on the couch, our legs tangled around each other like seaweed. Blues plays on shuffle in the background. Maddie leans her head back on the armrest and closes her eyes to let the music wash over her. She's mumbling something about her Bible study group, which is meeting tomorrow before church. Every week the women take turns telling their testimonies, and tomorrow is Maddie's turn.

"The other girls in the group just have such dramatic stories. One of them got into partying in her early twenties, like really into drugs, then she became a Christian, a *radical* Christian, and so her story was really 'Wow!'"

I ask Maddie if I can record her and she agrees. I place my phone on the coffee table next to us and press Record, sliding it the length of the glass toward her end.

Maddie's words trickle out like thick molasses, slowed down by wine and drowsiness. "I don't have an interesting life story like they do."

I remind her of her crazy ex-boyfriend, Greg, the one she thought was gay, and his bizarre, secretive behavior.

She keeps her head reclined and laughs. "Yes, that's true. Thanks for the reminder . . . But I also realized, who cares? I don't need a crazy, dramatic testimony."

It's quiet, and Maddie and I retreat to the corners of our own minds, gathering our thoughts like little stones before reuniting to show each other what we've found.

"Do you have any thoughts on the role of community?" I ask after a while.

"I don't know. Quite possibly. Why do you ask?"

"Because it keeps coming up in all my interviews."

"It's a really interesting topic," she muses. "I'm thinking of doing a series of paintings on the weird and wonderful ways people find community. It really is one of the most beautiful things about the church."

Maddie takes a sip of wine, and when I listen to the recording now, years later, I can hear the wine slide down back of her throat, the sound of it layered over Etta James's lulling voice, my murmurs, a car slowly driving by outside—a sensorial landscape filled with softness.

She continues. "What fascinates me is, I think sometimes, if I were to leave the church, how would I find this community? Of course, there are ways to find community outside the church, but I think the community is one of the most positive things to come out of organized religion. It's so entrenched; it's in place and it works."

I copy Maddie's position and recline my head on my own armrest and close my eyes. With the wine softening my defenses, I let myself remember what it was like to belong to the evangelical community, allowing the sweetness of belonging to lap like frothy surf around the edges of my body.

Maddie's voice takes on an urgent quality, sped up by the emotionality of her words. "I mean, you can have community at work, but you don't go deep with them. At church, it's like a family. You don't hold back with these people. You bare all. You don't have to put on a front. We are all putting on a front every day, but when you're with your Christian friends you can be your ugly self and they don't even care. To be known and connected, to be part of something and loved unconditionally—it's so *relieving*."

Eyes still closed, I respond, "I suppose the emotional depths that you are able to reach with these people is singular."

"Yes, exactly. For me, to sum up the Christian community in one sentence, I'd say it's to be known." Maddie pauses. "Even if it's just to be known truthfully by a handful of people . . . I don't think there's anything sweeter."

I agree, but I don't say so. I rock back and forth in the memory of the community, floating on my back in a wide, wide ocean, where I am held. I let myself be carried out.

We're both quiet now, and then Maddie sighs a contented sigh. I yawn. Etta James croons, unbothered, in the background.

"Thank you, Maddie."

I reach over and switch off the recorder.

Three years later, on an ordinary Sunday afternoon, while cleaning the house, I will find this recording by accident, buried deep in my computer archives, the file simply named "Maddie." I'll press Play, not knowing what I'm about to listen to, and when Maddie's soft, inebriated voice floats through my speakers, it will upend me. So much so that I will turn off the television, close the living room door, and sit down to listen. After the recording finishes, I'll play it again, and again, and again. Then I will think of what came later for Maddie, for me, for us, and I'll reach my hands to my face and find, much to my surprise, that it's wet with tears.

3

IN THE WORLD

*It turns out that detachment is not antithetical to attachment
but one of its styles.*

—Lauren Berlant

Around the age of twenty, along with many young American women, I discovered *The Vagina Monologues.* Its message of female empowerment resonated with me, and the essays were subversive, illicit, fresh. Late at night, other women from my evangelical college huddled inside my dorm room and listened as I read the essays aloud. I turned off all the lights, keeping just one lamp lit and casting its glow onto my face for dramatic effect.

But this wasn't your typical *Vagina Monologues* reading, the kind being performed, possibly at that very moment, at universities and theaters across the country. In my rendering, I omitted every curse word from the text and censored the parts I deemed too sexually explicit. I took on the challenging work of a translator, honoring the humor and intelligence of Eve Ensler's writing while appealing to my conservative evangelical audience. My performance improved with each show; I lowered my voice here and inserted a frustrated pitch there, goading my audience with suspenseful pauses and deadpan deliveries.

And that was just one example of the censoring that I undertook, that *we* undertook, every single day. Because life as an evangelical is a series of modifications. It's a constant negotiation of devout, conservative beliefs and the secular world evangelicals are obliged to inhabit. Some of these negotiations are predetermined and established, like the deep grooves of a hiking trail, making them easy to follow. Back at my evangelical high school, we were allowed to have a cheerleading squad but our skirts had to be to our fingertips, our movements had to be chaste ("No moving your hips!") and our chants needed to be Christian ("He is King!").

Eventually the time came for me to leave the confines of my evangelical nest and try these micro negotiations for myself out in the world. Luckily, I had been well trained, so that when I started attending yoga classes in my midtwenties, I promised myself that although I knew the risks involved—that it could open me to other religions—I would make the necessary adaptations to keep myself protected. As the other students in class closed their eyes and chanted in Sanskrit, I kept my lips tightly pressed together and conversed with my Christian God. Even once my deconversion process was under way, I continued to perform these little modifications. I went with my non-Christian friends to nightclubs but I monitored my dance moves. I listened to Rihanna and Lady Gaga, but not the songs with explicit language. I played drinking games, but while I reached the threshold of tipsy, I never slid into drunk. I left the shutters open so the light could keep pace with the darkness as it steadily filled the room.

Not so long ago, riding on a train into the English countryside, my friends discussed the music of their childhoods. "My mom always played Joni Mitchell," said one friend. Another said, "For me, it was Bob Dylan. I loved his music and listened to it so much that now, whenever I hear a song of his on the radio, it immediately brings me back to being eleven years old, sitting in my backyard as my parents barbecue." The Rolling Stones, Van Morrison. I remained silent. Growing up, I listened to Christian music—albums called *Jesus Freak* and songs such as "Heavenly Place." Another gap in knowledge, another absence that confirms just how cut off I was, and for so many years. When I think about these lacunae, I wondered what else I would have learned if I hadn't spent so much time memorizing scripture? If all of the Sunday school lessons and Bible classes I attended during high school and college were suddenly wiped out, what knowledge would take its place?

There are other knowledge gaps, such as about evolution. I was taught creationism, the evangelical teaching deriving from Genesis that God created the world and all life-forms in it over seven days.[1] And sex. Instead of learning sex education as a teenager, I learned about abstinence and purity.

These omissions, I've come to realize, are a result of the evangelical mandate to be "in the world but not of the world," an oft-repeated phrase based on a prayer Jesus uttered the night before his death: "My prayer is not that you take them out of the world but that you protect them from the evil one. They are not of the world, even as I am not of it" (John 17:15–16).[2] In high school, I printed out this verse and taped it to the inside of my locker, so that, every hour, in the hurried exchange of books and binders, I would "write these words on my heart," to use another evangelical phrase. Navigating the decree to be in but not of the world is tricky. A slight shift in semantics, just the exchange of a single preposition, makes all the difference in structuring the minutiae of an evangelical Christian life.

When I conducted research with single evangelical women, I found that it was tricky for them, too. Evangelical women practice their faith through the multiple social contexts they inhabit—the religious contexts of church and Bible study, but also the secular ones, such as work, family and non-Christian friends.[3] Their identities as Christian women are formed across all of these settings.[4] But the dividing line between evangelicalism and the world is fragile, shifting, unstable. The sociologist Courtney Bender refers to the boundary between the secular and the religious as "unfinished" and "overlapping."[5] The two spheres have blurry edges, according to this theoretical approach.[6] Not only that, but each context is mutually dependent on the other for fortification; they feast on each other to nourish their own solidity. "Our secularized societies are haunted by religion," writes the political scientist Olivier Roy.[7] The reverse is also true: religious groups such as evangelicalism are haunted by the secular.

Although the boundary between the secular and the religious may be porous, it still exists. The integrity of these categories and the demarcation between them are very real to evangelicals. Just consider the words of a woman I interviewed, who, in true evangelical fashion, had wandered away from her faith for a few years only to return to God in her twenties. "I wasn't doing any of the secular things during this time. It's not like I was sleeping around or doing drugs. Even though I had walked away, I wasn't going off and living a *secular* life." Another woman, who worked at Wellspring, told me about how she navigated the religious–secular divide: she loved Beyoncé but stopped listening because the music became too sexual; she went to dance clubs, but not ones with a pole; she attended exhibitions at art galleries, but not the "perverted" Alexander McQueen one at The

Met. She forbade her boyfriend to watch *Game of Thrones*, and likened it to hard-core pornography. "Basically, my whole life is church, and I love it being that way," she concluded.

Once women enter the door of evangelicalism, once they convert or reconvert and immerse themselves in the community, they face a new challenge: to be both modern and devout. They must stay involved in the world around them while immersing themselves in their religion. Evangelicalism is meant to impact every area of your life, yet navigating this on the everyday level, on both big and small issues, in a large city, is no easy task. Faith changes how women interact with the city, how they navigate all it offers. "Be my everything," evangelical worshippers sing in church services across the United States and the UK. But making God, and by extension your faith, your "everything" when you dwell in the unbelieving world is complicated.

Carys and I saw each other a lot in the summer of 2016. I called her every time I was in New York and we attended concerts and open-air theater performances together, enjoyed late afternoon walks in Central Park, and regularly exchanged online articles and think pieces about feminism and faith. Gradually, Carys became even more absorbed in the church. But she still carried vestiges of her old life: her job as a nurse, her improv comedy group, and her nonreligious friends. By the time fall came, I could see that Carys was torn. In order to access the intimacy that she so desired, she would have to immerse herself completely. At the same time, this immersion was consuming, and she started to resent the demands placed on her by the constant roster of events and activities at Wellspring.

"I've got some news," Carys announces, when we meet for coffee early one Saturday morning. She's wearing her cowboy boots as usual, this time pairing them with black jeans and a denim shirt, giving the impression she's headed to a country music festival.

I sit down in the empty chair next to her, still sleepy. "Yeah? What is it?"

"I'm thinking of getting ordained! Of becoming a pastor."

"Wow, exciting. Tell me more. When did you decide this?"

"Well, I've been thinking about it for a while actually. I think the church could really do with a working-class feminist pastor. And Wellspring started running sessions for people thinking about ordination, and I've started going—so actually I won't be able to stay long, because there's a meeting that starts at eleven o'clock." She looks down at her phone on the table to check the time. Then she slumps forward, both elbows landing on the table near her double-shot espresso, her hands cupping her face.

"Are you feeling okay?" I ask.

"Yeah, I'm just *exhausted*. You know I'm leading a Roots group, right? On Wednesdays. And my coleader—a man, of course—is absolutely useless. So basically I'm leading it alone. Then, on Mondays I attend another Roots group, not as a leader but as a sort of support to the group. And besides all that, work has been really stressful lately—lots of really gruesome cases. You know how it is . . ." She trails off.

"That's a lot of church," I say carefully. "Do you rest on the weekend?"

"Sundays I usually attend one church service and then help with the prayer team for another service. And last weekend was the Roots weekend away. But yeah, you're right, it *is* a lot of church," she says dryly. "In Christianity, as you know, friendship groups are pretty close. That's the nature of being in a church. You're living in deeper community than you would be if you were outside of church, so people are really in your life. One of the drawbacks, though, is that you can't be very discreet about things."

What kind of things? I ask. Carys reminds me that, ten years prior, it was actually the community that drove her away from Christianity—the same community that now pulls her back.

"I think I told you, back when I was engaged, some people at the church that I attended with my fiancé thought it was their business to become very involved in our relationship. Anyway, that's a whole other story."

"But you don't have to be going to all these things, right? Can't you just say no?"

She shrugs in response. A silent acceptance that this is just what it means to be a Christian within this evangelical community. "I do love my church though," she reminds me.

I think back to the interview I did the day before, with a spritely woman in her early twenties who had converted to Christianity just two years prior. She told me about the difficulty she had relating to her family, now that she was a Christian. For example, when her dad asked about her weekend plans, she'd tell him she attends healing ministry meetings, Bible study group, a homeless outreach ministry, and Sunday services—all of this in addition to working for the church.

"When I tell him all that, it's like his eyes are glazing over and he thinks we're nuts!" She laughed when recounting this exchange with her father. Then she turned serious. "But what he doesn't get is that my faith is everything. It's not a lifestyle; it's my whole *life*."

I look at Carys and I wonder if she is undergoing the same type of metamorphosis. Is her current absorption with Christianity just the zeal of a new convert, or is it something more long-lasting? The reluctance to dive into the community that she had less than a year ago is gone, and in its place is determination. I begin to wonder just how far in she will go.

As I followed Carys, Maddie, Liv, and Jo deeper into their Christian worlds, I also started meeting other evangelical women, such as Aurelie, who sat next to me at a dinner party at Liv's apartment. Tall and gangly, with perfectly crooked front teeth, Aurelie knew everyone there that night. Right before the food was served, she leaned in close and informed me that she had many food intolerances. This meant that her food intake that evening would be limited. She then provided me with a thorough overview of each intolerance and how each one had been discovered.

This is, without a doubt, the person you dread sitting next to at a dinner party. Yet, with Aurelie, the topic felt exciting. She explained in detail the pleasures of cooking, drilling down to the joy that comes with biting into the soft flesh of roasted eggplant. Every word swelled with enthusiasm and optimism. She animated without irritating. And it wasn't just food. Aurelie effervesced about everything: her French name, her newly restored Christian faith, the Chagall retrospective she'd seen over the weekend.

When I arrive at Wellspring to interview her a few weeks later, she is already at the reception desk, waving both arms back and forth like windshield wipers when she sees me approach. Aurelie has spread the news of my research like a contagion and has lined up six interviews for me that afternoon, starting with her. I gulp, grateful for the help but overwhelmed at the prospect.

When we sit down to talk, I don't need to ease Aurelie into the interview process or coax her to tell me things—she divulges freely. Listening to Aurelie speak is comparable to watching someone dance the tango without a partner. She requires little direction or guidance, just some background music to set the rhythm, and she's off, flitting across the dance floor on her own.

Aurelie starts off by saying she grew up in a loosely Christian family, strayed during her teenage years, and came back to Christianity a few years ago via Roots. Prior to her current role as outreach coordinator at Wellspring, she worked as an actress. And she certainly looks the part: chunky silver rings adorn every finger, her hair has been left hair loose and unkempt, and her oversize sweater falls nonchalantly off one shoulder.

"I don't hang out with my friends from my previous life as much anymore, because there were a lot of drugs and that kind of thing going on—well, I never *really* took part in the drugs anyway, but still. When I became a Christian, a few of them would make comments and jokes about it. At first I was able to just laugh it off, but then I just got bored of it. I didn't want to put up with it, so I distanced myself a bit."

My previous life. The phrase reaches out to me and grabs hold. She says it again: "Especially in my previous New York life, I would have been one of those girls in a club, dressed in hardly anything and grinding with lots of guys. And now I see that and I'm like '*Yuck!*'" Aurelie grimaces. Then she quickly transitions to a pensive facial expression. "Have I changed in other ways since coming to church? Well, actually, do you know what? I probably wouldn't seek out some art exhibitions that I would have done previously. A few years ago, when I was in theater, I was surrounded by lots of creatives, and if there were sex exhibitions or something like that, they would have probably loved it and I would have gone and been like 'Oh, this is so interesting.' Now, if a friend suggests one of those exhibitions, I would go along, but I wouldn't go out of my way to seek it out."

It's almost time for my next interview and I need to wrap this one up, but Aurelie seems to have lost track of time. In fact, it seems she's just getting warmed up. "Let's see, other ways I have changed . . ." She pauses to think. Now her eyes are narrowed and she's chewing on the corner of her bottom lip.

"Well, personally I don't like getting so drunk that I feel awful the next day, so I'm pretty good at having my own limit and knowing when I've had enough to drink. I don't get *drunk*, but I do enjoy alcohol. I love getting tipsy and having some drinks with friends. I still run in just a sports bra when it's hot outside—as long as it's not too skimpy. Honestly, I like that Christians aren't what people say we are. We aren't *boring*. We can go out and have fun. We can be normal and live within society."

Aurelie continues. She keeps the conversation light and level, cruising steadily, with the occasional break to catch her breath.

"In terms of my friends *now*, they are all Christian. Which is a little bit upsetting." She rolls her eyes. "So, I have a few friends who are non-Christian, maybe five or six, but no *close* friends who are non-Christian. And I think that is a shame; I want to try to change that. Because right now I work at Wellspring, and people know I am a Christian because of my job. But I'm quitting in a few months, and one of the things I am really excited about when I leave is being a Christian by my life rather than because I work for a church. I want to show people the Christian way of life and faith through my actions."

Suddenly, the door swings open and a group of people burst in the room, papering over their annoyance at being kept waiting with a veneer of Christian friendliness.

"Oh! We must've lost track of time!" Aurelie exclaims, eyes wide in surprise and hands in the air. We gather our belongings and shuffle out of the room.

Later that afternoon, I think more about what Aurelie mentioned at the end of our conversation. Not the part about having all Christian friends—most women I interviewed said the large majority, if not all, of their closest friends were Christians. Fellow believers were the ones with whom they felt the most intimate and meaningful connection; they were the ones who "had [their] heart," in the words of one woman. What struck me was the part about being upset about it. "I think that is a shame," Aurelie had said. "I want to try to change that." I wondered why it was something she felt she ought to change, and how she envisioned going about that. Aurelie wasn't the only one who felt this way. Another woman told me how all of her friends were Christians and then quickly followed it up by adding, "But I'm working on changing that!" As if she were embarrassed, or guilty of something.

Friendship, it seemed, was one of the thorniest aspects of the religious–secular divide. A woman named Alice told me that after she converted, in her early twenties, several of her friends got annoyed with her. "I wouldn't spend as much time with them as I did before, because obviously I got this new community of people and there's only so much you can do." But that wasn't the part that annoyed them. It was her Facebook posts.

"Well, when I first became a Christian, really crazy things happened to me. For example, one night I left a club because I just thought, *This is not fun anymore.* And I hailed a taxi—and I never usually get taxis. Anyway, the taxi driver said that he was a Christian, and he talked to me about his journey with God for about three and a half hours. And then he stopped the taxi and prayed for me. So I posted about it later on Facebook and some of my friends texted me and said, *What are you trying to do? Are you trying to evangelize to us? Stop sharing your views on God; no one wants to hear.*"

Regardless of their annoyance, she went on to say, it was really important to still engage with her non-Christian friends, to "meet them where they are at," whether that meant sharing a glass of wine or going to a nice restaurant. "But still," she added, somewhat remorsefully, "I don't see my non-Christian friends as much as I'd like to."

Evangelical women's insistence on having non-Christian friends arises because of the first part of the evangelical mandate to be "in the world," in order to evangelize. Other verses in the Bible support this practice. For example, Matthew 5:16 states, "In the same way, let your light shine before others, that they may see your good deeds and glorify your Father in heaven." In order to shine your light before others (nonbelievers), you have to actually be around them. And yet, at the same time, evangelicals are taught: "Do not be yoked together with unbelievers. For what do righteousness and wickedness have in common?" (2 Corinthians 6:14). The word *yoke* refers to the wooden beam that fits over two oxen, enabling them to carry a plow or cart. It connotes cooperation and intimacy. While some evangelicals apply this verse only to romantic relationships, others extend it to colleagues, neighbors, and friends. These opposing requirements—to maintain friendships with nonbelievers and yet keep your distance from them—is complicated for single evangelical women. The anthropologist Tanya Luhrmann captures this contradiction perfectly when she describes evangelicals' relationships with nonbelievers as "fraught."[8] It results in them simultaneously desiring non-Christian friends and distancing themselves from them.

I returned to Wellspring a few days after my six-interview stretch and interviewed another seven women—all arranged by Aurelie. From these interviews, I learned more about how single evangelical women navigated the religious–secular divide. As women immerse themselves in the community and learn to become *evangelical* women, they are supported and guided by their fellow evangelicals.

A woman named Tara, in one of the thirteen interviews I completed that frantic week, explained this to me. Tara felt that certain behaviors were not acceptable as a single evangelical woman.

"Recently, I noticed this one girl wearing a loose, sleeveless top. And she was wearing one of those frilly bras with lots of flowers, so, you know, it's not smooth. And the top probably showed most of her bra, and even as a woman you're going to notice that. As a guy, one hundred percent you'll notice it, because it's not even a plain bra . . . it's a beautiful, sexy, in-your-face bra. And I was thinking to myself, I would love to go up to her and say, 'I'm not judging you, but just so you're aware, your bra is kind of on show.'"

Tara then explained the someone had once done this informal version of accountability with her and had suggested she not move her hips when dancing, as her dance moves were "a bit too sexual." And Tara was grateful for the guidance, especially because she had only recently converted to evangelical Christianity.

As Tara's story demonstrates, evangelicals rely on each other, because knowing where the secular world ends and the Christian one begins is not always clear. Marie, another recent convert to evangelicalism, told me a story about being in a prayer group at Thames Gathering Place in London and making a *Harry Potter* reference. The vicar reprimanded her immediately, in front of the entire group: "We need to condemn magic and all these *Harry Potter* books that are coming out."

Marie rolled her eyes when recounting the experience. "And I was like, 'Oh, okay, so no point for Gryffindor then?'" She laughed. "I'd only been going to the church for about six weeks at that point, so I had no idea. It never even occurred to me that watching *Harry Potter* could be a non-Christian activity. Because, for me, that's fantasy. It's a story; it's not real life. It doesn't mean that I believe in magic; it doesn't mean that my faith in God is any less important for me . . . But I understand now that for other people that's very much the case. I think sometimes I find the boundaries of what makes a Christian confusing. I still have no idea, really, where those boundaries are."

Boundaries is a key word, and a woman named Greta later said these were important to maintain. When I arrived at Wellspring one afternoon after a quick lunch, I found Aurelie waiting in the reception area, standing next to a modest-looking woman wearing a navy blue cardigan and pearl earrings. "Katie, this is Greta. She's a good friend of mine," Aurelie said, exposing her crooked front teeth as she smiled. "I booked you guys into the room upstairs for one hour. Enjoy!"

Greta and I settle into a small room on the third floor, and almost immediately the atmosphere feels uneasy. Whereas Aurelie was generous and effusive, Greta is withdrawn and skeptical. She folds her arms across her chest and her eyes rove over me appraisingly. I begin to think that my role as researcher is simply a pretext for what is really going on here, that actually Greta is interviewing *me*, silently and without any questions.

"How did your lifestyle change when you reentered Christianity?" I ask.

"Um . . ." she says, by way of an answer.

"Or did it?"

"Yeah, it did. But, um, I'm trying to think." She pauses. I wait.

"I had a lot more stability because I had regular Bible studies and church on Sundays, so that gave me more of a structure to my week. But my *lifestyle*? I guess, as I became more interested in pursuing God, the other stuff I was involved in wasn't as interesting." Another pause. Words dripping out like water from a corroded faucet.

"I used to party a bit, and that didn't continue, because I just didn't find it interesting anymore. So that was a big change."

Greta tells me she completed a master's in fine art two years ago, where she created illustrations "focused on the Bible." The illustrations by other students at her art academy were dark, filled with scenes of suicide, death, and emptiness. As a result, she felt very alone at the academy and relied heavily on her Christian community. She joined a street ministry, run by Wellspring, which met after class and proselytized ("witnessed") to men and women living on the streets. I ask her what it felt like, going from art class to church ministry events.

"A relief," she says, exhaling. "I think it's definitely wise to maintain boundaries with the world. For example, if something is drawn from a really negative inspiration point, I wouldn't want to expose myself to it, because I am a very visual person. So if it's not positive, then I've really got to—"

She stops herself and I can see she's contemplating the next words she will say, aware that each and every one of them, along with every stutter and every hesitation, is being recorded on my phone, which sits between us on the table like a third person in the room.

"Make wise decisions."

Our time is up, and Greta calls it. I switch the recorder off and slip it into my bag, thanking her for her time. I give her my e-mail address and ask her to please contact me if she thinks of anything else or has any questions, though, as expected, I never hear from Greta again. Three years later, when I run into her at a Wellspring event, she smiles and introduces herself, offering an outstretched hand, as if we've never met.

Haredi, an Orthodox group within Judaism, is known for distancing itself from mainstream society. However, unlike the

Amish, who eschew all trappings of modern life, the *haredim* draw on many aspects of contemporary life, from cell phones and cars to civic responsibilities, making their relationship with the secular a complex negotiation rather than a full dismissal.[9] The majority of Talmudic scholars translate the Hebrew verb *haredim* as "to fear" or "to tremble." The name is based on a verse in Isaiah and is used to describe the relational condition of people to God—they are, literally, the ones who tremble before God.[10] But *haredim* also shares the same etymological root as *harada*, which means "anxiety." The Jewish scholar Samuel Heilman puts forward the argument that nineteenth-century Orthodox Jews changed the meaning of *haredi* in order to indicate their anxiety, their fear about infringement from the secular Jewish state.[11] In this sense, we can understand the Haredi Jews' desire to live separately from the secular world as a response to anxiety; we might even think of them as the "anxious ones."

If they are the anxious ones, then conservative evangelical Christians are the "embattled ones," at least according to Christian Smith. In his 1998 book, *American Evangelicals: Embattled and Thriving*, he states, "American evangelicalism is strong, not because it is shielded against, but because it is—or at least perceives itself to be—embattled with forces that seem to oppose or threaten it." In other words, evangelicals define themselves in opposition to what they are not.[12]

Popular evangelical leaders and pastors frequently utilize this language of separateness. John Piper, a well-known Baptist pastor and author, said in a sermon that Christians are "set apart in the spirit." He went on, "If you are sanctified by the spirit, making you holy, you become increasingly alien in Vancouver, Minneapolis, wherever."[13] During a recent sermon at Wellspring, the speaker listed three "set-apart practices" for believers, which included finding a "set-apart space" to encounter God. And Joel

Osteen, the megachurch pastor from Texas tweeted, "You're not everybody. You're the exception. The scripture says, 'You've been set apart. You are a chosen people.' That's saying, you're not common." There's even a gender-specific series of "set apart" books just for women, including *The Set-Apart Woman*, *Set-Apart Femininity*, and *Set-Apart Motherhood*.[14]

Like all groups and social movements who define themselves by pushing against and disavowing other groups, evangelicals establish their identities *in relation to* others.[15] They emphasize the differences between themselves and the secular world in order to strengthen their own collective evangelical identity, so that they can be identified as different, as embattled, as "set apart."[16]

Indeed, evangelicals also enact a process of differentiation within themselves. When reciting their conversion stories, their testimonies, they divide themselves into two separate people: the unbeliever who suffered in the past, contrasted with the believer who thrives in the present. As well as doing many other things, these narratives establish who they were before and who they are now. The differences are dramatized, the stakes are raised, and the comparison is sharpened, so that the old self becomes unrecognizable to this set-apart, evangelical version.

Donald Trump successfully tapped into this language of exceptionalism and difference to gather support from his evangelical base. In a 2017 commencement address at Liberty University, the conservative evangelical college founded by the late Jerry Falwell, Trump told graduates, "America is a nation of true believers." Later in his speech, he encouraged them to "relish the opportunity to be an outsider."

In all of these ways, boundaries are not only "wise to maintain" but also absolutely essential for evangelical survival. But it isn't enough to say that evangelicals battle with the secular, as

Smith claimed in the late nineties, or that they try to distance themselves from the secular, as their Haredi counterparts do.[17] Evangelicals entreat the secular, are seduced by it. They rely on it to affirm their own religious identity. There is a dynamic synergy between the religious and the secular, and evangelicals imbibe this synergy as they seek to simultaneously be in the world but not of it.[18]

By now, I'm a year and a half into my research and I've met enough women in both the United States and the UK to draw some conclusions. I've learned that being a Christian woman means learning the coordinates of where the world ends and Christianity begins, and then figuring out how to traverse that border. Church leaders and fellow evangelicals guide new converts through this process of habituation, ensuring that they learn what it means to be a believer and pointing out where the boundaries lie. It's a crucial process that I don't remember ever having experienced. Instead, learning how to be a Christian and engage with the secular was integrated seamlessly into my general childhood formation, along with learning multiplication and subtraction, reading and writing.

Sitting in my office, I type up these tidy conclusions. Each stroke of the keyboard elucidates the lifeworld of evangelicals and their complex relationship with the secular, how they deliberately construct and deconstruct boundaries between themselves and the world in order to define themselves as set apart.

And then Carys complicates my theory.

Carys, whom I haven't seen or heard from since the fall. My messages are unreturned and our regular encounters—picnics in the park, exchanging ideas about how to live a feminist life, comedy shows that make us laugh so hard we can't catch our breath—have ceased.

I write to her. *Hey! Where are you? Let's meet up! I miss you!*

Two days later, she responds. She suggests a date a month from now, on account of being so busy. We fix the date in our calendars and agree to meet in the morning, at a café near her apartment.

When that morning arrives, Carys is late. I sit in the café and wait for her, slowly sipping my coffee, watching the one I ordered for her grow cold. Ten minutes pass, and then Carys arrives. We greet each other—a flurry of apologies and reassurances—and then I ask her how she's been.

Carys rattles off all the church activities she's involved with: the Bible study gatherings and Roots groups, the prayer sessions and church services. The events for those interested in ordination. The weekends away.

"Next weekend, one of my friends from Wellspring—Have you met Julie yet?—Well, anyway, she's organized for a group of us from church to go away, on a retreat type thing. Just us and God. To recharge our batteries. I think it'll be fun. We all went to Florida recently; did you see the pictures I posted in Instagram? Here, I'll show you."

She pulls out her phone and navigates over to the photo app, pausing briefly to take a drink of her coffee. I nod as she flicks through the pictures of her and her friends at the beach, candid images of large straw hats, seafood, and sundresses. I'm hearing every word she is saying but feeling that I have lost her. But what have I lost, exactly? My friend or my research participant? The two roles have blurred together, and once again I am split in two.[19] I am both researcher and friend, observer and observed, self and object.[20] I study that object and the attendant feelings of sadness with great interest, mining it for intellectual import, wondering what it says about evangelical Christianity and about ethnography as a method.

Later that evening, Carys and I message each other to say how great it was to catch up, and she invites me to a dinner party at her apartment. *But just so you know*, she adds, the three dots of text message dancing on the screen before the rest arrives, *it'll mostly be other Wellspring people.*

A few months later, exactly one year after we first met, Carys makes a decision. She leaves the sill of the doorway of Christianity, where she's lingered for a while, and steps in.

We're crammed in the corner of a tiny Spanish restaurant with olive oil dripping down our chins when tells me she quit her job as a nurse in order to work as a personal assistant to one of the lead pastors at Wellspring. "It's a huge pay cut, but it feels like the right thing to do, feels like what God wants me to do."

"What about ordination?"

"Yeah, I'm still considering that, but this will give me good experience in the meantime."

"What about wanting to change the church, to make it more equitable for working-class feminist women?"

"That's still my plan. And anyway, I think the best change comes from the inside."

I want to rouse her awake and tell her she's selling out by assisting a pastor instead of being one. I want to say that she's lost her edge, that this is a big mistake. But the researcher in me takes over and holds me back.

As Carys takes a big bite of *pan con tomate*, I think about what her non-Christian friends must make of this transformation, what her family members and coworkers think when they look at this new version of the person they used to know. I wonder if they take any notice when she bows out of conversations about sex and politely declines the third round of after-work drinks, without giving an explanation. If they realize she's self-censoring, that her speech is swept clean of profanities now. And if they, too, feel that they've lost her.

Carys's transformation demonstrates how the organization of one's life along secular and religious lines can be rewritten again and again. On the one hand, this restructuring extended naturally from her immersion in the evangelical community. And she chose to invest time and energy into evangelical relationships because these were the people who nourished her fledgling faith.

Looked at another way, Carys was simply obeying the Bible. She was following the mandate to not be "yoked" together with an unbelieving world.

But a third explanation for Carys's transformation is that her desires actually changed. No one made her attend so many church activities or quit her job. She didn't consciously wrest herself away from her non-Christian friends, rejecting their invitations in order to follow a biblical mandate or because she felt compelled to fulfill church obligations. Instead, her interest in spending time with them simply diminished.

Similarly, when I censored *The Vagina Monologues* in front of an audience of wide-eyed evangelical women, no one *made* me do it. There was no obligation or rule, no obvious Bible verse to pinpoint. Sure, a certain amount of social pressure compelled me to edit, out of fear of what my friends would say (or think), just as social pressure induced Carys to attend so many church events. But I also *wanted* a cleaner version of the book. Back then, even when I read the book alone, I edited, skipping over every curse word and blatant reference to sex, enjoying the essays on my own, Christian terms. Similarly, Carys wanted to prioritize the Christian world over the secular one. She behaved in accordance with her desires, not in spite of them. I remember an interview with one of Aurelie's friends. "Very slowly, my appetites changed," she had said. "When I was in the world, I just lived for the week-end, I just lived for the next guy, and was trying to fill that void. It's not like that anymore."

Once fully integrated into the faith, many evangelical women cannot even disambiguate their own desires from Christian teachings. For example, a few women I met told me they didn't drink alcohol, and when I asked why, they had trouble answering. They couldn't tease out whether it was because of their faith or not. Jo explained that she didn't drink because she saw a friend get alcohol poisoning at age eighteen. Then she pivoted and said that she didn't drink because alcoholism ran in her family. Finally, she admitted that she didn't actually know whether sobriety was a "religious choice" or not. Another woman, in London, told me she stayed away from dance clubs and bars, though she couldn't be sure whether this was because of her Christian faith or her dislike for loud places.

There is a Bible verse instructing believers, "Do not be conformed to this world but be transformed by the renewing of your mind" (Romans 12:2). Transformation—true transformation of the type evangelicals seek wholeheartedly—requires pursuance and submission, in equal measure. Women invest in their faith by diligently attending church events, activities, and worship services. They study the Bible and pray regularly. They *practice* their religion. And then they let go. They let God transform their interior lives, shifting their inclinations and desires. These changes testify to their commitment to the faith while also demonstrating how powerful God truly is.[21]

Studies of other religious women report a similar phenomenon. In her book about Hasidic Jewish women in Brooklyn, Ayala Fader noted, "Women told me and their daughters that understanding and desire develop out of religious practice, not vice versa."[22] And Saba Mahmood's research on Muslim women

in Egypt reveals the same thing: women in the mosque movement train themselves to be pious, and their desires spring from
ongoing acts of submission and piety.[23] If, as feminists have
argued for decades, we can manipulate desire in such a way as
to subvert it, to not want what we are supposed to want within
a patriarchal society, then surely evangelical women can do the
same. With time and regular religious practice, they, too, can
desire different things.

But there is still more to this process of transformed appetites. On its own, this analysis risks privileging the self as an
agent and dismissing the role of the supernatural when evangelicals' religious practices occur within a deeply intimate relationship with the divine.[24] A more comprehensive explanation for
why evangelical women's appetites change is that, in concert with
human diligence, God bends believers' inclinations in such a way
as to align them with "his" teachings. After all, why not take
evangelical women's word for it when they say that God changed
them?

The relationship that believers hold with the secular world also
manifests itself physically. Think about Greta, a woman who created art while listening to worship music. She described the
"relief" that flooded her body when she moved from her art
college to her Wellspring ministry group every Monday evening, a relief that resurfaced even as she spoke about it during
our interview, causing her shoulders to soften. In her exhala-
tion, relief itself became an affective indicator of navigating the
religious–secular divide. Or consider Carys and the mixture of
exhaustion that stained her eyes red and the contented breaths
that flowed in and out, evidence of her immersion into the Christian world. The body serves as a language of its own, producing
"body phrases" that articulate the spiritual journey in a gram-
mar that words fail to capture.[25]

"Religion begins—and ends—with bodies," affirmed the sociologist Thomas Tweed.[26] Tracing the body's movements, enactments, and practices, especially at points where words fail, provides another means of deconstructing religion. These bodily affects expose a deeper understanding of evangelical Christianity and its permutations through space and time.[27] It allows us to study the body as a vehicle that crosses the religious–secular divide.

"There's New York life and then Christian life, you know? You have so much to do in New York, and then you have so much going on at church, and together it all becomes so busy," an evangelical woman named Andrea told me as we walked in a park near Wellspring one wintry afternoon. She went on to say how she had drifted away from her non-Christian friends from college.

"And I'm trying to see them as much as I can, but I can never make most of the gatherings where they all meet up."

"When did you last see them?" I ask.

"About a month ago, we had dinner at a friend's house. Because, you know, I think it's really important to still be normal. To show non-Christians that we can be normal and still live within society."

I heard the word *normal* often from evangelicals, and I smiled to myself every time it arose. It was like a private joke between two versions of myself: the past me and the present one, with their differing definitions of "normal." I chuckled at how much the word had morphed over time. In part, evangelicals' desire for normalcy is born of the desire for social acceptance, to fit in and prevent social ostracism. In part, though, the pursuit springs from the first part of the requirement to be *in* the world but not *of* the world. Part of being *in* the world means remaining intelligible to unbelievers, so as to reach them. After all, in order to convert the souls of unbelievers, you must remain connected to the world. Otherwise, there is no saving to be done. The mission statement of the Christian magazine *Relevant*, which targets twenty- and thirtysomethings, says, "Christians can't be complacent living in a Christian bubble and never engaging the world they live in. We want to live the way Jesus did. Through relationship and love, the world was changed."

But pursuing normalcy (or relevance), I thought to myself, as I watched Carys drift further and further into evangelicalism, was a meaningless contradiction. Meaningless because it stood in direct opposition to the other evangelical pursuit of maintaining boundaries with the world. After all, you cannot be both "normal" according to society's standards *and* set apart. To be relatable to nonbelievers is antithetical to the encasement involved with this demanding form of religion. The contradiction means that evangelical women strain for normal while clutching at the devout. Their arms stretch out across the two extremes, causing discomfort.

And yet, even after nearly two years of reimmersing myself in the evangelical Christian world, I still hadn't yet touched on the one area where normalcy was barred, where the topography of the religious–secular divide was most treacherous, where I myself had collapsed with fatigue, and where evangelicals have earned a famous reputation for weirdness.

Sex.

4

PURITY CULTURE

Cleanse me with hyssop, and I will be clean;
wash me, and I will be whiter than snow.

—Psalms 51:7

It's nine o'clock on a Monday morning and I'm settled in a busy café, talking about sex. The sun streams through the floor-length windows, and the sounds of milk steaming and clattering plates hum in the background. Liv, seated next to me on a wicker chair, is telling me her thoughts about her sexuality as a thirty-five-year-old single Christian woman.

As a lifelong Christian, Liv was raised in sexual purity culture. We bond as we recall our purity educations—decades' worth of books and sermons teaching us that our purity determined our worth—and the wounds left by these messages. We had both heard the analogy that our sexuality was like a flower: pluck too many petals off and you are left with just the stem. We both wore purity rings during our teen years, which we both took off sometime in our midtwenties. We both signed pledges that we would remain virgins until marriage. But unlike me, Liv had stayed the course, and, by her own definition, remained a virgin.

As we remembered, we rolled our eyes and laughed in a bid for those years to be banished far away from us, despite our feeling that they were so very near.

Liv drew in a deep breath. "Actually, I like owning my story and the fact that it doesn't follow the typical Christian pattern."

Before I can ask what she means, Liv continues.

"Christians always say, 'If you don't have sex before you're married, and you do this and you do that, then you will have a perfect life.' To that I say, 'Well, I've followed all the rules and I'm still single. And I'm actually okay. I'm not *angry* single; I'm doing amazing things! But don't try and preach that to me.'"

I nod in agreement, remembering the if/then promises that evangelical leaders peddle: if you wait, then you'll have a great marriage; if you abstain, then you'll have amazing sex later; if you follow the rules, then your life will be blessed.

"Because the truth is, I'm single and I've never had sex, but I feel I am a sexual being and I want to be open and honest about that. And it's really hard to get engagement with other Christians on that level."

I nod again.

"Let me give you an example." Liv places her tiny hands on my crossed legs and leans in close, eager to elaborate her point.

"So, I brought up vibrators with a group of Christian friends at dinner last week, and all but one of them went silent. They wouldn't even talk about it! And yet it would be normal for me to wake up and get a text from a non-Christian friend saying, *Hooked up with this hot guy last night. We tried anal. It was fun.* Or something like that. Why can't I get that kind of honesty with my Christian friends? I just hate that there is so much secrecy around sex!" Liv throws her hands up in the air for emphasis.

Like all the evangelical women I spoke to before and after her, Liv felt torn between two approaches to sex: the secular version that encourages sexual liberation and urges women to "have sex like a man," and the Christian version that calls for women's purity.[1] She grappled with how to experience herself as a sexual being within a religious-social structure that constrained the way she expressed that sexuality, especially while living in a large, metropolitan city.

A few months after this conversation, Liv would meet a junior pastor at church and they would start dating. In time, they would fall in love and consider marriage. She and I would continue to meet and talk about sex, and her straddling of two worlds, two approaches to sex, would intensify. In time, Liv's commitment to abstinence would be put to the test. But all of that came later. On that Monday morning in 2017, Liv remained frustrated yet a bit hopeful; searching but, most of all, committed.

Although sexual abstinence has proliferated in other religious and nonreligious settings, its largest proponents have been evangelical Christians.[2] However, now that Christianity is on the decline in the United States, and even more so in the UK, the question arises as to whether religious leaders can maintain such tight strictures around sexuality at a time when membership is waning.[3] For now, at least, the evangelical mandate to remain sexually pure before marriage shows no signs of abating.

Evangelical abstinence messages have evolved over the years, keeping pace with changes in mainstream dating culture that have proliferated in this era of speed dating, dating apps, and supper clubs where friends set up friends. And just like singles everywhere, the evangelical women I met are sampling from the feast that is modern dating culture.

Not too long ago, a new Christian dating app launched in the UK. The app, called Salt, in reference to the New Testament's exhortation for Christians to be the "salt and light" of the world, features a stylish interface and the same swiping mechanism as Tinder or Bumble. Similarly, in the United States, online dating sites such as Christian Mingle or Christian Connection, and the app United Young, are popular options for Christians searching for love.

The Christian dating scene has also experienced other, more subtle changes in recent years. In contrast to the late 1990s and early 2000s, when I was a young evangelical, women are no longer choosing "courtship" over dating, and going out for drinks with a guy you meet at Bible study is an acceptable first date activity. Of course, some aspects of the evangelical approach to sex and dating have stayed the same. Women today make small and sometimes large exceptions when it comes to sexual abstinence, just as my friends and I did during our years in purity culture. Their exceptions can include intense making out, dry humping, showering naked with a boyfriend, and even playing with sex toys, while still abstaining from intercourse.

In the United States, these Christian exceptions even have names and vary according to region. A woman I met in Seattle practiced JOP (just one pump) while another in Georgia favored JTT (just the tip). One evangelical woman I met told me that she and her boyfriend made the decision to only have sex on "special occasions." Pressed to define exactly what constituted such events, she replied, "You know, like birthdays." Another woman said that she and her boyfriend experimented with sex toys, such as dildos, but never had intercourse. "We're waiting for marriage," she reported proudly. As we saw earlier, women engage in a constant negotiation between the religious and the secular worlds that they simultaneously inhabit. Nowhere does this negotiation seem more pronounced, or thorny, than in the realm of romance.

What has also stayed the same is that the burden of sexual purity still falls heaviest on women.[4] The recent surge of writing by formerly evangelical women who feel traumatized by purity culture testifies to the way in which evangelical abstinence messages disproportionately target girls and women.[5] Soon after my sex talk with Liv, I stopped by the Wellspring bookstore to inspect the sexual purity literature they had in stock. Two books written for women by modern-day purity crusader Carrie Lloyd sat on a table near the front. There were other books written for both men and women, but I couldn't find a single purity book written exclusively for men.

At Bethel Church in California and Thames Gathering in London, I conducted the same informal bookstore surveys and found the same thing: most of the books and manuals on sexual abstinence were written for women. During a more recent search at Bethel, however, I found a series of books written under the aegis of their nonprofit organization, Moral Revolution, a group that calls itself "a company of radicals helping to define healthy sexuality." Moral Transformation's content is heavily gendered. The group provides separate "purity plans" for men and women in the form of YouTube videos, and they produced a six-week course called "Let's Talk About It: Sexuality," aimed at separate male and female audiences.

The gendered nature of these purity messages relies on hackneyed tropes from purity culture that equate men's purity with a show of strength and women's purity with virtue. In a blog post titled "Six Ways to Catch the Man of God You've Been Waiting For," a male pastor encourages girls to "be beautiful, but not sexy" as they "wait for Prince Charming." He goes on: "Contrary to popular opinion, dressing sexy says, 'I've got nothing else going on.'"[6] In another post, a female pastor encourages girls to wait for "the one" and not to lose hope. As of 2021, there aren't any posts detailing how men should dress or behave in the premarital period of their lives.

The Christian fixation with sex dates back to early church history. In the late fourth and early fifth centuries, Saint Augustine proclaimed that sexual desire was a sin, arguing that lust caused Adam and Eve's downfall in the Garden of Eden.[7] This conflation of sex with sin, even within marriage, influenced early Christian teachings, and it wasn't until 2021, when sexuality became a battleground issue during the Reformation, that Martin Luther rejected Augustine's idea of sex as sinful.

During the Enlightenment, even as Protestant leaders continued to teach that sex outside of marriage was sinful, people started to view it as more recreational, as something that could be liberated from the confines of marriage. This mentality toward sex was also prevalent in the Victorian era, even though that age has long been fabled to represent the epitome of sexual prudery. It was during this period that sex became a legitimate area of study.[8] About the Victorians, the French philosopher Michel Foucault wrote, "Is sex hidden from us, concealed by a new sense of decency, kept under a bushel by the grim necessities of bourgeois society? On the contrary, it shines forth; it is incandescent."[9]

Upon close examination we can see a few striking similarities between how Victorians treated sex and the way in which evangelicals approach it today. Now, as then, Christian leaders exhort premarital abstinence. And now, as then, Christians themselves do not exactly repress their sexuality; instead, they are absorbed by it. Over the past forty years, American evangelicals' relentless preoccupation with abstinence, channeled through policies, political agendas, church sermons, and books, testifies to this fixation.

In the 1970s, evangelical leaders in the United States decided to take a firm religious stance on abstinence in response to the sexual revolution tearing through mainstream society. But it wasn't until the 1990s that a shift from abstinence to *purity* occurred. Silver Ring Thing, a prominent American purity campaign that also operates a branch in the UK, was at the forefront of this change. Rather than abstinence alone, purity entails both physical and mental sexual conduct that aligns with what evangelicals believe is God's plan for marriage. As author and purity campaigner Dannah Gresh states, "You can abstain from sex and not be pure, I think. Purity is more all-encompassing. It's about your thought life. It's about your emotional life. It's about everything."[10] Indeed, the women I met spoke about mental purity almost as often as they did sexual purity—such as when one earnest young woman who worked for Wellspring told me she refused to watch *Orange Is the New Black* "because it's just too sexual." As Caitlin Zick of Bethel explains, "God's design is to be bonded, to be drawn intimately into our covenant marriage."[11]

In the 1990s, purity teachings mushroomed into a full-blown purity culture, with events, balls, films, books, and campaigns that urged boys and girls to pledge their commitment to chastity. Songs such as "Wait for Me," by Rebecca St. James, resounded from Christian radio stations, books such as *Passion and Purity* flew off the shelves of Christian bookstores, and girls slipped purity rings on their fingers. In 1997, Joshua Harris's *I Kissed Dating Goodbye* sold over a million copies, persuading a generation of young evangelicals to abstain from kissing until marriage and to adopt courtship instead of dating.[12]

Purity culture spread internationally during this same period. I met women from Australia, Canada, Hong Kong, Ireland, and

South Africa who all reported growing up with purity culture inside their evangelical churches. At a dinner party in London one night, a woman named Cheryl told me that her local evangelical church in Singapore had also promoted premarital purity. Then she ran upstairs and came back down with a small, square pillow she had made as a teenager. Flipping it around in a grand, revelatory gesture, she shoved it near my face. On it she had sewn a pair of white underpants dotted with tiny cherry decals. Across the top of the pillow she'd embroidered the words "Pure of Heart." Red velvet hearts and gold glitter floated around the edges.

These examples of purity culture's global reach are not merely anecdotal. Several purity campaigns aimed to spread the message of purity internationally. True Love Waits (TLW), a campaign run by Lifeway Christian Resources (the publishing arm of the Southern Baptist Convention, headquartered in Nashville), stood at the vanguard of the American purity movement. Recently rebranded as the True Love Project, the original TLW campaign started in 1987. In 1994, TLW expanded to such countries as Argentina, Australia, and New Zealand, holding summits at which evangelical youth pledged to stay pure until marriage. But it wasn't until 2004 that TLW really went global. As part of a $29 million program called Defining the Moment, created and bankrolled by Lifeway Christian Resources, TLW expanded to Kenya, Uganda, and seven other sub-Saharan African countries.[13]

Purity culture has also infiltrated American politics. The religious right has been at the forefront of endorsing abstinence-only education.[14] A confluence of factors accounted for increased attention to abstinence under Ronald Reagan's presidency, most notably the emergence of HIV/AIDS and the subsequent governmental pushes for condom use. During the late 1980s and early 1990s, successive administrations increased funding for religiously affiliated abstinence programs. In 2000, President George W. Bush substantially increased funding for avowedly faith-based organizations that advocate abstinence.[15] Then, from 2001 to 2005, federal funding doubled to $170 million.[16] In 2003, also under Bush's administration, abstinence education expanded to developing and middle-income countries such as South Africa, under the covering of the President's Emergency Plan for AIDS Relief, which set limits on contraceptive distribution.[17] This, combined with the expansion of evangelical purity organizations such as TLW to developing countries, meant that two concurrent abstinence-endorsing projects emanated from the United States.

President Obama put an end to abstinence-only education in 2010 and created the Teen Pregnancy Prevention Program, a comprehensive sex education agenda. Eight years later, however, President Trump overturned Obama's program and implemented the sexual risk avoidance education (SRAE) scheme under Title V. In combination with another bill passed by Congress, there was $110 million dedicated to the SRAE program, which was developed by Valerie Huber, the president of the nonprofit organization Ascend (formerly called the National Abstinence Education Association). Interestingly, Trump also appointed Huber as the lead for Title X funding, which provides family planning funds to organizations. Critics have referred to SRAE as a rebranding of abstinence-only education, and it's easy to see why. According to the Administration for Children and Families, "The purpose of the [program] is to fund projects to implement sexual risk avoidance education that teaches participants how to voluntarily refrain from nonmarital sexual activity." Despite data demonstrating a positive correlation between abstinence-only sex education and teen pregnancy, religious conservatives continue to advocate for the abstinence model.[18]

In the UK, the situation is markedly different. Although non-profit organizations such as Silver Ring Thing and Romance Academy seek to educate youth on sexuality and "the sanctity of marriage," abstinence-only education has not infiltrated the public education system.[19] Relationship and sex education is now compulsory in all English primary and secondary schools. The guidelines on how to implement sex education teachings, which include teaching on LGBTQ identities and safe sex, do make provisions for religious schools to adapt the curriculum as needed. And Church of England schools intend to do just that. On the official Church of England website, Nigel Genders, the church's education officer writes, "In Church of England schools, [relationship and sex education] will be rooted in the teachings of the Church, including the importance of trust, loyalty, fidelity and the Christian understanding of marriage as the context for sexual relationships, as well as the understanding of abstinence and celibacy as positive life choices."[20]

The entrenchment of premarital abstinence in evangelical culture also differs between the United States and the UK, as Carrie Lloyd affirmed. Writing from her home in California, she told me in an e-mail, "I'm aware, after being a pastor here for many years now, how much shame and damage the purity movement in America has brought many people. I didn't get to experience that in the UK growing up." Even if purity culture never reached full fruition in the UK, many aspects of it—including the books, teachings, and pressure to be pure—certainly made their way across the pond, as many of the British women I spoke to made clear.

I had my first brush with purity culture when I was only ten years old. My mom announced that we would start a special mother-daughter time every week, which would be focused around reading the book *Preparing for Adolescence*, by Dr. James Dobson. Dobson is a well-known evangelical author and psychologist who, in 1997, founded Focus on the Family, a politically conservative, antiabortion Christian organization based in Colorado Springs, Colorado. Every Wednesday night, I slipped into my parents' room, locked the door to keep my younger sister out, and read a chapter from Dobson's book with my mom. By week 3, we arrived at the chapter on sex, where Dobson writes, "My strongest advice is for you to decide *right now* to save your body for the one who will eventually be your marriage partner. If you don't control this desire you will later wish that you had."[21] After this is a section break, and the next paragraph is headed with the boldface subtitle "Venereal Disease."

Three years later, on the eve of my graduation from middle school, my parents presented me with my purity ring. The delicate yellow gold ring shone in its velvet box, a tiny diamond sparkling in the center of the band. I slipped it on my left ring finger as my parents instructed me to do and nodded my head as they told me this ring symbolized my purity commitment not only to God but also to my future husband, even though, at the time, I didn't really even understand what sex was.

Purity rings may not have gained as much traction in the UK, but the teaching that women ought to remain sexually abstinent until marriage certainly did. All the London-based women I met knew that their church leaders wanted them to remain pure before marriage, yet few could recall exactly *how* they knew this. Single women in both countries knew that the ideal Christian woman, as detailed in the next chapter, waited for marriage to have sex. Many believed that God desired them to guard their minds, hearts, and bodies from premarital sex, and some believed the Bible explicitly commands purity. Some believed in modesty, checking before they went out that their skirt wasn't too short or their blouse too transparent, so as not to cause men to "stumble" in lust. They all somehow knew that same-sex attraction and homosexuality were strictly forbidden—so forbidden, in fact, that in all the years I have conducted research, not one woman has ever mentioned same-sex attraction.

Many evangelical women I met complained that their church leaders never really addressed sex. But at least, the women conceded, the pastors did speak about dating. The Wellspring annual church retreat a few years back included an evening event called Meet My Friend, where everyone brought a friend in the hopes of meeting someone new. Jo, who attended that year, told me drily that the room was packed with hopeful young evangelical women—and very few men. The following year, Wellspring initiated a three-week dating course to teach people how to "date well," though they still shied away from the topic of sex. Currently, in addition to the dating course, the church runs a two-week program called The Single Life, aimed primarily at "people who want to explore finding fulfillment in single living."

A few months into my research, I noticed that the women were right: pastors rarely mentioned sex or purity during Sunday services. This led Liv to fume, "No one is talking about it!" So where did these women receive instruction on sexuality? To find out, I needed to track down purity crusader, writer, and pastor Carrie Lloyd.

Originally from Britain, Carrie moved out to California several years ago to take up a job as a pastor at Bethel Church. The author of two purity books, *The Virgin Monologues* and *Prude*, which are widely read by single Christian women, she is considered the definitive source on modern evangelical women's sexuality. One magazine called her the "Christian Carrie Bradshaw," referring to the lead character in *Sex and the City*. In addition to her books, Carrie Lloyd writes a blog called *Her Glass Slipper: The Trials and Tribulations of Christian Dating* and hosts a podcast called *Carrie On.* The Christian women I met spoke of her adoringly, their respect palpable, as if she was the cool older sister they aspired to be someday.

Carrie grew up as a pastor's daughter in the south of England, but she left the faith in her late teens, soon after her father's sudden death. Those were wild years, according to her. She slid from Christian to atheist, from abstaining from sex to having sex, and from attending Sunday school to attending drug-fueled parties. After several years of this lifestyle, she came back to God and to Christianity. "I decided to hang up my Agent Provocateur negligees," she writes. A self-declared "neo-virgin," Carrie began teaching other women how to recommit to sexual purity.

In both of her books, Carrie writes tantalizingly about orgasms, porn addiction, and how much she enjoyed sex—and how good she was at it—before she began to practice purity. (When I spoke to her on the phone, she said that her Christian publishers edited her original manuscript for what they considered vulgarity.) Having been sexually active and then returning to purity, Carrie reported that abstinence brought true freedom. Rather than feeling constrained by abstinence, Carrie said, "I'm too free, too aware of what is good for me, too in touch with God's heart to want to purposefully hurt it."[22]

Christian teachers often use language of liberation and freedom to encourage evangelicals to practice purity. This line of thinking proposes that abstinence offers freedom from the worries of dating and sex, as you can leave your love life up to God.[23] But not all evangelical women view purity as liberating, of that I was certain. My own experience of it, especially as I grew older, was of dogmatic rules that unfairly applied to girls. In a *Guardian* article entitled "True Love Waits? The Story of the Purity

Ring and Feeling Like I Didn't Have a Choice," author Amy Deneson recalls the pressure and coercion she felt to remain pure as a young American evangelical. How could sexual purity be simultaneously freeing, as Carrie declared, *and* constraining? I decided it was time to start asking evangelical women uncomfortable questions about sex.

I started with Jo. By now, she'd left her job at the teen group home and taken up a position with Wellspring's youth ministry. We met at a park near her apartment one afternoon, and, following a brief stroll, settled on a bench where we could watch passersby. Forthright and feisty, Jo admitted to me that it was very difficult to reconcile her commitment to purity with her sexual urges.

"There are days of the month that I can barely go outside," she stated drily. I studied Jo as she spoke, trying to discern if she was being serious. She created a visor with her hand, shielding her pale face from the sun. Thick strips of platinum blond highlights ran through her frizzy brown hair, lighting up her face like a halo.

At a church retreat a few months before, Jo said, she'd taken it upon herself to educate two twentysomething Christian men about women's sexuality. All purportedly virgins and trying to stay that way, the three of them sat around the dining hall after dinner, discussing their faith and sexuality. Suddenly, one of the boys interjected, "Well, it's easier for girls to stay pure because you aren't as visual as guys are. It's much harder for us."

Tired of having her sexual desires discounted, Jo shot back, "I'm just going to interrupt you here for a second, because I think it's really important for you to know that women definitely have sexual feelings."

The two men fell silent, and Jo continued.

"I mean, I'm not trying to be awkward, but sometimes I'm a nasty horndog and I would fucking jump on anything. I am just being honest."

The other man, a friend of the first, wrinkled his face in disgust. "You're making me never want to get married!"

At this, Jo's small round eyes began to sparkle, something that happened whenever she sensed a feminist fight approaching.

"I hope you never do get fucking married, until you can sort out your piss-poor attitude toward women and sexuality!"

"Hey, that's really harsh," argued the first man, a red sweep of agitation flowering across his cheeks.

Jo pressed on, undeterred. "I think it's harsher to relegate half the population of the planet to being nonsexual because *you* don't fucking like it!"

The boys stood up abruptly and cleared their plates, leaving Jo alone in the empty dining hall.

Hearing a twenty-nine-year-old virgin and church employee use the word *horndog* to describe her sexuality made me giggle. I admired Jo's straightforwardness and her ability to speak openly about her sexual desires, even as she committed herself to premarital purity. Rather than embracing purity lock, stock, and barrel, Jo had found a way to reconcile her sexuality with her Christian beliefs about sex.

As we sat in the weakening sunshine, Jo squinted and told me how angry it made her that her sexuality was ignored. That single women were oversexualized *and* undersexualized simultaneously in the church.

I asked if she had dated much and she told me she'd had one long-term relationship with a non-Christian guy that ended a few years ago. She trailed off and became very quiet. I started to ask more, but before I could, she cut me off. "Hey, I've got to run! I'm late for worship team practice."

At the time, this abrupt ending seemed natural, unremark-able. It's only years later that I recognize these conversational detours and body phrases for what they are. The stiffening of a torso, eyes that shift downward, a clenched jaw—the sudden announcement that it's time to go . . . These are clues that one misses when one is not looking for something, when you don't even know there is something to find, or when a person has a secret buried so deeply within them that *they* aren't even con-scious yet that it's there.

I walked with Jo over toward the main road and waited for her bus to arrive. Soon, a long accordion-like bus barreled around the corner and Jo waved her arm in the air, signaling for the driver to stop. As we hugged good-bye, Jo suggested I speak with her friend Naomi, from London, whom she met years ago dur-ing a visit to Thames Gathering Place. "She *does* have sex, and is still a committed Christian, so it'd be interesting for you to hear what she has to say." With that she was off, a mischievous grin spreading across her face as she climbed onto the bus.

The next time I'm in London, I pay Naomi a visit. Naomi is dignified, circumspect, polite. The child of Jamaican parents, she grew up in London, attending African Pentecostal churches. In her early twenties she joined Thames Gathering Place, at the suggestion of a friend from university, and had been there for a decade. As she speaks, she gestures with her hands so that her diamond engagement ring flashes back and forth in front of my eyes, hypnotizing me. We sit in the living room of her elegant town house in North London, sipping Earl Grey tea from bone china mugs, and I start to wonder how I am going to broach the topic of sex with a complete stranger.

I feel a familiar tightening of my chest as I subtly angle the conversation from Jo to Naomi's upcoming wedding to church.

After several minutes of small talk, I spot a *Magic Mike* DVD resting on a bookshelf and interrupt Naomi to ask if it's hers.

"Oh yes!" she gushes. "I love *Magic Mike*, and I love Channing Tatum. I would watch it every week if I could." The transition from speaking about Naomi's role on the church worship team to Channing Tatum stripping feels jarring, but I decide to go with it. She continues, "And I must say, that's something I really can't stand. I just hate how the church deals with sex."

Relieved that the topic had arisen without me even having to ask, I encourage her to tell me more.

"So, the message I received at church was just basically 'Close your legs.' Essentially, don't do it. It's always a *'Don't, don't, don't* do it.' And it's dangerous, because the message is don't do it, because if you wait, there's a reward waiting for you, which is that the sex after marriage will be very good."

I tell Naomi that I received similar messages growing up in American evangelicalism, noticing that the more I share, the more she reciprocates by opening up.

"A few years ago, I decided I only want to have sex with people I'm in love with. And that was my other issue with the church. I felt like the church gave me two options: either you close your legs or you sleep with everyone. The world sleeps with everyone; we don't sleep with anyone, they'd say. And then I met James, and I waited for about five or six months to have sex with him."

In her first relationship, Naomi had also had sex, she says, but back then, it caused her to feel tremendous shame.

"I used to cry after sex all the time, because of the guilt that I felt. Not feeling guilty about what I was actually doing, but feeling guilty about what I'd heard, that somehow I was going to be punished. As if I'd done something bad. And it was really stressful, because it didn't *feel* bad. Nothing bad was actually happening in my reality, but I was told that it was bad. I was very, very confused."

I ask her if she ever receives criticism at church for this choice, especially given her position on the worship team.

"Well, there was this one time we had a sex talk at Thames Gathering, and afterwards I went down to the front to get prayer for something. A lady started praying for God to 'revirginize' me and 'clothe me in white,' which was a bit weird."

Naomi grimaces and pulls her mug of tea closer so that it rests on her chest. Then another memory rears its head.

"And there was this other time . . . I mentioned to a girl on the worship team that I have sex and she said, 'Oh! We need to have a conversation about this!' I said, 'No we don't. This is the choice I've made and I'm happy with it. You don't need to save my soul. I'm fine.' I never did end up talking to her, and I just laughed it off."

Naomi tells me that a few friends warned her to keep her views on sex quiet when church leaders were around, "just in case." I marvel at how lighthearted she seems as she recounts these experiences. She'd found a way to have sex while still remaining embedded in the evangelical community. And as she had told her worried friend at Thames Gathering, she was happy with her choice. An hour later, as we neared the end of our conversation, I tossed in a question that I asked nearly every Christian woman.

"How comfortable would you say you are with your stance on sex, on a scale from one to ten, with one being 'Very uncomfortable' and ten being 'Very comfortable'?"

Naomi considers my question, absentmindedly sliding her engagement ring up and down her finger.

"You know," she starts, "funnily enough, I think I would say five . . . Because I don't think I can ever say that it's fully right, but at the same time I don't think I can say it's fully wrong. And I think I'll always respect someone who is able to stay abstinent before marriage."

Even Naomi, who appeared so self-assured and confident in her sexuality, so sure that the church had it wrong when it came to sex, reflected a perfect ambivalence. During our entire two-hour conversation, I thought that I was observing a woman unburdened by the church's mandate to remain pure, but in reality, Naomi—just like me, just like the other women I had met—had internalized these teachings, and despite her rationalizations to the contrary, they remained.

In an attempt to understand the Christian fixation with sex and purity, some scholars propose that sex serves as a crucial boundary for evangelicalism's relationship with secular culture. In the general American population, only 3 percent of women aged twenty-five to twenty nine report being virgins (defined as having never had intercourse), and the number drops to less than 2 percent for women aged thirty to thirty-four, which is the age of most evangelical women that I met.[24] It makes sense, therefore, that evangelicals would seize upon sex, as it provides them with a strong line of demarcation, given how rare it is for women in their twenties and thirties to remain virgins.[25] Certainly, Christianity isn't the only religion or cultural group to fortify its collective identity by promoting abstinence before marriage, yet it remains the most politically vocal in the United States.[26]

Feminists provide a more cynical explanation for the endurance of Christian purity teachings. They argue that evangelical Christianity's focus on female purity reflects the sexism that pervades churches. Feminist Jessica Valenti put forth this idea in *The Purity Myth*, a searing account of how evangelical purity norms harm women. Five years ago, my evangelical cousin handed me this book at a family gathering. "Read this," she instructed me in a hushed tone, as she pressed the book firmly into my hands. It wasn't until Maddie mentioned it again, while I was doing my research, that I revisited the book in earnest and found the following passage: "There's no room in the virginity movement's analysis for the idea that young women may *want* to be sexy, to have sex, or to express themselves in ways that don't include wearing ankle-length skirts and finding husbands." Valenti is correct that the purity movement doesn't create space for women's sexuality. (As Jo once asked, "Where do I *put* my sexuality, if I'm not having sex?") On the other hand, Valenti's argument that purity culture encourages evangelical women to be "blank slates" clashes with my observations of how evangelical women navigate their sexuality.[27]

Moreover, as Naomi mentioned, there are some convincing reasons to abstain. The promise—or at least the hope—of a strong marriage with a beautiful sex life entices many evangelical women to hold out for marriage. Evangelical sex manuals and websites promise that mind-blowing sex awaits those who respect premarital purity.[28] The True Love Waits website used to provide a tidy pamphlet called *Ten Risks of Having Sex Before Marriage*. The lure of good marital sex was there, among the ten bullet points outlining risks: "Sexual purity before marriage is the first step to *incredible* sexual fulfilment after marriage" (emphasis theirs). Evangelical churches such as the now defunct Mars Hill in Seattle even go so far as to explicitly describe sexual acts—all within the bounds of heterosexual marriage. Mark Driscoll, the former pastor of Mars Hill, preached on "biblical oral sex" and told his ten thousand congregants, "Men, I am glad to report to you that oral sex is biblical . . . Ladies, your husbands appreciate oral sex. So, serve them, love them well."[29]

Many of my friends, believing this if/then promise, practiced purity right up until they got married, in their early twenties. When a friend called me six months into her marriage to talk about sex, I clutched the phone to my ear, eager to hear the secrets of this forbidden act. But to my surprise, she admitted that she hated sex. Sex was painful, she said, and was one of those things you just had to "get through," usually by vacating your body and letting your mind drift off. My face drained of color. Why was I guarding my purity with such ferocity, I wondered, if there was bad sex waiting for me on the other end?

The Bible study group I joined at Wellspring provided fertile ground for discussing sex and dating. The four other women in the group were all single thirtysomethings, and like most New Yorkers of that demographic, they tried to navigate the maze of online dating in a city of more than eight million. One Sunday, before she started dating her boyfriend, Liv announced that she had been up late the night before chatting with a guy on Tinder. The other women snickered and showed interest, especially Tina, who had set up Liv's profile. Liv stood in the doorway of her living room to tell us the story, as we, her devoted audience, listened from the couch. Suddenly, her face began to darken as she told us that an hour into their chat, her Tinder match had invited her to come over to his apartment to "hook up."

"I quickly unmatched him after that and turned my phone off!" She flopped down on a nearby armchair.

"Ugh, I'm so disillusioned with dating," Tina confessed wearily. "Why is it so hard to find a decent Christian guy?"

"The problem is that you just can't date casually in the church. Guys just *don't* ask girls out," Liv interjected.

As the conversation evolved, I noticed how closely the conversation at Bible study mirrored those I had with my non-Christian friends, whether in New York, California, or London. It was the spinning uncertainty of *Whose turn is it to text?*, *Are they into me?*, *Am I into them?* The only things distinguishing the conversation at Bible study were the focus on finding a Christian guy, and the absence of sex.

A few days later, I met up with Fiona, one of the women from our Bible study group. She invited me to her apartment after work and we sipped herbal tea in her darkened living room, the wind howling outside. When she referenced Liv's experience on Tinder, I asked if she was on any dating apps.

"Not anymore. I was for a few months, but then I got really convicted a couple of weeks ago, and I said to God, 'Actually, this isn't how I think I'm going to meet my husband or my partner or whomever.' For me, it's not about the visual; it's about heart-to-heart connection. So I just got rid of it. And I believe as women we need to fully trust that God will bring us someone."

In evangelical Christianity, to be "convicted" is to feel a prick of guilt or a heavy remorse that you've done something wrong, usually prompted by the Holy Spirit.

"What made you feel convicted?"

She rolled the question around in her mind, trying to select just the right words.

"I think because I was selling myself short. I diminished all of my faith, and my history with God, to 'No ONS,' which is an acronym for No One-Night Stands. And the fact that it says 'Christian' on my profile, that doesn't mean much in the Christian dating world or the dating world in general. I was on a Christian dating site recently and the guy said, 'When are we gonna sleep together?' I couldn't believe it! I thought he was a Christian!

I mean, this was a Christian site, so which part of the Bible was he reading?"

Fiona shook her head, and I could feel her resolve strengthening. "I'm sure I could meet someone and go for a nice drink with them, but their ulterior motives would be there, so I am just going to be patient and wait."

Torn between her desire to date and her desire to honor what she believed God wanted, Fiona settled on waiting. Then she rushed to tell me that she didn't judge women who took different paths. But judgment comes from somewhere. Otherwise, evangelical women wouldn't feel crippling guilt when they transgressed, and Naomi wouldn't have cried regularly during her first sexual relationship.

I thought back to our Bible study session the previous week. The conversation around sex had seemed harmless and open, yet this was the same group of women that Liv told me wouldn't talk about vibrators. And even during our conversation at Bible study, I had censored myself, reluctant to admit my own views on sex, even after all these years. The social pressure to be pure was always there, like a floating specter, invisible and ever present.

I started to realize that maybe the reward of waiting for marriage is not an eventual wild sex life but the validation that comes from church leaders and fellow Christians. Maybe it's acceptance. Maybe the real reward of abstinence is the avoidance of shame.

Six months later I found myself at another café, this time close to Wellspring, where Liv worked. She had just met her boyfriend, Jonathan, an up-and-coming junior pastor in the church.

I raised my cappuccino to my mouth and, feeling the warm milk burn my lips, set it back down again. "So, tell me about this new guy."

"Well," she began, unable to stop herself from smiling, "he's a bit older, and he adores me. He's an amazing preacher, and very sexy . . . We are going away together to the Catskills next week; I found this very romantic resort for us to stay." I raised my eyebrows in surprise and wondered how Liv planned to approach sex, now that she was in a relationship. Noticing my reaction, Liv rushed to clarify.

"Oh, well, we aren't having sex. We want to wait for marriage."

Well practiced at posing uncomfortable questions to evangelical women, I barely hesitated before asking, "And by sex, you mean intercourse, right?"

She nodded. "But we do other things . . . We're very attracted to each other."

"Such as?"

"Oh, you know, we spend the night together and make out naked . . ."

"Do your other Christian friends know?"

"Well, so, that's the thing: I don't really tell anyone. He's a high-profile guy in the church, so I'm trying to be careful with who I talk to about our relationship. I feel comfortable with my choices, in and of themselves, but I do worry that other Christians will judge me, so I tell very few people."

Liv felt guilt, not because she violated her own beliefs around sex but because she violated *other* evangelicals' beliefs. It was as if her fellow Christians foisted the guilt upon her and she could either receive it with open arms and change her sexual behavior or resist it by keeping her sexual life a secret. I had a strong hunch that other Christian women were also feeling guilt, not from within but from without, so I messaged Jo again. Of all people, I knew she would give an honest opinion.

When we met at a bar a few days later, Jo arrived at eight o'clock sharp. We both ordered cranberry juice, much to the bartender's surprise, and found a secluded table near the back. Soon after we sat down, I bluntly asked if she ever felt an imposed muteness around sex. She nodded her head and swallowed her juice, clearing her throat before speaking. A few months prior, she recounted, she was talking to a friend and had casually inserted the topic of masturbation into the conversation. Her friend had interrupted Jo midsentence. "Wait, what? A Christian girl who masturbates?"

"Um, what Christian girl *doesn't*?"

"Um, most of them," her friend answered, her certainty starting to wither as she spoke.

"And so I told her, well, they are either lying or they are fucking dumb!" Jo roared with laughter after this final pronouncement and emptied her glass.

Jo's friend's assumption that evangelical women did not masturbate was understandable. As Linda Kay Klein notes in her book about the evangelical movement, "The purity movement teaches that *every* sexual activity—from masturbation to kissing if it elicits that special feeling—can make one less pure."[30] Although I had never heard a pastor at Wellspring speak about masturbation, leaders at Bethel Church, in California, certainly did. On day 11 of the "Purity Plan" on YouTube, Caitlin Zick and Jason Vallotton explain, in separate sexual purity messages, that masturbation is a "painkiller" that people use when they feel disconnected from others. They articulate the standard evangelical stance clearly: masturbation violates God's plan for purity and connection.

Having spent years studying evangelical women (and a lifetime being evangelical), I knew that masturbating did not necessarily mean that Jo had changed her mind about sex. I also recognized that it had been a while since we had first discussed it, and that beliefs change. I proceeded with the acuity of cross examiner. "And where exactly would you say you land on the issue of premarital sex now?"

Jo straightened up her shoulders as she readied herself to reply. "I still don't want to have sex before marriage because, well, that is just my belief. I also think, I have waited so long, I might as well keep going. At the same time, I don't think it's the biggest deal."

She went on to tell me that even though she was a virgin, she loved to talk about sex.

"Yeah, I probably talk about it *too* much for someone who doesn't bone. My non-Christian friends think I'm a pro at sex. They just assume, because when we talk about sex, I'm very vocal, because I find it so interesting."

What did Jo's non-Christian friends think about her being a virgin at thirty?

She gasped. "Oh fuck. They don't know! I would *never* tell them." She shook her head as if my question had bordered on the ridiculous. "They would think I am a psycho!"

I remembered that she'd dated a non-Christian several years ago. "How did you maintain your purity standards in the relationship you had?"

Jo's body stiffened, just like before, at the park, when I had mentioned her past relationship. She stood abruptly and suggested another round of juice. By the time she returned a little while later with juices in hand, her demeanor had changed. The stiffness had softened and she was back to her confident, crass self.

"Oh, I wanted to say, it's almost like there's this unwritten rule in Christian circles where it's like you can do whatever you like, just don't have sex. And sometimes I think, fuck it! I'd rather just sleep with a guy and feel convicted and ask forgiveness as opposed to saying, oh this isn't as bad. And I think with sex it's like you can dabble with other things, but just don't have sex, and as a result it becomes so blown up, so huge."

Later, after we finished our second round, we left the bar and said our good-byes. I walked for a while, eager for the cool night-time air to clear my head. I thought about Jo, about our conversation, about the contradiction between speaking about "boning" all the time and resisting sex. Jo not only self-censored with her Christian friends, she also did so with her non-Christian friends. She was caught between two forms of shame and two conflicting attitudes toward sex. And she had found a way to handle the cultural clash by hiding her virginity from certain friends and hiding her vibrator from others. Jo was not sexually repressed, despite what some feminist critics might conclude, nor did she accept all aspects of purity culture—including the word *pure*, which she told me she detested. Instead, sexuality prompted a deep ambivalence, which she, along with many other evangelical women, managed in creative ways.

As I advanced along the bustling streets of Lower Manhattan, I thought of Foucault's repression hypothesis, the idea that power operates not by repressing sexuality but by controlling it, adjudicating the lines between good and bad, right and wrong. Lines that often get crossed, intentionally or unintentionally. "People will be surprised at the eagerness with which we went about pretending to rouse from its slumber a sexuality which everything—our discourses, our customs, our institutions, our regulations, our knowledges—was busy producing in the light of day and broadcasting to noisy accompaniment," Foucault wrote.[31] Rather than resting in a deep slumber, sex and sexuality are wide awake in evangelical Christianity, under the careful watch of church leaders and fellow evangelicals.

In order to preserve their place in the community, women navigate the slippery, confusing world of sex in silence. As much as they still choose abstinence, it's often a fragile choice, one that is selected because the other options are steeped in shame. And it is a choice that brings disastrous consequences for those who err.

I met Jamie only once, and despite (or because of) the intimacy of what she shared, we never spoke again. We met in London near Thames Gathering Place, where she volunteered in the children's ministry, on a late summer afternoon.

Early in our conversation, Jamie started telling me her story. She was raised in a strict Pentecostal family in Scotland and was required to attend church at least twice a week. Growing up, she was taught by her church leaders that going to the movie theater, playing video games, drinking alcohol, and having sex all were sinful. While at university, Jamie became engaged to another Christian. When we approached the topic of their relationship, Jamie's breezy, upbeat manner vanished.

"I was severely depressed at that time. I was very suicidal. I was hurting myself. It was a horrible, horrible period." She uttered each sentence laboriously.

"Why?"

"I wasn't comfortable with the level of intimacy we had. I look back on it, and I can't even recognize myself. I just feel completely separated from that time in my life. I hated the whole experience; I hated *myself*. At that point, I was sliding into a depression, and I got mononucleosis. Thankfully, we split up not too long after I was diagnosed, so at least I wasn't ill and having to deal with all that."

I asked if her depression was related to crossing sexual boundaries.

"I think that was a big part of it. And I find it incredibly hard to even get to the point where the Lord can forgive me. I couldn't accept that for a long, long time, and I still struggle with that. I mean, it's not something that I talk about a lot. And because my Christian friends at the time wouldn't talk about it, I *couldn't* actually talk about it. I couldn't say anything. A couple of them knew what was happening, because I was breaking down, but it wasn't like they could offer me support, because they were also Christians, brought up in Christian families . . . you know."

Then Jamie looked up to face me squarely, her face contorting to hold back the force of emotion that swelled within her. "How do you deal with somebody who's not done something . . . perfect?"

I never found out exactly what Jamie and her ex-fiancé had done sexually, or what purity line they had crossed. By repeatedly substituting the word *it* for *sex*, the silence from Jamie's past reappeared in our present conversation. Jamie had received the harshest punishment possible for her violation: estrangement from her Christian community. And being denied the approval and connection she sought from others caused Jamie to turn against her own body. She had experienced the dark side of purity culture.

The following day, Maddie and I went for a run, as we sometimes did on Saturday mornings when I was in London. Afterwards, we found a quiet spot near a row of trees and began to stretch. She asked how my research was going and I admitted I had just done a difficult interview covering the consequences of breaking purity standards. Maddie remained quiet and nodded solemnly.

I reached for my feet, folding my achy body in half.

"Where do you stand on the whole issue of sexual purity?" I asked, from upside down.

"Well, I think it's a good idea to save sex for marriage. For one, because I feel like it reduces complexities."

"What do you mean by that?"

"You know, if you break up with the person, then having not had sex can limit the emotional damage . . . But that being said, I have started to question it all a bit. Just the way the church ties a woman's worth to purity."

"Yeah, I know what you mean."

"I really felt that after my last relationship," Maddie admitted.

Soon after recommitting her life to God, Maddie had started dating a Christian man she met at church. She and her then-boyfriend had crossed their sexual purity line several times over the course of their two-year relationship. Although they didn't have sex, they got pretty close: showering together, sleeping in the same bed, and "doing everything *but* sex" (by which she meant intercourse).

"Thankfully, by the grace of God, we didn't go so far where I have massive regrets. And even though I know that no matter where we go, there's redemption from God, well, you just really beat yourself up afterwards, you know? You think, *I've done it again. I let myself down, I let my boyfriend down, let God down, let everyone down.*"

Her former boyfriend didn't internalize as much guilt as she did, she said, perhaps knowing that Maddie, as a woman, carried the major responsibility of the purity mandate. When I asked how she felt when she crossed these boundaries, Maddie became very still. By now she was seated on the grass, the soles of her running shoes pressed together so her legs formed a diamond shape. She ran her fingers through her scalp, which was still matted with sweat, in an attempt to maintain her poise. Then she paused and whispered, "Awful."

That word, *awful*, rattled around my head for months. Every time I heard it, I saw Maddie's posture: her slender shoulders pushed downward as if a heavy woolen shawl had been draped over them, her eyes filled with remorse. *Awful. Awful. Awful.* I was unable to shake it.

I called my sister, and she suggested I write letters to the women as a way to excise the heavy emotions stirred up by fieldwork. The first letter I wrote was to Maddie. I apologized for asking her about the past, for calling forth the memory of that shameful time in her life. I assured her that her worth was not tethered to what she had done or ever would do sexually.

I kept writing. I wrote letters to Jamie, Liv, and Naomi. And then I wrote one to myself. I reached into the past and wrote to the version of myself that had needlessly felt ashamed of an ill-fitting school uniform, which had earned me a detention for being "sexually provocative." I wrote to the self who felt dirty after making out with a college boyfriend, and to the present version of myself whose only recourse in the face of these painful stories of purity was to sleep with strangers. As I wrote, a more recent memory surfaced, one that I had try to ignore.

Years before this research, despite having reconciled a healthy sex life with my continued affiliation with (and occasional participation in) Christianity, it was a romance gone awry that had finally secured my exit from the church. A friend introduced me to a man at a birthday party in late summer, and despite my reluctance to date a Christian again, especially one so involved with church leadership, I willed myself to remain open-minded. Early on, I told him my stance on sex—that it was an important part of a relationship—and asked if he would have a problem with that. Although he was a virgin, he assured me that he saw the merits of premarital sex and was open to changing his mind.

I dated this worship team guitarist for only a few weeks before it all went horribly wrong. For what would be our final date, he invited me to an art show his friend had produced in a buzzy neighborhood of East London. I searched my closet for what to wear, and I settled on a cobalt blue sundress with a high neckline and buttons down the front. When I met my Christian date out front of a large steel warehouse, he admired my dress and complimented me on how beautiful I looked. We interlaced fingers and walked into the show together. Two hours later, tipsy on free wine and abstract art, we stumbled outside onto the street. Dusk saturated the city, and, pulling my hand toward himself, he invited me to come back to his house to spend the night. I debated, knowing I had to get up early the next morning to catch a train out of town, but I decided to go anyway, the thrill of summer in London urging me onward.

We arrived at his apartment, tumbled on his bed, and began kissing. When he tried to take things further, I told him to stop, that I wanted to take things slow. He continued, and I protested. We repeated this cycle again and again, until he finally gave up and we fell asleep. In the morning he kissed me and asked if I wanted to take a shower with him.

"I think it's a bit too soon for that," I responded, remembering that he had done very little sexually. Reinvigorated from a full night's sleep, he resumed his begging, and I my protests. We showered, separately, and then he walked me to the front door, bidding me farewell with a casual kiss on the forehead.

I didn't hear from him for several days after that. After a week, I became worried.

"Maybe he lost interest," my friend proposed. Finally, I called him and suggested we speak in person, because by then it had become obvious that something was very wrong.

When we finally met, I told him I was confused. "I don't understand. What happened?" He stayed distant and cold throughout our encounter, refusing to meet my eyes.

"The other night was inappropriate," he stated, matter-of-factly. "You should never have tempted me that way. I sought counsel about the situation, and they agreed."

"But you were the one pushing for us to go further!" I exclaimed, glossing over the mention of "they" for the time being.

"*You* shouldn't have put me in that position! With both of us tipsy, in bed . . . especially knowing your sexual history."

A smile slowly extended across my face, because suddenly it was clear: even though he had violated his own purity values, it was my fault. It was the same message I had received time and again in American evangelicalism, and here I was sitting in a park across the world, hearing it from a British boy that I barely knew.

Years later I would even hear it from women in my research. Speaking about "breaking boundaries," a twenty-seven-year-old American woman told me, "I would say that sexual purity is more of a woman's duty. I think even walking with God, women have no idea what power they have over men. And just because men love the Lord doesn't mean they don't have hormones. More and more I have such sympathy for men . . . Most women I would say can shut down desires very quickly and are less likely to be led into sexual mistakes. Whereas men, as soon as you start going down a road, it's harder for them to stop. And so, I think women need to be careful how they are around men."

The idea that sexual purity is primarily a woman's responsibility has been internalized by Christian men and women alike, and in the process, women's sexual desires are diminished, or at least distorted.

I went to church one last time after the incident with the guitarist, refusing to stay away on account of one sexually confused Christian man. And as I watched him up on stage, playing along to the worship songs, his body engrossed in the act of adoration, I felt rage. I looked around for the senior pastors, all men, and wondered which one had instructed him to speak with me. Which one had absolved him of any wrongdoing and twisted our story into an Adam and Eve narrative of a women's sinfulness?

How many people sitting in the chapel knew the intimate details
of that night?

Before the service even finished, I knew that it was over. I had
no more fight left in me. This incident provided just the nudge
I needed to march out the door of evangelicalism and close it
firmly behind me. For good.

In August 2016, a Christian version of #MeToo broke out.
Similar to the movement that preceded it, #ChurchToo brought
women's stories of nonconsensual sex, sexual harassment, and
overall sexual misconduct to light. Two American Christian
women, Emily Joy and Hannah Paasch, launched #ChurchToo
in order to shed light on the sexual secrecy and shame that per-
meates evangelical circles as well as to expose the countless stories of churches mishandling sexual abuse. According to Emily
Joy, there are multiple roots of sexual misconduct in Christianity, and one of them is purity culture. Little did I know, when I
first learned about #MeToo and #ChurchToo, the impact it
would have on one of the women in my research, one who had
become increasingly closer to me.

Today, women continue to share their stories of pain and
healing on Twitter with the hashtag #ChurchToo. It has spawned
other online movements, including #ThingsOnlyChristianWom
enHear, where women document instances of sex discrimination in church. Purity messages feature heavily in this hashtag.
As one user tweeted, "Every time you go too far with a boy,
you're chipping away your worth and giving it to him. #Things
OnlyChristianWomenHear."

These movements, along with Time's Up, an organization
against sexual harassment, are built on women reaching their
limits—from Hollywood to academia to evangelical Christianity. As these movements bloom, they create new opportunities

for women to lay claim to the equality and fairness that is their due. They also provoke women to recognize systematic discrimination and alter the very architecture of their social environment. Linda Kay Klein, still a Christian despite her difficult years in evangelicalism, started an organization called Break Free Together to help other women heal from the shame of purity culture.

Similarly, the 2019 book *Shameless: A Sexual Reformation*, by Pastor Nadia Bolz-Weber, aims to rectify decades of purity messages taught by evangelical leaders. Upon its release, the book shot onto the *New York Times* best seller list and was sold out on Amazon UK for months. Bolz-Weber also invited women to mail in their purity rings. In return, she promised to send them a "certificate of impurity" and to melt the rings down and make a statue of a vagina. True to her word, on February 8, 2019, Bolz-Weber presented the vagina statue, adorned with a collection of tiny purity rings just like mine, to feminist activist Gloria Steinem.

These books, movements, and female crusaders are advancing a new sexual ethics outside of purity and providing alternatives for Christian women who want to have sex *and* stay in the church. And they now compete with purity culture for authority over Christian women's sexuality.

After a year together, Liv and her boyfriend broke up. Like so many couples, they realized the relationship just wasn't working. I didn't know what state I would find Liv in when we met soon after their breakup. Another café, another Monday morning, but this time so much had changed.

I arrived at the coffee shop early and found us a spot near the windows. When Liv finally arrived, she entered the café absent-mindedly, as if she'd just been blown in by a gust of wind. Dressed in a bright fuchsia dress, Liv had foregone makeup and left her long hair loose and free. Her eyes darted around the café until she found me and smiled.

It turned out that Liv was just fine. A bit sore from all of the emotional talks and crying spells that often accompany the end of a relationship, but otherwise, in good spirits.

"Do you regret anything?" I asked her, in the moments before we parted ways.

"Nothing," Liv replied firmly, shaking her head.

I wondered if that included the sexual aspect of their relationship, but in the end I decided not to ask.

I glanced down at her tiny hands as they rested in her lap and saw the naked finger where she had once worn a purity ring. I thought about the concessions she had made, the ongoing wrestling she had endured. Most of all, I admired Liv's persistence in forging her own sexual ethics, in spite of the conflicting messages she received around sex, and in spite of the conflicting cultures she inhabited.

Religion is not easily separable from other areas of social life, so religious practices such as sexual purity constitute a way of life, not just obedience to a religious law. Evangelicalism's treatment of sexuality touches the most intimate moments and private bodily experiences of the people who come under its influence. In an environment where adherence to sexual purity is so intimately tied to an evangelical identity, women stand to face very real consequences when they don't conform to the purity model. Some women, such as Jamie, transgress and suffer the fallout in silence. When silence becomes too much to bear, others, like me, leave the church. Whether the effects manifest in frequent crying spells, a dull, internal sense of self-reproach, or the muteness one is required to maintain in exchange for the sexual activities she enjoys, few evangelical women come through the purity machine unscathed. The purported freedom that accompanies sexual purity more closely resembles what the poet Claudia Rankine calls a "complicit freedom," the kind of freedom that injures at the same time as it seeks to emancipate.

The church's approach to female sexuality caused me to finally snap and leave Christianity, but this was preceded by decades of being in a highly circumscribed environment. A "snap" is a moment with a history, Sara Ahmed reminds us.[32] It's a moment preceded by so many other moments. Like the slow, steady layering of limestone, I had accrued years of resentments that had calcified over time.

But although Maddie, Liv, Jo, and Carys held certain grievances with the church, they hadn't left. And so I started to wonder, if it wasn't the pressure to remain sexually pure, what might make these women snap?

5

THE IDEAL WOMAN

*What must I be in order to be recognized, and what criterion
holds sway here at the very condition of my own emergence?*
—Judith Butler

There's so much bullshit around mental health in the
church. There's so much *Oh, joy of the Lord!* With my
depression, I want to just say to those people, 'Would
you fucking say that if my leg was broken?' As far as I'm concerned, honesty begets honesty, and I feel like there's a lot that
I can do just by being honest and saying that depression and anxiety are part of my story, they are part of where I'm at right now,
and the Lord can use me."

Jo and I are in the living room of her basement apartment on
a Saturday afternoon. She's telling me how she grew up as a pastor's daughter near Chicago. Her father, a stout, lively man took
up the call for ministry after three decades in the police force.
He joined the Foursquare denomination, a branch of Protestant-
ism founded by Aimee Semple McPherson, which emphasizes
a supernatural engagement with Christianity and, importantly,
is one of the only denominations that theologically supports

women in leadership. Consequently, Jo's parents taught their three daughters that they were equal to men, whether inside or outside the church. The girls grew up reading books with strong female protagonists—*Little Women* and *Anne of Green Gables* when they were younger, transitioning to Germaine Greer as they grew older. In fact, Jo was named after the strong heroine in *Little Women*, she told me proudly.

Jo was the eldest of the girls and the most spirited. She inherited her energy and irreverence from her father and her sensitivity and dedication from her mother. The combination seemed perfectly suited to church ministry, and Jo entered college with the aim of studying psychology to help provide counseling to church congregants. She joined the Christian club on her secular college campus and immersed herself in the local church, where she led worship.

Soon after graduating, Jo moved to New York. A friend of hers from college had started working at the growing Wellspring Community Church, whose mission was to spread the gospel and revive a de-Christianizing city. And so, with very little money, Jo moved across the country. ("I said to myself, *Fuck it, I'm gonna go!*") She started working at a group home for troubled youth and spent the rest of her time at Wellspring. As one of the only Christians at her job, she often faced criticism for her conservative evangelical beliefs, including her abstention from alcohol and sex. *How can you be both a feminist and an evangelical?* her coworkers would ask her, during the all-night shifts. *And how can you be part of a church without any female leaders?* Confusion and contempt dripped from their mouths.

These questions never ruffled Jo, and she replied with steady, sure answers. Her faith was solid, as was her feminism. Her parents had raised her with the natural fusion of the two, so she hardly knew one without the other. *Honestly, more women need to step up to the plate*, she'd reply. *As women, we are often hesitant to put ourselves out there, and Christian women need to go for these positions more.* Jo spoke authoritatively and with confidence, knowing that she was one of the women that Christian feminists had been waiting for. She was the woman who would go for these leadership positions, who wouldn't be deterred. Like a large ship smoothly breaking the water, she advanced forward.

A few years after she arrived in the city, Jo left her job and started to work for Wellspring. The pay was bad and the hours weren't great (she often had to work weekends), but she felt certain that God wanted her to be part of the change from the inside. She started singing and playing guitar on the worship team, just as she had done all through high school and college. During a particularly charismatic worship service one Sunday, where people were "slain in the spirit," miracles were performed, and tongues were spoken, Jo was "spiritually head hunted," as she calls it. One of the pastors slowly approached and stopped just far enough away that when his hands stretched out, they still remained inches from her body. And then he spoke these prophetic words over her: "I see you speaking in front of masses of people. Delivering a brand-new teaching, a new revelation. You will be a great leader."

Jo stood motionless, her arms out wide to the sides, palms up, as if to catch his words in her hands, to hold onto them for safekeeping. Her head was bowed, chin to chest, silent tears streaming down her face—tears of happiness that she finally was being recognized for the calling she'd felt for so many years. She was grateful for the rebellious spirit that she had inherited from her father, for her commitment to her faith, for fighting through those depressive episodes.

When I interview her, about six months after this event, she's gearing up to become a worship leader. Though she feels equipped and ready ("This is my calling"), she's also terrified.

"I've realized that if I wait until I'm not afraid anymore, I'm just not going to do it. I am always going to be afraid and so I just need to push through. One of my friends is mentoring me around worship stuff now. He's being really supportive. Frankly, it's just amazing to have a man in church who isn't afraid that people are going to sexualize our relationship. I think that's a big reason why women are not in leadership roles. It's because male–female relationships are so often sexualized that men don't want to mentor women. And anyway, Christian guys never go for me . . ."

She shakes her head vigorously, her curls bouncing unfettered around the edges of her face. "If I say this to my guy friends, they say, 'Oh you're really great; you'll find someone,' and I say, 'Yeah, but you're only looking for a Scandinavian Barbie who is eight years younger than you.'"

In evangelical circles validation is often conferred via recognition from men, and women who look a certain way achieve that recognition. Women gain many benefits from this recognition, including the possibility of marriage, which can lead to leadership roles. In evangelicalism, it is easier to *marry* a pastor than to try to become one yourself, single women often told me. This is true because, first, once you are married you are no longer sexualized and thus no longer a temptation for men in the church. Second, you are seen to be fulfilling God's plan for marriage and the expected role for women. And finally, if your husband has a position of leadership—say he's a pastor already— then you are automatically ushered into a role of leadership, serving with him as co-pastor or as "pastor's wife," a role which carries its own authority.

Yet the deck is still stacked against women. In the United States, 55 percent of evangelicals are women, while only 45 percent are men.[1] In the United Kingdom, the ratio is roughly three

women for every two men, though informally, many evangelicals I spoke with estimated that the ratio is four to one in some
churches.[2] Evangelical women often described the difficulty of
finding a marriage partner, given the scarcity of single men in
the church, and the tremendous pressure they felt to marry.[3]

"I don't know what it is that means Christian guys don't like
me . . . Maybe it's—" Jo hesitates, searching for possible expla-
nations. "I don't know. I wish I knew what it was. But the fact is,
at the end of the day, I am who I've been created to be. That
doesn't mean that there aren't some changes that the Lord might
want to make in my heart, but the essentials of who I am—the
fire, the passion, the honesty, the deep value of integrity—those
are not things that the Lord wants to change in me. And he does
not want to change me into a quiet, gentle little wifey. That is
definitely not who I was created to be! And so actually, you know,
even though part of me wants to know what it is that means that
Christian guys don't want me, actually, the essentials of who I
am and who the Lord made me to be, I will not fucking change."

"How does this experience with dating and guys in the church
affect your relationship with God?" I ask.

"It makes me frustrated, to be honest. This issue . . . Oh gosh,
I'm actually pretty emotional now. This particular issue, I find
it so difficult to even pray about it because I'm so frustrated. I
find it so hard to even bring my frustration to the table with God
because I just don't see any evidence of decent Christian guys
who want to date anyone besides a twenty-two-year-old skinny
blond who is so young she hasn't quite figured out who she is. It
doesn't make me not believe in God; it makes me not believe in
men. It makes me not believe in men at all."

Jo remains quiet for a few seconds while she wipes the corners of her eyes. "It's really hard . . . it's just really hard. At the
end of the day, I know that I can have a great life without a

partner. I do know that. But that doesn't mean it's not incredibly frustrating sometimes."

Just then the living room door swings open and Jo's roommate walks in. Silence descends as she takes in the emotional mise-en-scène: Jo sniffling on the couch, surrounded by scattered tissues, and a stranger with a recorder leaning in close.

"Oh, hi Emily!" Jo turns around to greet her roommate. "This is Katie. She's interviewing me."

She turns back to me. "We can just keep going, because I've had all these conversations with Emily anyway."

Emily says hello and then starts rummaging around in the kitchen while Jo continues to tell me how difficult it is to date in the evangelical context, and how heartbroken it leaves her. "I don't have a single Christian friend who hasn't been dicked around at this point," she says. Jo keeps protesting that she doesn't want to be anything other than her feisty feminist self, with an imperfect, pear-shaped body and short curly hair that turns frizzy on humid days. The pitch of her voice rises, gathering vehemence like a swelling storm.

"I can't give a rat's ass about being liked if it means compromising my values. Fuck being liked! I don't care. And the thing is, that means I'm not a 'cool chill girl' anymore—because cool girls have to be chilled out and everything, right? I used to be a big guys' girl, but I'm not chill anymore because I challenge stuff. And I'll say to people in the church, 'You're full of shit.' Sometimes it feels like singleness is a self-perpetuating thing, because I refuse to stay silent on this stuff and that makes me unattractive. I'm not really wife material for them."

Emily's head emerges from a cupboard at this last sentence. "What was that about being wife material?" She laughs drily and abandons the kitchen, taking a seat opposite me in a sprawling armchair.

"Emily, you've got to explain to Katie," Jo says, and I nod vigorously. Emily launches right in.

"Just last week my Bible study leader, a guy named Rick, described what he calls 'wifey material.' You know, a woman who is subservient, quiet, patient, kind—more in the shadows. The type who lets her man take charge." Emily rolls her eyes.

"But the thing is, there are a lot of girls I talk to who strive to be those things, who want to be those things, who want to be 'good Christian women' . . . It's just not me."

"Or me!" Jo chimes in, taking back the reins of the conversation. "Anyway, I just think people in the church should be allowed to date normally, without so much pressure. The church puts so much pressure on you to get married, to find someone, and it means that no one asks anyone out because they're in a fishbowl. Guys just need to relax."

Soon after this interview with Jo, it's time for another Women Rise event. The group is gaining momentum. They have 1,500 Facebook followers now and more than two hundred women at each of their monthly events. The group is designed to inspire and support women at different career levels, and Liv has rebranded it an "association." The aim, she tells me, is to create a girls' club to rival the boys' club tribalism that pervades evangelical Christianity. They have launched monthly mentoring luncheons with prominent women leaders—politicians, financial consultants, CEOs—as well as a website and merchandise bearing the Women Rise logo.

As I write this now, many years later, their Facebook page, website, and past events remain on the internet, suspended in time, like a mausoleum for the hopes of a group of earnest evangelical women. Last summer, at the yearly Wellspring retreat, I overhead two women speaking about it as I waited in line for lunch. "Hey, whatever happened to that Women Rise group?" one of them asked. The other shrugged in response and they moved on to a different topic of conversation.

But that would all come later. Back then, I found myself stricken, as if with a fever, with the enthusiasm of Women Rise and the optimism that the sexism in the church was about to change. Finally, boys' clubs would become girls' clubs, women would reclaim their rightful place in church leadership, and my own history of being silenced by evangelical male leaders would be redeemed through the collective action of Women Rise.

As often happens when one loads an experience with certain expectations, the Women Rise event turned out very differently than I anticipated. The theme that night, Super Soul Sunday Night, a variation on Oprah Winfrey's television show, revolved around making time in the new year for a relationship with God alongside women's plans and dreams. A woman named Jessa, who directed an anti–sex trafficking organization, was speaking on God's timing.

On my walk into the church, along a dark, nameless lane that led to the back of the grounds, I met a friendly woman wearing pinstriped trousers and a navy blazer. She matched my stride and introduced herself, explaining that she worked at Jessa's organization and had come, along with her other coworkers, to support her boss. I introduced myself and told her I was there as a researcher, studying single evangelical women.

"You should meet Jessa. She's *amazing*," the young woman gushed. "She just does so much, and does it all so well, you know?"

"Yes, I'd like to meet her. Could you introduce us?"

"Sure. I'm sure she'd love to hear about your research," she replied.

As soon as we entered the church's main meeting room, my new friend spotted a crowd of women clustered in a group and strode over to them. I trailed behind dutifully. The huddle fanned open as I approached, and there in the center stood Jessa. In her late twenties, white, attractive and thin, Jessa wore a black leather jacket and tattered skinny jeans. Her long hair was slightly untamed and her face was made up, but imperceptibly so. We shook hands and said hello. Almost immediately after, the women closed ranks around her, turning back to each other and resuming their previous conversation, leaving me literally and figuratively outside the circle.

Affronted, I wandered over to Jo, who was working the front desk, checking people in and handing out canvas bags. "Did I tell you that I got promoted at work?" Jo exclaimed, as I commandeered the seat next to her. Ignoring her registration desk duties, she said that her boss had called a meeting the week before and told Jo he saw her advancing into a more senior role in the church. I congratulated her, just as Liv's voice floated over the loudspeaker, announcing that the event was about to begin. Jo and I said good-bye and I hurried over to the main stage to find a seat. The crowd of women around Jessa dispersed and she took her place on a bar stool next to Liv, scooting it in close to the microphone.

Liv introduced Jessa and the theme for the evening and then launched into her first question.

"Jessa, one of the things we talk about a lot here at Women Rise is the difficulty in managing multiple roles and responsibilities. I know this is something you have a lot of experience with, so I wondered if you could tell us a bit about how you do it all."

"Well, I'm not sure I do it *all*!" Jessa's eyes roved over the audience, which laughed in response. She pulled her shiny chestnut hair over to one side and straightened up her shoulders.

"No, but in all seriousness, by God's grace I am the director of an NGO, fighting the injustice of slavery, and it's my dream job. But I'm also a co-pastor with my husband *and* I'm a wife. So, to keep everything in balance, it all comes down to following God's agenda. And making time every day to be in conversation with him so that I can really listen. Nothing is more important than starting the day with the word of God."

Several women in the audience murmured in agreement and nodded their heads. As Jessa started speaking about her husband, I thought about Jo, sitting just a few rows behind me, who had lamented that Christian guys never noticed her. I remembered the frustration she felt around being unnoticed, and how it had caused her to well up when talking about it in her living room a few weeks back.

The next month, I was in London for a visit, so I called up Maddie and she invited me to stop by her art studio. When I arrived, we hugged at the doorway of her tiny, cramped studio, and I noticed flecks of cornflower blue paint dotting her hair and neck.

"Let me just grab my bag and we can go out for a wander. Fresh air would be nice, wouldn't it?"

"Sure," I replied, smiling at that British way of turning a statement into a question.

Maddie smeared red lipstick across her bottom lip, blotted her lips together a few times, and slid on a pair of sunglasses.

As we wandered down the busy sidewalk, I asked her about the figure of a "good Christian woman" that Jo had described, and if it existed in the UK.

"Well, she's somewhat paradoxical because she's wholesome yet hot, strong yet submissive," Maddie began. "Definitely doesn't have sex before marriage, yet is still sexy, in a modest, Christian sort of way." I thought back to Jessa—she certainly demonstrated strength and acquiescence in equal measure. That night at Women Rise, she spoke effortlessly about managing her multiple roles. She mentioned her husband often and affectionately, their romance seeming as fresh as ever. I observed how the leaders of Women Rise introduced Jessa and interviewed her, and how the hundred-odd women in the audience responded so positively to her. The rest of the night she was surrounded by throngs of women; everyone wanted to be around Jessa—or maybe everyone wanted to *be* Jessa, I wasn't quite sure. Much to my irritation, I even found myself wanting to know her and to gain access to her inner circle, aggrieved about being rebuffed earlier in the night. My thoughts floated over to Maddie, walking next to me.

"Well, why aren't *you* the ideal woman?" I asked.

Maddie sighed. I knew by now that a sigh could mean so many things with her. It could mean she was readying herself to disclose personal information; it could serve as pivot to a different topic, one she felt more comfortable with; or it could be a response in itself.

"I'm just too edgy, too alternative, too . . ." she trailed off. "I remember when I first came back to Christianity and went on a church retreat, I was rooming with a group of other girls who had been at the church for a while and they just all seemed so *perfect*." Maddie punctuated this last word with disdain. "After the retreat, I even went shopping and tried to align my dress style more with theirs. To capture that perfect 'wholesome yet hot' look. Obviously, that didn't work out!" She gestures to her outfit: scruffy black Converse sneakers, black leggings, and a black blouse buttoned all the way up to her neck.

"I've stopped trying now. And actually, I've started distancing myself from the church a bit, now that I started this art program. I just don't have time anymore! I still go on Sundays, but that's about it."

She went on to tell me all about the new friends she'd made at her art institute and the painting she was currently working on.

After Maddie, I checked in with other Christian women, in both countries, about this ideal figure. They chuckled in response to my question, then went on to describe her with formulaic precision.

"I think *calm* is a word that I would not associate with myself and I *would* associate with people I look at that are good examples of a good Christian woman," Aurelie said. "And they dress very formally, not too revealing, don't draw attention to themselves," she continued, glancing down at her exposed midriff and low-hanging jeans. "They put everyone apart from themselves first." I nodded as she spoke and scribbled down shorthand summaries in my notebook: *modest, selfless, humble.*

"Very middle or upper class," a working-class woman in London told me.

I gathered more descriptions, treating them as artifacts that I could later line up neatly on the shelf and scrutinize in detail.

"Let's see," Naomi started, as we sat side by side on a park bench in London, an icy spring breeze blowing past us and inducing a shiver. She rubbed her hands together to keep them warm, and I noticed her chipped nail polish, a hint of disarray on this otherwise perfectly groomed woman.

"The perfect Christian woman is blond, thin . . . a little artsy on the side, something with kids, *very* Christian." She pulled in a deep breath. "And white, definitely white." It was true: all of the women in any sort of leadership role at Wellspring, including all the pastors' wives, were white, even as the congregation became more and more racially diverse.

"Is this something that comes up for you a lot, going to a church that is predominately white?"

"Well, weirdly, I'm used to it, because I went to a private school where I was the only Black kid. I grew up in an environment where most people don't look like me. So in a weird sort of way that feels normal. But anyway, Wellspring does have a lot more Black people now. The service that I go to has a good mix of people, and there are definitely more Black people coming to the church now than when I first started."

Then, Liv: "The ideal woman is definitely not ambitious or career-oriented. She works at something nonprofit-related, but only until she gets married and has kids. The job is never the main focus; it's like biding her time until she meets her husband, and then she drops it and supports him in church ministry." Liv spoke with the same antipathy as Naomi, Jo, Maddie, and Carys, yet they each had their own reasons for despising the archetype.

After interviewing women across both countries, I inspected my collection of descriptors: "works at a charity," "only has one or two glasses of wine when she goes out," "is powerful but not *too* powerful," "subservient," "mousy, quiet, stays in the kitchen," "doesn't hold strong opinions," "a bit more in the shadows." Exemplarity also surfaced through the body: the stilled body that expressed an internal calmness; the body stylishly yet modestly adorned; the agreeable woman who conveyed her compliance through her smiling, receptive face, her acquiescence to the status quo. When I put all these adjectives together, the figure of the ideal woman appeared so circumscribed that I wondered who could possibly inhabit her.

And then I met Rachel.

We sat next to each other at a breakfast event run by a Christian organization in London. Within the first five minutes, I found out that Rachel attended Thames Gathering Place and that she knew Aurelie. Our common acquaintance enabled a sudden and unearned intimacy. She told me she felt nervous to start her new job at a Christian charity in a week; I told her about the difficulties of finishing a PhD. Later, when the event finished and Rachel left the table, I watched her expertly navigate the maze of tables and chairs, her long honey-blond hair sashaying after her like a trail of ducklings. As I watched, I realized Rachel ticked all of the boxes. *She* was the ideal woman. I looked down at the scrap of paper in my hand, where she had scrawled her phone number, and I folded it carefully and tucked it inside my purse.

I messaged her the next day, and soon we met up at a small neighborhood café for toast and tea. As she spoke, I studied her and ran through the ideal woman checklist in my head. Works for a charity—tick! Expresses support for women's role in the church, but somehow manages to never come across as forceful—tick! Beautiful, young, white—tick, tick, tick! Rachel so perfectly fit the good Christian woman figure that I nearly asked her how many glasses of wine she usually ordered on a night out. And although she certainly carried a certain strength, it was a fragile strength, one that might yield or fold at any moment.

I shifted in my seat and looked into Rachel's greenish-blue eyes. They weren't searching eyes like Carys's or furious eyes like Jo's. Instead, these eyes seemed to convey a yawning contentedness. *I want nothing more than this*, they said. *My desires are simple, my demands spartan.*

Oh, to be content with one's conditions, I mused afterwards, as I rode the Tube in silence, willing my face to take on the arid quality of Rachel's, to see what it felt like. Maybe that had always been my problem with evangelical Christianity: I had always wanted more. Wanted *too much*. I had suffered from chronic dissatisfaction, and my dissatisfaction eventually led to an outright rejection of the very architecture of evangelicalism, prompting my exit.

Poststructuralist theorists have a word for the creation and sustenance of an ideal: normativity. According to Foucault, normativity is created through discourse—language, text, images, art, and symbols—and it is heavily invested with power. Using Foucault's analysis, the theorist Stuart Hall asserts, "Power, it seems, has to be understood here, not only in terms of economic exploitation and physical control, but also in broader cultural and symbolic terms, including the power to represent someone, or something in a certain way—within a 'regime of representation.'"[4]

Both Foucault and Hall argue that norms are not imposed upon us in a top-down fashion. It is too facile to say that the TV we watch, the books we read, or the advertisements we see create the ideal and that humans, in their robotized state, then replicate and reproduce the norm.[5] Rather, these discursive fragments are *diffuse*; they circulate and spread around the social world like particles of pollution, and we breathe them in, internalize them, and exhale them back out again, filling the figurative airspace with our own replications of the norm, which in turn become discursive particles, ready for ingestion.

We can see how this plays out among the evangelical women I met and their varied responses to the ideal norm. Some, like Maddie, try to emulate her, changing their clothing to align to the dominant style. Others, such as Liv, look up to her while retaining their own sense of self. And still others, such as Jo, outright reject her. But regardless of the response, the ideal holds sway. She is the woman that men desire, pursue, and later marry. She is the exemplar, and as such she holds her own authority and power, even within a context that restricts women from authority roles.

The evangelical world, like all subcultures, has its own classification system of what it means to be an ideal Christian man or woman, which differs slightly from mainstream ideals and paradigmatic figures in other subcultures. And the representation of the ideal circulates through various forms of Christian material culture, including sermons, books, magazines, Bible study texts, and, of course, social media. Take *The Virgin Monologues*, for example, the purity book written by modern-day abstinence advocate Carrie Lloyd. Even though there aren't any images in the book, the references to certain clothing brands (Miu Miu and Prada), nail polish (OPI), and places (Jeffrey's in New York) make it clear that Carrie is writing to an audience that is familiar with these brands, an audience of a particular social class.

Another popular book is *And the Bride Wore White*, written by Dannah Gresh in 1999. When I was growing up, this book was a standard text for American girls hoping to keep themselves pure before marriage. In it, Gresh describes "gorgeous girls" who are waiting for marriage to have sex. In one passage we meet Jenny, a woman who "came to her marriage bed a virgin—physically and mentally."[6] The story describes Jenny's "creamy, white complexion" and cotton pajamas. The next passage praises Jenny's fortitude in resisting sexual temptation. By identifying Jenny's skin color as white and connecting this to innocence, as conveyed through the reference to pajamas, the text aligns purity with whiteness.[7]

Now consider the magazine *Magnify*, which appeals to evangelical women from Los Angeles to London to Lagos. The images and stories in *Magnify* are certainly more racially diverse than most American evangelical purity books, yet they carry some of the same values of Christian womanhood, especially with regard to youth, beauty, social class, and marriage. A recent issue featured an interview with the American Christian woman Courtney Lopez (née Barry). Lopez, president of the digital media marketing agency West of Fairfax, coleads Hillsong California with her husband, Sam. She also has a large social media following, in part due to her close friendship with Selena Gomez. Lopez is young, stylish, successful, and—at the time of the article—engaged to be married. In one image, Lopez, who is white, poses in a red suit and leans her arm against an olive-green door, her brown hair slicked back, and eyes heavily made up. She ticks all the boxes for ideal Christian womanhood in terms of age, race, social class, beauty, and—importantly—the movement out of singlehood.

And then we have the examples of the ideal proliferating through music. The most popular Christian recording artist in 2018, 2019, and 2020, according to *Billboard* magazine, was Lauren Daigle. Winner of two Grammy awards and two Dove awards, an accolade from the Gospel Music Industry, Daigle's album *How Can It Be* went platinum in 2015. Blending her evangelical faith and Southern roots with a hippie aesthetic, thirty-year-old Daigle presents a slightly different version of the standard Christian ideal. Yet, if you look closely, she still meets all the key markers: pretty, thin, young, middle class, and white. As of June 2021, she's single—but she's young, so there's still time for her meet and marry a Christian man, leaving her squarely within the remit of ideal womanhood.

All of these different textual and visual forms work together, like links in a chain, to craft the figure of an ideal Christian woman and reinforce the power of the norm. These days, one of the most common channels of representation is digital media, made popular by the numerous Christian women bloggers,

Instagram stars, and influencers. This, in turn, has expanded the avenues for normative profusion. One click on your phone and suddenly images, words, and representations of the ideal Christian woman pour forth.

Growing up in my American evangelical community in the 1990s and early 2000s, I learned about the good Christian woman through books (*Let Me Be a Woman*), magazines (*Brio*), and musicians (Amy Grant). Today, with the popularity of digital media, Christian women have an ever-expanding array of examples to which they can compare themselves. Moreover, these images transcend the local and contribute toward a global understanding of normativity. An evangelical woman in London may follow a California-based blogger, just as one in Miami might emulate a Christian influencer from Caracas. The image of the ideal woman has multiplied and spread, making her nearly inescapable, yet also nearly identical. In other words, the integrity of the ideal has withstood the profusion. But the advent of digital media has also expanded opportunities for religious women by threatening traditional forms of authority and opening up alternative channels of power, especially for women who have been denied church leadership. This leads some scholars to suggest that social media poses a threat to traditional Christian authority structures.[8] But is digital media a threat, or is it just a replication of the norm? I flew to California to find out.

It was a sure sign that I had strayed from evangelical culture when, much to my surprise, my sister introduced me to the world of female evangelical influencers. I knew about Carrie Lloyd's books, and I had read *Magnify* and browsed through articles in *Relevant*, a popular online magazine for Christians, but Christian influencers?

My sister, Natalee, who prides herself on keeping a close pulse on the American celebrity world, pokes me in the side as we sit next to each other in Starbucks on a particularly hot summer afternoon in Sacramento. "There's one of the Christian women influencers!" she hisses. I follow her eyes over to a blond-haired, blue-eyed woman who takes off her sunglasses as she walks into the air-conditioned coffee shop. My sister and I watch her in silence, our gaze unrelenting as the woman walks to the counter to order.

Natalee reaches into her purse and pulls out her cracked iPhone. Her fingers tap the screen, inputting the passcode and then clicking on Instagram. Within an instant, the woman a few feet away from us appears on my sister's phone. "Alyssa Quilala is her name," Natalee whispers, as if we are colluding as undercover agents instead of observing an evangelical Christian woman at a popular coffee chain.

When I return home later that day, I sit down to the computer and begin exploring the realm of online evangelical influencers. I find a deep, deep rabbit hole with no exit and a dense web of connections. Alyssa is married to musician Chris Quilala, of Jesus Culture Sacramento.[9] Jesus Culture is an offshoot of Bethel Church in Redding, California, where Carrie Lloyd pastors. Alyssa is also friends with Caressa Prescott, the wife of Ben Prescott, of Free Chapel Church in Orange County, California. This Free Chapel branch is one of seven sites ("campuses") led by head pastor and televangelist Jentezen Franklin, Caressa's father. Caressa and Alyssa both follow another Insta celebrity, DawnCheré Wilkerson, who is co-pastor, with her husband, Rich, of Vous Church in Miami. The couple gained fame after Rich performed the marriage of Kim Kardashian and Kanye West. And in 2015, DawnCheré and Rich were featured in TV docuseries called *Rich in Faith*, which detailed their lives as pastors in Miami. I do some more digging and learn that Vous Church spun out of megachurch Trinity, also in Miami, run by the senior Rich Wilkerson and his wife, Robyn.

The web of female evangelical influencers spreads across the country. It turns out that DawnCheré is friends with Jessa, the ideal woman who spoke at the Women Rise event I attended in New York. At a church conference in London, DawnCheré posted a video on Instagram of her and Jessa pushing their strollers through Hyde Park on a particularly sunny afternoon, joined by some evangelical women who attend Thames Gathering Place. And in June 2019, DawnCheré, Rich Jr., Jentezen, and the Bethel worship team all came together at the Forward Conference in Atlanta, which an estimated thirteen thousand students attended, making the event a veritable who's who of the evangelical world.

Standing just one notch higher, however, is the biggest female Christian star of all: Rachel Hollis. With more than 1.7 million Instagram followers and two *New York Times* best sellers to her name, Hollis is the paradigm of a successful Christian woman. However, she also differs from other social media stars—first, because she isn't a pastor's wife; and second, because even though she professes to be a Christian in her books and social media, Hollis doesn't use her faith as her platform. Her focus is on helping women to achieve financial success and career advancement, rather than on faith, a reversal of how other evangelical social media stars use their Instagram accounts.

It doesn't come as a surprise that these social media stars all share the characteristics of the ideal woman as described to me by the evangelical women with whom I spoke. They are all white, attractive, and young; their lifestyle, habits, and hobbies signify middle- to upper-class tastes; they are stylish but not overtly sexy in how they dress. And they are all married (to men). Several identify themselves as "wife of" or "mother of" in their social media bios. And yet there are some features that women didn't mention. For one thing, they all work out. A lot.

In an Instagram post from February 2019, Prescott is lifting weights and doing crunches outdoors at a boot camp–type setting. Underneath the images, she writes, "Trying to get my best body and doing it in the most comfortable @varley set. Strong is the new skinny." The hashtag #ad lets viewers know that the post is a paid advertisement sponsored by the athletics brand Varley. Users comment favorably on Prescott's body and appearance, writing messages such as "You should be a model!," "Stunning," and "What's your diet?" Elsewhere, Courtney Lopez, who was featured in *Magnify*, posted a series of shots from her bachelorette party in Cabo San Lucas, Mexico, where she and five other women, including Selena Gomez, are wearing white swimsuits and posing on the beach. In the comments section, Prescott wrote, "I'm dying at these photos!! You look insane." Beneath that, Lopez responded, "My first year consistently working out. I'm posing 1000 photos lol," to which Prescott wrote, "It shows!!!" Another user asked, "What is the regime?! You look so good!"

Similarly, Rachel Hollis uploaded a picture of herself working out, which gathered more than thirty-three thousand likes. She captioned it with, "We workout everyday [*sic*] not so we can LOOK good but so we can FEEL good." Other posts feature Hollis and her husband training for a marathon, or selfies in the gym—which, she notes, she sometimes visits twice a day when preparing for a public speaking event. Again, as in Prescott's post, Hollis attributes her motivation to exercise as a desire to feel good rather than to look good. But by aligning working out with "feeling good," or promoting being "strong" rather than "skinny," Rachel Hollis's and Caressa Prescott's exercise pictures extend the pressure for women to be beautiful from the outside to the inside.[10] It's no longer enough just to look good on the outside; now evangelical women must *feel* good as well. What's more, "feeling good" about one's body, as these images imply, is only possible when one has a slim, middle-class, white body.

Many of the social media stars' pictures feature them with their husbands, who they describe as "hunky" or "sexy," sometimes in intimate kissing poses that make you feel like you are intruding. Other times they are smiling and declaring their undying love. Their husbands are usually pastors, though in Hollis's case, her husband is the cofounder of Hollis Company, their multimedia, lifestyle, and coaching enterprise. And the women's role of wife is central to their identity. Caressa Prescott calls herself "Wife, Mommy, Pastor + Friend" on her website, Leo & Luca, whereas Quilala writes "Wife to Chris Quilala" on the first line of her Instagram bio. (Later, when I mention this to Liv, she says, "They need to get a job!")

In November 2018, Wilkerson posted a Polaroid photo of herself and her husband embracing in the sea. The caption states simply "Us." Similarly, Quilala praises her husband for supporting her to have a fourth child. In one Instagram post, she writes, "He told me I was beautiful when I felt like a blob," next to a heart and a fire emoji. The image that goes with the text is a photo of her, heavily pregnant, wearing a long cotton dress with a high slit, embracing her husband as she leans on the kitchen table. On Prescott's Instagram feed, romantic photos with her husband are common—whether they are frolicking on the beach in Florida or wearing strappy sandals while vacationing at five-star resorts in Cabo San Lucas. Such images link beauty with heterosexual marriage and suggest that beauty is achieved not only by makeup and clothing endorsements but also by the approval of your husband.

In the "Lifestyle" section of her website, Prescott even provides suggestions for Valentine's Day gifts "for him" and "for her." A "sexy teddy" and Yves Saint Laurent lipsticks are listed as gifts for her, while for him, Prescott writes, "I will just say this, the best you can give a guy is sex. I think thats [sic] pretty universal for every type of personality. If you want to do more than that I would suggest these things to go along with it :)"[11]

What is particularly interesting about these sexy marital posts, and others like them, is that they are embedded within an evangelical context in which single women (and, to a lesser extent, men) are urged to maintain premarital purity. Purity messages, as the last chapter showed, argue that *if* you wait, *then* your marriage will be blessed. Thus, these posts become part of the purity ecosystem by providing single evangelical women with a visual representation of what awaits them if they postpone sex until marriage.[12]

As I fell further down the rabbit hole of social media stars, flicking through their Instagram pages for hours on end, I also started attending services at Quilala's church, Jesus Culture Sacramento. I slipped discreetly into the back of the dark high school auditorium where they met on Sundays. The rock band on stage belted out songs of praise and I observed worshippers' bodies swaying as they confronted transcendence. I chatted to congregants before and after services, while waiting in line for coffee at their pop-up café or browsing the bookshop. And every Sunday I watched Alyssa, dutifully present in the front row, as her husband sang from the stage. I thought about her life and wondered about the real woman behind this image of perfection.

One Sunday, I decided to skip Jesus Culture and visit their mother church, Bethel, a nondenominational megachurch in northern California, with its dedicated worship music school—the School of Supernatural Ministry—where believers from all over the world train in the "gifts of the spirit." The church has a congregation of eleven thousand and estimates that another thirty thousand listen to their online livestream.[13] In a city of ninety thousand residents, Bethel now holds tremendous influence: Redding's mayor is part of Bethel's leadership team, the church donated $500,000 to the Redding Neighborhood Police Unit to keep it from closing, and they were influential in convincing Delta Airlines to open a nonstop flight from Los Angeles to Redding.[14] Given their close ties with the city council, the church leaders faced controversy in 2017, when the Redding Planning Commission approved Bethel's plans for a $96 million expansion, which some residents protested on the grounds that it would increase traffic congestion, lead to water shortages, and further drive up housing prices.[15] Bethel also has been in the news for its controversial supernatural practices, such as praying for God to raise the dead and worshipping under swirling gold dust, which they call a "Glory Cloud" and attribute to God's presence.[16]

Back in London, the evangelicals I met at Thames Gathering Place spoke of Bethel positively and passionately, as a sort of mecca for evangelicals to visit and experience a revitalization of their faith. Maddie had spent a few months at the School of Supernatural Ministry one summer, and although she criticized some aspects of their theology, she held the church in high regard.

Driving along Interstate 5 north from Sacramento to Redding, a two-lane freeway with golden-brown fields on either side, I angled the air-conditioning vents of the car toward my face. There was nobody else on the road that warm Sunday morning, apart from a few truckers hauling their cargo on the lengthy thoroughfare that stretches from the north of the state to the south. A news story about urbanization and architecture droned on in the background, but my mind was elsewhere, anticipating this church that I had heard so much about.

My phone hummed and Maddie's name flashed across the screen. *Have fun at Bethel! Let me know how it goes. I loved it out there . . .*

At the turnoff to Redding, I slowed the car and prepared to brake at a rusty stop sign. Only a three-hour drive, and yet the setting had changed dramatically. American flags filled my line of vision, rippling in the breeze, poking out of mailboxes, affixed to front doors, rising like tall redwood trees from scorched lawns. Located just two hours from the Oregon border, Redding is a fertile region, which attracted growth during the twentieth century due to its two large dams. Because of Bethel's popularity, the city has experienced enormous growth, and visitors from all over the country and the world now make the journey up to what was once just a sleepy city in the north of the state.

As I entered Bethel's campus, I noticed more flags, but not just American ones. Flags from other countries lined the newly paved asphalt road winding up to the church, extending out of tall metal poles and stretching into the cloudless sky, so that the entrance felt more like a multinational organization than a church. I parked in an overflow parking lot, directed there by men and women in fluorescent vests. My car rattled across the uneven gravel, searching for a spot among rows of minivans, their windows covered in dirt and dust, attesting to a long journey.

Walking into the main church building, I passed by the prayer room, a circular wooden hut with windows all around, and saw more flags, including the blue and white flag of Israel. A middle-aged man with a crooked smile and a balding head greeted me at the entrance. The main auditorium was full, he said, as was the spillover room, so I was very welcome to go into the second spillover room to watch the service on a live feed. He handed me a church bulletin and pointed a knobby finger in the direction I needed to go.

I found a seat in the back of the second spillover room, already crowded with young families. The head pastor, Bill Johnson, a slick-looking man with graying black hair and a long face, spoke to us from two large screens. Johnson was dressed casually that day, and he perched on a bar stool as he addressed the audience, just as the pastors at Thames Gathering and Wellspring often did. He invited everyone to stand up to pray for the tithes and offerings, a standard procedure in evangelical services, so I rose with the rest of the congregants and closed my eyes in preparation.

"Dear Lord," Johnson began, beseechingly, "we pray you would give us checks in the mail and bonuses at work . . ." My eyes popped opened in surprise. Everyone continued reciting the prayer along with Johnson, but there were no words on the screen. I grabbed the leaflet that the bald man had handed me and riffled through it, searching for the words to the prayer.

"And we pray you'd give us favor with our bosses and commissions from sales." A middle-aged man in front of me wrapped his arm around his daughter, pulling her in close to his side. Someone behind me shouted "Amen!," off the cuff. I still couldn't find the words.

"Lord, we ask that you bless us and bless our tithes and offerings, that they would be used to further your kingdom. In Jesus's name—amen!" The churchgoers stamped this final *amen* with enthusiasm before opening their eyes, sitting down, and readying their wallets for the offering basket, which was shortly passed around.

I remembered this prosperity prayer months later when Johnson came out in favor of Donald Trump. He defended his candidate in a written statement by arguing, "God gives us the ability to make wealth, and that merely giving people money without work can create a lifestyle of dependency that is dangerous for them and our government."[17] And I remembered it when, after my trip to Bethel, I noticed how luxurious the evangelical social media stars' lives appeared.

In 2012, Esther Houston, a former model from Brazil, married Joel Houston, coleader of Hillsong New York. Hillsong NYC is an offshoot of Hillsong Australia, a megachurch founded by Joel's parents, which has expanded to branches all over the world. In one Instagram photo, Esther Houston smiles as she wades into the ocean wearing a white shirtdress. She's tagged various expensive items in the post, including her dress, sunglasses, jewelry, and a Chanel purse.

In addition to promoting brands, evangelical social media stars shared pictures of their large and well-decorated homes and their shopping trips. Caressa Prescott's social media feed features an image of her carrying a shopping bag from the high-end designer Alexander Wang as she walks down a street in New York. In another, she simply posts a picture of a Celine shopping bag in a hotel room in Paris. And in November 2015, she posted selfie in a dressing room, wearing a floor-length beaded gown. The caption reads, "Oh you know just getting a dress for church tomorrow. #Sundaybest #casual #saturdaysareforshoppingwhile benstudies."

Similarly, Quilala has a series of dressing room selfies from Saks Fifth Avenue in San Francisco. She writes that she is trying to find a dress for the Grammys, which she will attend with her husband, who, along with the band Jesus Culture, was nominated for the Best Contemporary Christian Music Album award. Like Prescott, Quilala fuses her role as Christian woman and wife with wealth by writing, "I ended up catching a designer gown on flash sale for under $200. WHAT?! The Lord loves me, guys!" Even though they don't attend churches that are considered "prosperity churches," by linking their identity as Christians with shopping, these women perpetuate a prosperity gospel theology that suggests that obedience to God results in affluence, similar to the tithing prayer recited at Bethel on the Sunday when I attended.[18] And through social media, these evangelical stars conflate notions of ideal womanhood with Christian values and upper-class sensibilities.

Whether endorsing a political candidate, attacking a Senate bill, or rallying behind a particular issue, evangelical social media stars also use their influence to promote politics. At Quilala's church, Jesus Culture Sacramento, Pastor Banning Liebscher invoked politics during one of the Sunday services I attended. I knew that the lead pastors at Bethel publicly supported Donald Trump, but I wasn't sure how or if this extended to other policies.

That morning, Liebscher, a casually dressed white man in his thirties, spoke about SB 1146, a bill proposed by California senator Richard Lara that would close a loophole allowing religiously affiliated private universities that receive federal funding to discriminate against students and staff on the grounds of gender identity and sexual orientation. "We prayed for it to be shot down," Leibscher told the congregation that Sunday, "and they withdrew the bill from the Senate." The congregants clapped and cheered in reaction to this news. He went on to emphasize that, as a church, they had a "responsibility" to shape politics, because "what happens in Sacramento affects the nation as a capital city."

The evangelical women I interviewed also saw political engagement as a spiritual duty. And a key issue that concerned them was human trafficking. Jessa, the ideal woman who spoke at Women Rise, directed an antitrafficking organization. Wellspring even dedicated an evening service to the issue, featuring a female congregant who volunteered with an anti–sex trafficking charity. And several of the evangelical social media influencers posted selfies with a red cross on the back of their hand, a symbol for the End It Movement, which calls itself "a coalition of the leading organizations in the world in the fight for freedom [from slavery]."

American evangelicals' interest in anti–sex trafficking activism represents an attempt to rescue so-called defiled women, argues the scholar Elizabeth Bernstein.[19] Indeed, there has been disproportionate attention to trafficking as a social justice issue within white evangelicalism, where the language of "freedom" and "restoration" resonates with biblical parables such as the prodigal son, Jesus's atonement for human sins, and indeed, the entire conversion process, which promises freedom from one's previous life.

Politics, gender, and evangelicalism certainly collided in 2016, when 73 percent of white evangelical women voted for Donald Trump for president.[20] Sandra, whom I interviewed in August 2016, before the presidential election, told me she knew that the leaders at her evangelical megachurch wanted her to vote for Trump. Even still, she had hesitations. A former high school support worker who had only recently converted to evangelicalism, Sandra had left her job in San Francisco and was studying for a degree in pastoral counseling when I met her. Because of her line of work, she struggled to reconcile voting for Trump with her beliefs about equality and social justice.

Since 2016, evangelical social media stars have also expressed their political allegiance to Donald Trump. Just a few weeks before the 2016 presidential election, Prescott alluded to her support for Trump via an Instagram post. She wrote, "There are things that are apart [sic] of the foundation of my faith that I can't ignore. The sanctity of life . . . If this was the only reason why I have decided to vote it's enough of a reason to me. I understand there are many other important issues facing our country today but I choose to vote on the one most important to me . . . my precious innocent baby and his future, along with all future babies just like him." She cited Psalms 139:13–16, Bible verses often used by evangelicals to oppose abortion.

Two and a half years later, in May 2019, Prescott posted a picture of herself with her mother, Cherise Franklin; Ivanka Trump; and Paula White-Cain, pastor, speaker, and chairwoman of Trump's Evangelical Advisory Board. Prescott captioned the photo, "This administration is doing more than any other has in history to invest in women's economic empowerment and the next generation. I am so honored to have had the opportunity and seat at the table." The next day, Prescott uploaded a photo of herself standing alone in front of the White House in a brown dress and heels.

Apart from supporting Trump, there are other key conservative issues that white evangelical social media stars rally behind, such as antivaccination and military intervention. On April 7, 2017, the day after the first American attack on the Assad regime in Syria, Esther Houston shared a picture of herself laughing in a windowsill and wearing a silky pink dress that could be mistaken for a negligée. Her blond hair is tousled, as if she's just woken up, and her right leg is hiked up, exposing her thighs. "Don't be solely caught up in an image of a pink satin-wearing careless girl: I have my eyes wide open," Houston writes under the image. She continues, "At what point do we decide its [*sic*] enough injustice to idly witness? At what point do we stand up to other's [*sic*] lives at the risk of ours? At what point do we start denying lives in fear of losing ours? How much is too much? When do we protect ourselves and our loved ones and when do we actually and literally love others and somehow step in? If not this, then what is our Red Line?"

Previous studies documented evangelical women's involvement with right-wing politics through antiabortion advocacy and lobbying for abstinence-only education; contemporary evangelical women exercise their conservative political beliefs via social media.[21] In this sense, their social media activity represents a complementary extension of the political activities of their churches. And it adds another dimension to the figure of the ideal Christian woman: conservative political beliefs. "The virtual is also political," the scholar Monique Moultrie claims.[22] And nowhere is that more apparent than in the social media accounts of female evangelical influencers.

When I got back to New York, I asked the three women about these images. "This is not Christ's message!" Carys exclaimed, throwing her hands up in the air. Liv rolled her eyes and told me she had stopped following Prescott after her post with Ivanka Trump at the White House. Some of her friends followed Wilkerson, Prescott, and Quilala and were influenced by their version of Christian womanhood, she said, but she outright rejected that kind of thing.

And then I called Jo. When I spoke to her about the evangelical influencers, she didn't scoff like Liv did, nor did she reject them on theological grounds, like Carys. Her rage, which had so visibly motivated her words during our interview about the ideal Christian woman, the "Scandinavian Barbie," had dissipated. In its place I heard sorrow. Years of feeling like she never quite measured up to ideal Christian womanhood, of trying and failing to fit the norm, of being rejected by men again and again, had left Jo defeated.

The act of seeing is mutable and highly contested. We see images in specific ways, shaped by our own particular social environments and the political moment in which we find ourselves.[23] For example, a nonreligious woman skimming through Alyssa Quilala's Instagram feed would respond differently than an evangelical Christian woman, especially one from Sacramento or Redding. And looking at these images during Trump's presidency, with the knowledge that these women belong to churches that endorsed him, also changes your relationship to the image and the way you interpret it.

Images also elicit different affective responses. Carys, Maddie, Jo, and Liv reacted to evangelical social media stars' images with varying emotional expressions, from laughter to scorn to disgust to sadness. But other evangelical women respond with admiration, and that is what makes these stars so popular in the first place.[24] These specific ways of seeing make images relational as well as dependent on social context for meaning.

More importantly, these social media posts dynamically interact with other discursive material, such as magazine articles, sermons, purity books, and Bible study texts. These discursive parts link with one another and build the seemingly coherent figure of an ideal woman. The art historian Giselda Pollock writes, "These combinations interact and cross refer with other discourses, accumulating around certain points to create so dense a texture of mutual reference that some statements, and some visions, acquire the authority of the obvious."[25] And this is exactly what has happened: what it means to be an ideal Christian woman has become so *obvious*. The eye rolls and snickers that Carys, Jo, and Liv performed when I mentioned the ideal weren't just because they had tired of her; it was because she was so glaringly recognizable.

Female evangelical stars' use of digital media upholds the racial, class, and gender inequalities that many single evangelical women I met experienced in their churches. Of course, evangelical influencers are not all to blame, and their social media posts articulate and reinstate ideals of Christian womanhood that circulate in evangelical churches on an everyday relational level. They offer visual representations of normativity, a picture that connects to words that connects to videos that connects to real-life experiences of exclusion and invisibility. In a feedback loop of representation and response, ordinary evangelical women themselves shape the ideal just as social media celebrities do through the images they post. The material and the figural exist in copresence. But alongside this critique, I also have sympathy for the ideal Christian woman. Believe it or not, there's also pain on the other side, not just for those who are denied entry into ideal womanhood.

Growing up with my father, the Pastor, meant that the rest of us were also given roles for which we never applied. My sister and I were the Pastor's Daughters and my mother was the Pastor's Wife, a role she never would have wanted, as a shy and private woman who preferred to remain inconspicuous. Among her Pastor's Wife friends, women in whom she could confide about the pressures that came with the job, was Annette. Annette was the antithesis of my mom. Originally from the South, she was gregarious and feminine. She always wore lipstick—varying shades of pink—and she baked a lot. She mentored younger women in the church and stood on stage next to her husband during prayers, smiling widely into the bright white lights. In many ways, she embodied a 1990s version of the ideal Christian woman.

I recently called Annette and asked if I could interview her about her years as a pastor's wife, now that she had retired from the role. Speaking in her characteristic rambling way, Annette admitted that actually those years in the church had been hard.

"You know, there was a lot of pressure back then to look a certain way, to *be* a certain way . . . even though my husband never put that pressure on me . . . I mean, bless him, he never would have done that."

And then she made a startling confession: at the age of fifteen, she'd gotten pregnant and had an abortion. Her home life had been difficult, she said. Her dad was an alcoholic, and after he had an affair with his secretary, he abandoned the family. Then, a year later, she became pregnant again, and this time she hid the pregnancy until it was too late to terminate it. She had the child and gave him up for adoption.

She'd kept these pregnancies and the baby a secret for nearly thirty years, in order to support her husband's ministry, in order to squeeze into the role of the unblemished pastor's wife. But the secrecy had taken a toll, she explained, one that no one even knew was being taken. She'd suffered bouts of debilitating depression and at one point had even considered suicide.

"Don't worry, honey, your mama knows all this already. I'm fairly open about it all now," she reassured me.

It wasn't until her husband passed away, years later, and her secret was released into the wild that she finally found peace. In her words, "I stopped performing, and I started actually living."

After speaking with Annette, I started to wonder whether the pastor's wives who have become social media influencers were also performing. What secrets were they harboring? It would be another three years before I found out.

The ideal woman is crafted from lines of exclusion, which cut across age, beauty, and marital status, but even more intractably, the ideal cuts across racial and class lines. In an environment where womanhood is so circumscribed, the question arises, What about those who do not fit the ideal? And a second, more sobering question is, What about those who *cannot* fit the ideal, no matter how hard they try?

6

WOUNDS THAT NEVER HEAL

Because yes *is a small and sacred and savage word all at the same time.*

— Cristina Rivera Garza

The first thing you notice when you attend an evangelical church, whether in America or Britain, are the smiles. These smiles stand out from the everyday, expressionless faces that greet you in supermarket aisles or stare back at you in stalled traffic. In evangelicalism, smiles abound. And you have a variety: the toothy type that greets you when you first walk in the door; discreet, unimposing ones that acknowledge you as you wait in line for the bathroom; generous smiles that brighten an entire face, radiating from every pastor, worship leader, and congregant.

These were the smiles I encountered when I walked into Wellspring in early November for Awaken, an event for women interested in church leadership. Unlike Women Rise, Liv's unofficial association of feminist women, Wellspring sponsored Awaken, and two female pastors-in-training hosted the event. Over a hundred women filled the church lobby that day—mostly white; mostly in their twenties and thirties.

It had been a while since I'd been to Wellspring. This was partly on purpose—I'd needed some distance—and partly on account of other demands for my attention. But this Saturday morning I caught an early train to meet Carys and take the pulse of evangelical women's fight for equality. I could tell from Carys's messages that this event filled her with hope—hope because it was happening, and even more, hope because Wellspring had sponsored it. This hope no doubt rode on the heels of news that Willow Creek Community Church in Illinois would soon be co-pastored by Heather Larson, making it one of the only mega-churches in the United States led by a woman. (*THE NEW PAS-TOR AT WILLOW CREEK IS A WOMAN*, Carys had texted me, upon reading the news.) Carys was not optimistic by nature. If anything, she veered toward cynicism, a character trait she'd developed over many years working as a nurse caring for dying children. Yet, in her newly restored Christian state, she continually wrested herself from pessimism and reoriented herself toward hope.

When I walk into the grand building with its high ceilings and wooden beams, the first thing I see are Carys's cowboy boots. She's standing near the buffet table with a coffee in one hand and a blueberry muffin in the other. Two pretty brunette women with identical haircuts flank Carys on either side. She introduces me to them, and one, the more talkative of the pair, tells me she attends an evangelical church near Washington, DC. They're both considering ordination, she says, and they view this event as a taster session to see whether they will pursue formal church training. I want to get Carys alone, to see how she's been, but the brunettes don't give us a chance. At this point, Carys has been working for the church for nearly nine months, and from the intermittent messages and phone calls, I've gleaned that it hasn't been easy. But she always assures me that she's finding the work meaningful and remains certain that this is what God wants for her.

The four of us take our seats and I scan the room. The all-female audience is abuzz. Nervous excitement swerves all around us, bouncing off every oak panel and stained glass window. Voices climb louder and louder; laughter gushes out. One of the pastors organizing the event, a tall, slim woman named Jane, takes to the stage, carrying a microphone. She welcomes us to the event, underlining its importance in the church's history, and without further ado, introduces the pastor of a "sister church," who sadly cannot be here in person but wanted to share his remarks via a video recording.

The lights cut out and the image of a fresh-faced man in a denim shirt appears on the screen.

"Hey everyone!" he starts. "I'm so sorry I couldn't be there, but I just wanted to say how glad I am that you've come and how important the issue of women leadership is to us here. At our church, we actually don't have any women in leadership roles yet, *but* we are desperate for that to change. And we are actively encouraging women to rise up and receive the support they need to be leaders."

I fold my arms and stare back defiantly. I'm not sure what bothers me more: the way he uses the word *desperate* so beseechingly or that I am being addressed by a white male pastor first thing in the morning, at an event organized for women.

"Personally, I am all for female leadership in the church. I say, 'You go, girls!'" he exclaims.

The audience, already perched on emotional tenterhooks, erupts in applause and gleeful shouts.

Then it's back to Jane, who reminds us about the different panels we have to choose from throughout the day, all arranged in a tidy table on the paper handout we received when we arrived.

Carys tells me she wants to go to the talk on theology. After years of studying scripture and memorizing Bible verses, I decide to pass, and I stay for the "Relationships and Family" panel instead. We promise to meet up for lunch.

The talkative brunette has also decided to stay behind, and as the session begins, she abandons her chair and moves closer to me. Jane is coleading the session, along with younger and much tinier pastor named Alice. The women take turns sharing, in unscripted streams of consciousness, how they manage the demands of being pastor, mother, and wife.

"My identity bounced from church intern to girlfriend to fiancée to associate pastor," says Jane. She keeps her legs crossed and leans so far forward that I worry she may topple over.

Alice speaks very quickly, in a sugary sweet voice. She tells us her husband is a full-time paid pastor right now and she has stepped away from ministry to take care of their two small kids. It would be a big ask for her husband to look after two small children so she could go back to work, she says. "Besides, it's such a gift to make my children my full priority right now."

When they solicit questions from the audience, a young woman with a messy bun and a forest green hoodie shoots up her hand.

"What I find is that men support women in leadership on a theological level but not in practice. They have their little locker-room banter, their snide, sexist comments, and when I speak up about it, I end up feeling like either a doormat or a bulldog. How do I raise issues without being slotted into one of these categories?"

Jane takes the mic and clears her throat. She tells the woman that raising an issue doesn't have to mean you are a "bra-burning feminist." In fact, she continues, she often has to speak up in meetings at Wellspring and ask where all the women are. "It's quite men-heavy at Wellspring," she adds, by way of explanation.

When we break for lunch, I wander through swarms of cheerful women and search for Carys. I find her in line for a sandwich, in deep conversation with a pleasantly plump middle-aged woman whose commanding presence gives the appearance of a matriarch. Carys introduces us and then quickly runs off to find her friends.

"This is a watershed moment, you realize," the matriarch declares. Before I can state whether I do or do not realize this, she continues, "I've been a pastor for years and it is really unprecedented to have this event. It's very important to have the male church leaders stand up there and name this problem." I smile a weak, perfunctory smile, one that is diluted by skepticism. *Is naming the problem enough, when the problem continues to persist?* I think to myself. But I don't say it aloud because I imagine my question will be met with platitudes such as "At least it's a start" or "You have to name it before it can change." I'd heard these types of phrases from evangelical women and church leaders ever since I'd started this research more than two and a half years before.[1]

At the afternoon session I attend, called "Raising the Next Generation of Female Church Leaders," I hear more optimistic refrains. A row of four church leaders, an even mix of men and women, sits before us in white plastic chairs, holding pads of paper and pens, looking like an interview panel or some kind of hearing.

"You're at a turning point here today, a key moment in the history of Wellspring and its sister churches," says a man named Paul, who sounds sincere, unlike the pastor who opened up the day's events. He says he wants to figure out how to empower women to enter ordained ministry, and to address the glaring lack of women leaders. But how to do so?

One of the key barriers, we learn from a female pastor who seems beleaguered and tired, is women themselves. "A lack of self-confidence is a particularly female problem," she says. "We need to encourage girls and women and raise their confidence. They aren't going for ordination roles because they aren't *believing in themselves.*"

This, too, I have heard before. At a Women Rise event the previous year, an entire evening had been devoted to helping women see their value and combat perfectionism. The speaker that night, a male church leader, pleaded for women to celebrate their successes. He started to well up as he shared his sadness over society's beauty standards, which he called "unjust and debasing" to women. Women in the audience whooped and shouted "Amen!" in agreement.

And it was what Jo had said, when I first met her. "Women need to step up to the plate," she'd told me, with her characteristic bluntness. "We hold ourselves back by not believing in ourselves."

By identifying women's self-esteem problem as a key barrier to reaching leadership positions, this line of thinking rests the church's problem with gender inequality squarely on the shoulders of Christian women themselves. It blames women's own lack of confidence, rather than blaming majority-male leadership teams at churches, who consistently select men instead of women for ordination.[2] By centralizing individual barriers, it erases structural ones.

Later that day, as Carys, her friends, and I walk toward the subway station, I ask them what they thought of the event. One of the brunettes says that, as a bisexual woman, she was irritated with the assumption that all the women present were straight. (The "Relationships and Family" panel, for example, sought to help women considering ordination balance their ministry with a husband and children.) Carys was discouraged by the speakers' overwhelming tendency to put the responsibility on women for not achieving leadership positions. I agree with both their complaints, and there is a pause in our conversation as the four of us march down the sidewalk in silence.

"At least it's a start," Carys says at last.

But *was* it a start? Who is to say where, in the long battle for women's equality in evangelicalism, this event falls?[3] For some, it might have been the start; for others, the middle. Looking back now, more than four years later, to me it actually looks more like the end.

The summer before the Awaken event, there had been more women and women of color speaking at Wellspring's annual church retreat. Carys and Jo texted me this news, separately, from the retreat. They'd laced their messages with buoyancy and hope, conveyed through an abundance of exclamation marks and capital letters. I read these messages with interest from my family home in California. In recent years, Bill Johnson, the vocal Trump-supporting pastor from Bethel Church, had been one of the keynote speakers. At least *he* wasn't speaking this year, Jo added.

After the retreat, Carys pointed out that Wellspring had also started a singleness ministry. It aimed to eradicate the stigma associated with being single, a stigma that grew more acute as women got older and remained unmarried. By themselves, each of these occurrences wouldn't have meant much, but taken together—the Awaken event, the popularity of Women Rise, the female lead pastor at Willow Creek Community Church, the women of color speaking at the retreat—they coalesced into expectancy, an indication that change was under way, or at least imminent.

But at the same time that these promises shot up from the earth, like fledgling sprouts reaching toward the bright spring sun, a silent opposition thundered forth. Not the obvious type of opposition—the kind where church leaders outright prohibit women from holding any authority, because of the Bible. This enemy was shapeless and formless, diffuse and destructive, everywhere and nowhere, deeply felt and yet untraceable.

"Power is tolerable only on condition that it masks a substantial part of itself," asserts Michel Foucault. "Its success is proportional to an ability to hide its own mechanisms." He implores us to discover the "local power relations at work," to understand how power, as a dispersed yet ubiquitous phenomena, shape shifts according to its microclimate.[4]

I first became aware of this localized form of power at the Awaken event, in a passing comment said so swiftly and lightly that it could have drifted right past me unnoticed: "Give me a Catholic opposed to women in leadership any time over a church leader who theologically supports it but doesn't practice it." This was said by a woman in her early fifties, an associate pastor from a different church, who knew Carys, as she reached across me to grab an orange, avoiding my eyes, and then walked away.

After this, I became more attuned to how this slippery opposition worked. I became attentive to its machinations; I learned its tactics. I start taking note when Carys complains to me that she's been left off a group e-mail at work and missed a meeting as a result. When she follows it up with her superiors, she's told it was a careless mistake, a harmless oversight. But it doesn't feel like a mistake, she tells me. It feels purposeful. And then it happens again. She starts to wonder if maybe her e-mail is broken, if it's just all in her head.

Or when Jo calls me from the Midwest, having recently moved home to be near her family. The line is scratchy and our words keep cutting out, the connection made worse by the merciless wind that wraps around me as I cycle to work.

"I was never utilized at church because I was a certain type of woman. A *single* certain type of woman. A woman of a certain ilk," she says, evaluating her decision to leave Wellspring. She tells me that many people recognized what a good singing voice she has ("one of the best in the church, to be honest"), and yet she was never promoted to worship leader, despite the mentoring she had received for the role. Despite the prophetic word she had received during an emotional worship service. Despite the calling God had placed on her life.

One Sunday, a few months before she moved, during a break in worship practice, Jo's friend had told her that she'd just discovered her boyfriend was cheating on her. "Well, I hope someone rips his nut sack off!" Jo replied, louder than expected. The rest of the worship team immediately halted their conversations to look at Jo and her friend. The senior pastor, who was present that afternoon, glanced from Jo to the worship leader. "You need to get your team under control," he said tartly.

"Don't cheat on my friends," Jo retorted.

"And that's why I was never promoted," she says to me now, as I angle my head away from the wind, straining to catch her words, to deposit them into my head like coins in a piggy bank. "That's why I was relegated to backup singer, despite having one of the best voices in the church. I mean, what did he think, that I actually go around ripping off nut sacks in my free time? Just for fun?"

I laugh. *A woman of a certain ilk.*

With the lens of what I now know about this type of power, I reexamine Liv's interview, conducted several years ago, when I barely knew her. Doing so brings me fresh insight.

"What I found really frustrating when I joined the church at twenty-six and was identified as an all-star with heaps of potential, was that time and time again I would see men join the church at the same level and get put straight in with the church leaders. They would be taken to football games, flown over to Napa on a private plane to go to a winery. They would be supported, you know? One of the male church leaders started doing all these leadership weekends where he would take fifteen men away to a cabin in the woods and really invest in them. And nothing like that was happening for women."

When I relisten to her story, it's two years later. Liv has been allowed to carry on with Women Rise, though not as a church-sponsored ministry, and she's maintained her high-level job as director of communications. The church leaders have even matched her with a mentor—a woman just a few years older, with two small children—but so far, Liv hasn't hopped on any private planes to Napa or lounged in a cabin in the woods at a leadership weekend.

But why not? More than eight years have passed, eight years in which church leaders at Wellspring and Thames Gathering have been "desperate for more women in leadership" and women have been eager to take up more senior roles. Women have started feminist groups, put themselves forward for ordination, quit their jobs in order to work for the church. They've complained publicly in staff meetings and privately to senior pastors that there aren't enough women, let alone enough women of color or working-class women, in positions of authority. A Black American woman I spoke to said, "For people who feel the need to go to somebody in leadership to talk about spiritual stuff, it's really disproportional not having any people of color—*any* color—and not having any women. And I know that Wellspring is trying like crazy to address it. But I also know that, within the congregation, there is a ripple feeling of *Is there a racism issue here?*"

Now, it's been nearly a decade since I started this research, yet the majority of leaders at Thames Gathering Place in London are still male. The same thing continues at Bethel Church: the senior leadership team is composed of either married couples or men. And though some women occupy senior roles at Wellspring, the lead pastor is male. Again, all white.

"We are desperate for that to change."

"I am all for female leadership."

"You go, girls!"

Why aren't things changing?

As I write this, I'm seated outdoors in a garden in Istanbul, far away from American or British evangelicals, seeking refuge in distance, endeavoring to write myself out of a story that is almost too painful to write—more painful than if these promises had never been made. If only I could reorder time and space and send these four women to the evangelical church I attended growing up, where women weren't even permitted to pray out loud, let alone get up front and speak from the pulpit, and where the very idea of a woman pastor remained outside the bounds of possibility. At least then, they wouldn't cling to hope. This is a perverse wish, and an impossible one, because these four women would never attend a church that prohibited women in leadership. This is exactly the problem. And as the call to prayers rings out over the humid city, I start to think that maybe evangelical leaders know this.

A woman I spoke to a few years ago, a Black British woman who had recently married, reflected on her experiences in a majority-white evangelical community. "I suppose I've always been on the edge of the inside," she told me. I liked this metaphor. It connoted a very specific location that was neither at the center of church life nor fully outside it. It described a sort of borderland, a region on the outskirts, characterized by tension and contradiction. According to Gloria Anzaldúa, "A borderland is a vague and undetermined place created by the emotional residue of an unnatural boundary. It is in a constant state of transition. The prohibited and forbidden are its inhabitants."[5] In the Christian context, a borderland is an in-between place for women who don't fully fit but don't leave the church. It's the place where the four evangelical women I came to know well spent large amounts of time, where they were exiled every time they tried to move closer to the center and bumped up against resistance.

As a symbolic location, the borderland engenders various emotions: paranoia, self-doubt, confusion, pain. Indeed, when I reread my fieldwork journals, those unlined pages of observations and analysis, I am struck by how often the word *pain* appears. In many of these instances, it is unclear whether I was writing about the women's pain, my pain for them, or my own pain from the past. Sometimes the word *raw* or *pain* stands alone on an entire page, circled, underlined, the word traced over several times with ballpoint pen, thickened with pathos.

Heidi, another Black British woman, who had attended Thames Gathering Place for a few years but had already moved on to another evangelical church by the time I met her, said, "I am constantly fighting against who I actually am." I transposed the quote onto a blank page, writing in haste on the street corner outside her office after our interview. Next to it I wrote, *Pain: It was that she felt so not okay with herself.* Again, it's unclear, looking over these notes now, whether I was referring to her pain, to mine, or to a confluence of the two, like two estuaries that merge together, forming one furious rush of water.

Anger also germinates at the borderland. And as time went on and she continued to battle a shapeless enemy, Liv grew angrier and angrier.

"The other day I was told, once again, that I'm intimidating. I'm *not* intimidating! I'm a warm personality, I'm very open, I'm very personable. I'm a seven on the Enneagram [personality test], the fun-loving type that loves socializing, loves interacting. I know that I'm not an intimidating person. I know that, because I'm successful and I speak up, they rephrase that as intimidating." It's a Friday night and we're at the movie theater, chatting in our seats before the film starts. Liv lowers her voice and looks around her suspiciously before continuing. "Some things I've spoken out about for the last year at Wellspring—I'm not sure if anyone is listening—is where are the people of color? And where are the women preaching? Why is it that every time a man gets on stage to give a sermon, he is introduced as a husband and a father? How is that relevant to what he's preaching? In staff meetings, they always celebrate engagements and weddings, so there is this silent message of 'All the single people better hurry up!'"

"Why are you looking around nervously?" I ask.

"Well, you just never know who might be here listening!"

I shake my head and then ask her if these grievances ever cause her to question her faith.

"It makes me angry; it doesn't make me question my faith. For example, I also think that homosexuality is fine. I get angry that the church doesn't agree, but it doesn't make me feel angry at God; it makes me feel angry at the church. I feel very comfortable—and I know a lot of people don't—but I feel very comfortable holding doubt, criticism, and anger in one hand,

and in the other hand holding my faith, and not feeling like I have to make a choice between the two."

She tucks a foot underneath her, so she's propped up higher, and straightens her bright yellow sundress. I tell Liv that I can't recount how many times evangelical women have told me they are considered intimidating—and there have been some surprising cases. There was the thirty-year-old financial consultant in London who refused to pursue ordination, even though her pastor encouraged her to, because she hadn't decided if it was biblical or not. She had very few male friends, she told me, because "they haven't known how to handle me. They've been a bit suspicious, challenged, and intimidated."

There was also Courtney, an American evangelical woman who worked for the church and said, "Maybe I'm too intimidating. Maybe because I'm a pastor here and I've got strong opinions about stuff, even though I'm always waiting to listen to the other side, I think some guys just find me intimidating."

The most surprising was a gentle, soft-spoken white woman from New Zealand, in whose presence I felt instantly calmed. "Two guy friends have told me 'Sarah, sometimes you can be intimidating,'" she reported, delivering the indictment with a breathy sigh. "At first, I thought, Okay do I need to dull things down? Do I need to change? And then I thought, Well no! I am strong, and I'm not going to stop being a strong personality . . . I am a passionate person, and I can't tone that down. I've tried, and it doesn't work. And I am independent, but I'm not above asking for help, I'm not above saying 'Hey, I can't do this.'" Her voice drifted off in something resembling what the poet and philosopher Denise Riley calls a "lachrymose wrath," that heady mix of fury, powerlessness, and despair.[6]

The borderland is also a very lonely place. Precisely because it is unaccounted for, unindexed, outside the norm, it isolates and separates its inhabitants. Blighted by a dense fog, women stumble along in this liminal space without a road map, and often without knowing they have company.

Brianna, a Black American woman in her late thirties, told me, "I like to try and be on the periphery." When I asked her why, she responded, "I feel like I shouldn't really be there, or I should be there with a male figure and he should then be my husband, because the first thing they'll ask you is 'So how's your dating life going?'" Brianna's single status took on a life of its own and became an "it"—as in, "I don't want *it* to be highlighted." In a setting where marriage and motherhood are so highly esteemed, Brianna experienced singleness as a concealed injury that must stay hidden. This injury oriented her toward the margins, the outside of the inside.

At the end of our interview, as I packed up my recorder and notepad and prepared to leave, I offhandedly remarked that her answers were very common.

"Wow," she replied, her eyes wide with surprise and pleasure. "I thought I was the only one."

After we drop the other women at the subway station, Carys and I finally have time alone. We wander to a nearby coffee shop and she tells me that it's hard being a working-class woman in this evangelical environment. Even if there are other working-class people around, middle- and upper-middle-class culture has so deeply burrowed into the very upholstery of the church community that it has become the unspoken, codified texture of the place; it pervades speech, language, gestures, and social interactions.[7]

How does this texture show itself?

"The fact that everyone here has at least a bachelor's degree. Where I come from, no one does! Here, their parents might be doctors or lawyers, or at least have master's degrees. My mom is a preschool teacher and my dad works at a grocery store. And I guess little social interactions that you learn when you go to certain schools and move in certain circles. There's a particular way of speaking that comes across as fairly cultivated, and it's usually very subtle."

And what does it feel like?

A pause, and then a careful answer.

"It can feel pretty lonely. When I think about the people I'm good friends with here, no one comes from the kind of background I come from."

It will take six more months for Carys to find companions at the margins. First, she'll meet another working-class woman who also works for the church. ("Finding her, it feels really powerful, like a big relief.") A few months after that, she will meet another misfit, an outspoken feminist who also champions LGBTQ+ rights and complains about Wellspring's treatment of women. But even before she meets her companions, while she endures long stretches of isolation at the interstices of exclusion, Carys clings to hope.

"The leadership are desperate for that not to be the case," she tells me, as we take drawn-out sips of tea. "And they promote the church being very inclusive and welcoming, and I think in many ways it is, but I think equally, when everyone you encounter is pretty privileged and not necessarily aware of that privilege, it can be really isolating and not how the leadership would want it to be."

Like Liv, Carys was able to hold doubt and anger in one hand and faith in the other. Both women interpreted the leaders' pleas for inclusivity as messages of hope—hope that stretched out like a membrane over time, becoming so thin, so tenuous, that it nearly snapped. But it didn't snap; it sustained them. Believing that the church leaders would not want working-class women to feel marginalized held Carys in place. It sustained her, but it also deluded her, in time causing her to doubt her own senses, leaving her to wonder why she was left off work e-mails, why she wasn't invited to meetings.

One afternoon, I received several missed calls and a panicked text message from Carys. When I called her back, she told me that a pastor had called her into his office and questioned her about a recently discovered affair between a male church leader and a female congregant.

"Are other people being questioned about it? Why was I called in? Is it because I'm blue collar? Is it because I'm a woman?" Breathless questions rushed from her end of the phone line to mine, and I stepped outside my office to address them, to reassure her that it probably wasn't anything personal. Still, she needed to check, *just to be sure.* And even as I soothed her, I began to doubt myself. Could I really be sure that she wasn't being singled out?

Self-doubt is a low-grade, durational, and persistent emotion. It is infinitely sustainable, not dramatic enough to propel women to leave the church but also lacking any cathartic release.[8] It is produced by an adversary who promises you everything you want yet time and time again fails to deliver. It is an amorphous regime of power whose success, in the words of Foucault, "is proportional to an ability to hide its own mechanisms."

The poet Cathy Park Hong calls the dismissal of one's perception of reality and the resultant self-doubt a "disfiguring of senses."[9] The word *disfigure* comes from the Old French word *disfigurer,* meaning "to alter, to disguise." Being fed promises that never materialize—or worse, being blamed for them not materializing—certainly disguises the truth of the situation and conceals the machinations of power. But another, more fitting, definition of *disfigurer* is "to destroy." This definition shows how events such as being left off of work e-mails, being questioned unnecessarily, and never being promoted to worship leader carry the repetitive force that not only disguises but also destroys women's senses. It destroys their perception of reality, severing them from what they know to be true.

Recently, Liv invited me to her birthday party. I entered the backyard, wearing my most summery dress, and quickly found myself talking to two strangers who told me, in depth, about their very important jobs in finance. My eyes roved over the crowd, searching for an escape hatch. Then I saw Tina, one of the women from the Bible study group I'd been part of, standing on her own. I rushed over to her and we hugged, quickly resuming the intimacy we'd once shared.

"I am writing a book about single Christian women now," I said. "You'll be in the book!"

Tina raised her eyebrows in surprise. "A lot has changed," she replied. "My views are very different now from what they were back then."

Tina then told me that she'd stopped going to church more than a year ago. "I just got so *tired*," she said, drily. "Going there felt exhausting."

I knew exactly what she meant. Consistently trying to resubjectivize yourself, to be a subject that the community values, is exhausting. Back on that windy day, when Jo told me about the nut sack incident and the church she'd recently joined in Chicago, I had asked her how she carried on in the face of what she called "quite deep-rooted pain."

"It's tiring," she replied, the usual sarcasm and humor draining from her voice. "I'm very tired, and I sometimes don't know if I can go on."

There are times, when it's dark and dreary in England, or at Christmas, when I miss my family, when the longing to return to church asserts itself. I imagine finding an inclusive and supportive Christian community—like the one I briefly experienced in Madrid—full of other misfits like me. I picture my rancorous spirit finally settling down, like boiling water collapsing to a simmer. How peaceful it might feel. I don't know if a community like this exists, and even if it did, I conclude, before this reverie progresses too far, I'm too tired to go looking for it.

Women like Tina are exhausted because they've been fighting for equality with men, and to be valued on their own, without a husband, for a long time. A recent report found that only 3 percent of American evangelical congregations are led by women, the same percentage as in 1998, even though 35 percent of the churches surveyed actually support women in pastoral leadership. Evangelicalism has among the fewest female leaders of all the religions surveyed, second only to Roman Catholicism.[10] In England, women make up only 28 percent of paid clergy, despite the Church of England authorizing female ordination in 1994. And less than one in fifty of the largest churches in England are led by women.[11] (Jo translated these statistics as "Basically, a lot of white dick up on the stage.") Even so, female churchgoers far outnumber men in both countries.

The "feminization of the church," a phrase often touted in American and British evangelical churches, directs the blame for the low number of men attending church on the overly feminine nature of church services.[12] Targeted ministry groups, such as Band of Brothers at Bethel and Bacon, Bible, Brew at Wellspring, aim to augment the gender imbalance and draw men into the church. However, if the recent trend toward evangelical women's disaffiliation continues, church leaders may need to pay more attention to keeping women in the church, rather than just to attracting men.

Unsurprisingly, the women most likely to leave are those who feel discriminated against for their gender, for their sexuality, or for being single and having career ambitions.[13] A study from 2008 reports, "Women who work full time, are not married, who have feminist orientations or are not heterosexual will be most likely to be marginal church attendees and disaffiliate."[14] Another study finds that, for career-focused women, traditional religious groups like evangelical Christianity "are more likely to prove a hindrance to women than a help."[15] This makes sense, considering that almost half of British evangelicals believe that a woman's main role is in the home, with children.[16] American evangelicals feel similarly.[17]

Zibby, whom I mentioned in the preface, attended a popular church in Austin, Texas. In many ways, she fit the characteristics of the ideal Christian woman: stylish though modest, beautiful though not overtly sexy, white, and solidly upper middle class. But Zibby was also ambitious. She studied communication at college and after graduation quickly found a job at a top advertising agency, where she rose up the ladder to creative director by the age of thirty-three. This posed a problem for her fiancé, a teaching pastor at her church, who believed in traditional gender roles. In fairness to him, Zibby argued at the time, the fiancé was just regurgitating what he heard from their senior pastor, who thought that women should remain in the home. She brushed off her fiancé's concerns, hoping in time that he'd realize that, given his low-paid church position, her income was integral to their livelihood.

I met Zibby, her fiancé, and another friend of hers for drinks one night in a swanky cocktail bar. We toasted their upcoming wedding—just six months away—and Zibby's fiancé pulled her close for a kiss. Later, when speaking about their future plans, the fiancé shared with the entire table that he felt called by God to be a missionary in West Africa.

"We'll see about that!" Zibby quipped playfully, swiping him on the shoulder and shaking her head. The conversation moved on, but I kept my gaze fixed on the fiancé as I tried to decode the strange look on his face. It wasn't discouragement or deflation, I realized afterwards, as the image of his narrowed eyes and lifted chin returned to me again and again. It was defiance.

Over the next few months leading up to their wedding, the tension between what the fiancé wanted—a homemaker wife, a submissive wife, a missionary wife—and Zibby's career ambitions escalated. Five weeks before their wedding, Zibby's fiancé messaged her, asking for an impromptu dinner at an old-fashioned diner near their church. *It's important*, he wrote simply.

As soon as they sat down, he told her he'd made up his mind: upon the counsel from senior pastors at the church, he'd decided that Zibby needed to quit her job after they got married. He was to be the sole breadwinner. In addition, within the next few years they'd be moving to West Africa. She'd have to learn French. And she needed to get on board with what God had called him—the pastor, the man—to do. His words unfurled with a new sense of resoluteness that startled Zibby.

She stood up, shaking, slid her engagement ring off her finger, and placed it on the table. A few weeks later, I accompanied Zibby to collect her wedding dress, which had already been paid for—along with the rest of the wedding. I carried the dress out myself as she wept behind oversize black sunglasses.

As painful as the experience was, the worst was yet to come. After she called off the wedding, Zibby's entire community of friends from church, including one of her bridesmaids, turned their backs on her. Text messages went unanswered, calls unreturned, eyes were averted, invitations revoked.

"I was exiled," she says dispassionately, when we reflect on the experience now.

Today, Zibby still calls herself a Christian. She took a few months "off" of church and then found a small liturgical congregation near her new apartment. Like so many other women I met, Zibby slipped into the pews at the back every Sunday, just as the service started, and slipped out during the final prayer, hoping to avoid meeting anyone. In time, she married (a Christian), and together they found a new church, which they attend regularly. She maintains her high-status job as creative director.

Zibby's relationship with Christianity changed after her experience of marginalization, but she didn't disaffiliate. However, many women do leave, especially when it comes to the issue of sex. Research in the UK suggests that women who are sexually active or hold nonnormative views on sexuality outside of abstinence (including queer women) are more likely to leave evangelicalism.[18] In my research with evangelicals, I found that women who were considered opinionated, feisty, or "difficult" also felt like they didn't belong. This was especially true of women of color and of working-class women.

Vanessa, a mixed-race, working-class British woman in London explained the marginalization she encountered: "I just think that for Black people, when they go into the church, unless they are in really nice clothes, they feel they don't fit, because all they are seeing is a lot of white middle class. But then again, I guess it's the church you choose to go to. It's not like the church leaders are saying 'No Blacks allowed' or, you know, 'Please let us see your credentials before you go in.'" After she said this, she became contemplative, slowing down the velocity with which she spoke. "I think for the longest time I've felt like I am a square peg trying to fit through a round hole. And now I've realized that I need to figure out, where do I fit? What do I love? What do I want to do? And where will I feel comfortable?" Vanessa explained that she had tried a majority-Black Pentecostal evangelical church but didn't feel she fit in there, either. Recently, she'd found a small, diverse neighborhood church, composed of just forty people.

Of course, Vanessa's marginalization didn't stem just from her racial positioning. Instead, it was a complex interplay of her gender, her single status, her race, and her class. These different axes of inequality dynamically interact to produce unique experiences of oppression.[19]

Misfit women, women who don't fit the ideal, who are incongruent with the norm, articulate their marginality through the language of the body—the hunched shoulders, the lowered eyes, the angry words that spew out of twisted mouths when talking about not being seen, about being rendered *unseeable*. I remember a woman I met in Maryland, who, after growing up in evangelicalism, finally stopped attending church in her late twenties on account of the church's treatment of women and the judgment she received. She told me that now, every time she stepped into a church building, she suffered from panic attacks, which consisted of tears, sweating, escalated breathing, and searching for an exit. As a result, she'd only gone back twice in the past five years.

Women's bodies serve as both the cause and the expression of woundedness. "What about us? Are we then to be devalued by the church?" demanded Vanessa during our interview. "There's no space for me here." Her pain so thoroughly saturated the air around us that afternoon that it was only after I finally stepped outside her house that I could really breathe.

As someone who resided in the borderland for a long time before leaving, I locate myself alongside these stories. I also write this as a white, middle-class, straight woman whose injuries were acquired from far less fixed markers of difference than women who remain anchored to the margins due to their race, social class, or sexual identity. And although leaving Christianity did not heal my wounds completely, it did stop reinfection. On the other hand, women who experience marginality and remain in the church incur wounds that never heal, that structurally *cannot* heal, as long as they stay in such spaces.

Exactly one year after my windy phone conversation with Jo, the time period in which Carys began doubting herself and Liv continued to rail against the sexism in the church, I meet Maddie for dinner in London. It's winter and her paintings have just been featured in a major art magazine. She is busy planning her first public art exhibition and the critics are already predicting it's going to be a big success. She's also fallen in love, and it shows in the way she carries herself—her confidence, her breezy insouciance.

I arrive early at the Indian restaurant and wait outside. A few moments later I spot Maddie from afar, rounding the corner with her elegant, leonine stride. Her hair is cut very short and dyed platinum, giving her delicacy a decided edge. A long green scarf, the color of a dazzling emerald, clings to her neck, the tail escaping down her back. As I watch her steadily approach, I realize how much I've missed her.

We settle into the restaurant, and after the waiter takes our order, we segue from inane topics to more substantial ones. She tells me about the feature in the magazine, her big exhibition, and her new boyfriend, whom she's planning to move in with soon. Then I ask if she's still going to church. Maddie shakes her head no. She presses her lips together, and I can't tell if it's an expression of remorse or resignation. Perhaps both; the line between the two is so fine.

"So, what made you finally leave?" I ask.

She glances over at the vacant table next to us. "I just felt like a fraud going there, and I couldn't stand that feeling like that any longer. It was like my body was still sitting in the pew but mentally I'd already left."

The waiter returns and places steaming dishes of basmati rice and dal in front of us. We stare at the food, not bothering to touch it, as if it's been put there for display.

Maddie tells me that she started to feel worse after church services than before them, that when she started dating her boyfriend, an atheist, and they started sleeping together, she kept it a secret because she feared the judgment of other Christians.

"It's my best relationship though," she hurries to tell me. "And I'm so much happier than I ever was with my Christian boyfriend, the one who pressured me to lie in bed naked with him and then guilted me about it afterwards."

I nod my head, remembering.

"Even though it wasn't like anyone was *doing* anything or telling me I couldn't be there, I always felt so out of place in the church." She takes a sip of water, her long, graceful fingers seizing the glass with such force that I fear it may shatter. "I guess I was just tired of not fitting the mold."

So one day she reached it: the breaking point, where she knew she had to leave.

"Do you still consider yourself a Christian?"

She smiles compassionately, as if to temper the news she's about to deliver. Afraid to say the words aloud, to make them real.

"I don't think so," she responds at last. Her words are weighed down with bitterness, with sorrow.

I sit back in my chair, contemplating Maddie afresh. Maddie the apostate. I wonder if I should give her an induction into this new life. The first thing I would say is that you have to accept that you lost a lot of time and can never get it back. You gave a lot of control over to the church, for a long time, and when that realization hits you one morning, you'll likely feel enraged. Especially when you consider all those promises you made to do better, to be better, all those efforts to dampen down your own desires and ambitions, to be wholesome and pure, to perform compliance, done so repeatedly that it became like second nature and then it ceased being a performance and it became *performative*. It became you.

On top of all that, think of all the sex you gave up! Think of the time wasted worrying about whether God was okay with anal sex and oral sex as long as it wasn't *sex* sex. Whether you could still see your gay friend from college or you should keep your distance. The micro ways you altered your entire life to conform to the evangelical model, only to sit here, in an empty Indian restaurant at the start of winter, and renounce it all.

But remember, I'd say, evangelicalism also gave you so much. A sense of belonging, a rootedness, a warmth, a community— one that you have lost, now that you've left. And you should know that you'll never find a suitable replacement, no matter how hard you look. Anyway, it's too late to go back now, because the lights have come on at the party and as you look around you see the destroyed living room, the floor sticky with booze, the stale chips in brightly colored plastic bowls, the rest of the partygoers still enchanted.

Did you think it would end like this?

An uncomfortable silence metastasizes between Maddie and me, filled with all the things unsaid, the words that cannot be spoken, that we don't let pass through our lips.

Eventually we begin to spoon dal into our mouths and, bodies warmed from the inside, we speak again, carefully choosing a topic that promises us surer footing.

Battling an amorphous power regime gives rise to emotions that move contagiously among bodies; more importantly, these emotions *move* bodies.[20] They moved Maddie out of the church and out of an entire religious system. For other women, self-doubt, anger, fatigue, and a deep sense of not belonging redirected them toward the margins of the evangelical community, toward the borderland.

Some women endured these feelings by not investing very much in the church, even if they continued to attend. After I ran into Tina at Liv's summer party, I went back to my interview with her to try to figure out what she might have meant when she said that her answers would be very different now. Back then, she described herself as a "reluctant Christian." Why? I had asked her at the time.

"I feel like I don't really fit in. That's very dramatic. I don't mean on a daily basis I walk around thinking I don't fit in. But I don't really feel like I fit in with the church, particularly, because there's not much opportunity to engage with the issues that I want to engage with. It's kind of like they try to conform people rather than transform people. There's too much conformity. And now that it's the information age, we've got so much information, so we are aware of so much more. We have a lot more thoughts and are more independent thinkers, but I don't think the church really allows for that."

She told me that although she still attended weekly Sunday services, she came and went quickly from church so as to avoid social encounters. She physically embodied her misfit feelings by hovering in the background.[21] But now, even minimal exposure to the evangelical community, safeguarded by coming late and leaving early, is too much. Now Tina has migrated from the borderland to the outside.

Simone, a single woman in North London who did not fit in because of her views on feminism and sex, also told me that she resided "on the outside" and felt like "an observer." She elaborated: "I just think it's really important to know that if you are going to be a Christian, it's really lonely and it's really hard to do stuff when you are by yourself. Beliefs die, you know?" Simone located herself on the periphery, and her strategy—to not invest much in the church and to participate minimally—mirrored Tina's.

I e-mailed Simone recently to tell her I'd moved to London and asked if we could meet. She wrote a quick e-mail in reply: *A lot has changed. I'm moving abroad with my non-Christian boyfriend to live in sin. Good luck with the book!*

The borderland is not built for long-term residence. In time, Simone, like Tina, like Maddie, and like me, opened the door of Christianity and walked out. But not everyone leaves, because although they are temporary lodgings, the borderland also blooms with opportunity. Without the constraints of a harsh border or the need to maintain the status quo, a certain type of freedom swells. This location provides a safe enough distance to preserve anger, which can animate and motivate. It allows residents to repurpose their wounds and bring about change.[22] The borderland can be an energetic space, one that fosters resistance, that births insurrection.

A 1994 study about Catholic and Protestant feminists in the United States found that many were "defecting in place," meaning that women embraced their feminist beliefs within their patriarchal church environments by staying and finding strategies to make it bearable. Some mentally checked out. Others actively continued to be part of their church communities, despite their alienation.[23] While such an account might sound inspiring, it is also disheartening to realize how little ground has been gained in the twenty-five years since the study was written. The disparity between promises made and outcomes delivered continues to wound single evangelical women. It drives some women out of the church. But for others, like Liv, it fuels their fire.

The sweet fragrance of jasmine floods the sidewalks, and even though it's eight o'clock when I step off the bus, a soft glow lingers in the sky, lighting up the English gloom. As usual, I'm late. I scold myself as I turn left, then right, down wide, heavily populated streets. I take a chance and sprint across three lanes of traffic, dodge a speeding motorcycle, stop, breathe, rearrange my shirt, and then charge up the stairs leading to a brutalist cement building, quickly but smoothly pushing past the glass doors. Second floor, east wing, Maddie had told me.

I arrive on the second floor, but instead of Maddie, I find her paintings. Six large canvases, unframed. She's filled them with the colors of summer, of an Italian island, of conviviality and heat. There are paintings of farmers feeding their goats, an old man sipping coffee, and various still lifes: a slice of fruit tart on a lace tablecloth, paper-thin flower petals brightening up a dusty road. But it's the painting in the center of the wall facing me that captures my attention. It's of a woman entering the sea. She's no bigger than my hand, and I imagine Maddie arriving early to a seaside cliff that bright morning, carrying her sketch pad and a big bottle of water.

We can only see the woman from behind. She's pulled her straw hat down low on her head and its baby blue ribbon flaps wildly in the wind. Wrinkles line her back and her arms, which are spread wide to steady her as she wades farther into the crystalline water. Concentric circles ripple out from her body—perfect, undisturbed, smooth circles that start at her waist and continue outward, growing in diameter, in magnitude, endlessly and effortlessly. Stopping only when they meet the edge of the canvas.

7

REPRISALS

*Don't laugh. Just tell me the story / again, / of the sparrows who
flew from falling Rome, / their blazed wings. / How ruin nested
inside each thimbled throat / & made it sing*

—Ocean Vuong

It all started with a knock at the door. Bony knuckles rapping lightly, insistently. If Liv could have known then what that knock meant—that it wasn't the sound of arrival but of exit, that it was the vault from which the darkest, most painful three months of her life would spring—would she have answered it?

"Come in."

Her boss's cheerful face peeked around the door. "Hey, Liv, I want to talk with you about something. I thought maybe we could meet tomorrow morning?"

Liv's hands hovered over the keyboard, suspended in space.

"Sure. Is everything okay?"

"Oh, yes," her boss responded reassuringly. "The senior management is making some organizational changes and I thought we should sit down and discuss them."

"Okay."

"Great. So, see you in the morning? Just come into my office when you get in."

The following morning, Liv learned that her role as director of communications was being terminated. It wasn't that she was being *fired*, just that the *role* was no longer needed.

"What about the forty people who work for me?" asked Liv.

"They'll be reassigned," her boss replied, voice dry like a slab of concrete baking in the sun.

"What about the twelve years I've put into this church?"

"Your service and devotion to the church have been so appreciated. But there is a major restructuring afoot, and anyway, you've said for some time that you plan to move on eventually. It's just come sooner than we expected. Remember: change is *good*."

By the time she left the meeting, Liv's hands were trembling. She walked unsteadily back to her office and regarded the empty chair in front of her desk, unsure what to do next. She picked up her phone, fingers shaking, and texted Carys. *Can we meet? Something's happened.*

In March of my junior year at an evangelical college, I started receiving frightening phone calls. For Liv it was a knock at the door; for me, the ring of a telephone—sounds that we naively mistook for the harmless din of everyday life, when in fact they were the soft whispers of alarm.

Three rings and I lunge for the ivory handset.

"Hello?"

Silence.

"Hello?" I ask again, my voice prickling with suspicion.

Still nothing.

A police car passes by outside, casting its swirling red light across my room, penetrating the still, black night with color.

Just as I prepare to hang up, there is a voice. A robotized voice; male, low, gravelly.

"You've been very very bad."

"Who is this?" I demand.

"You've been very bad," he repeats, and I realize I'm hearing a voice synthesizer.

This must be a wrong number, I think. Wires must have gotten crossed somewhere. But then he says my name. My full name. The way it's said with pageantry, a year later at my college graduation, as I rise to accept my diploma.

"Katie Gaddini, you've been bad, and you need to be punished."

Silence. Unfiltered fear surges through me, causing my breathing to slow. I place the phone back in its cradle, my movements careful and quiet. Then I drop to the carpet and crouch down next to the front door, waiting for my roommates to come home.

Shortly after hearing that her job would be terminated, Liv learned that a nearly identical role would soon be opening in an adjacent department. The news reached her via the weekly e-mail that went out to all staff members at Wellspring.

"I just can't believe this," Liv hissed, turning her face away from Carys and toward two unruly children who ran around the restaurant where they were eating. "I feel like I'm being betrayed, like I'm being stabbed in the back—by my own family. I've given everything to this church. For twelve years! I've made them my family. And now they're discarding me, just like that!" She snapped her fingers in the air.

"You know what you should do," Carys said, leaning back in her chair. "You should apply for the new position. Show them that you aren't going to be messed around like this."

"But it's *my* position! Just in a different department. Do you know how humiliating it is to apply for my own job?"

Carys nodded and narrowed her eyes. The two women sat quietly as they strategized, neither bothering to touch the plate of soggy nachos before them.

"That's all you can do," Carys said at last. "Apply for the position, see what happens. Then at least we'll know if they just want to get rid of *you* or if it really is the role, like they say."

Liv went home and created a résumé, something she hadn't done in more than a decade, and drafted a cover letter. The next morning she sent her application to human resources, and then she waited. A week later her boss's boss called her in for an interview. Liv forwarded the interview request to Carys, and a minute later a reply arrived in her in-box: *Good. Now we wait.*

A few days after the first phone call, I receive a second one. This time it is eleven o'clock at night and my roommates and I are bustling around our apartment, brushing teeth and washing hair, moving through our bedtime rituals. The first ring, we ignore. At the second, we glance at one another without exchanging any words. A third, a fourth, the sound forceful and insistent, refusing to be ignored. My roommates watch as I slowly walk toward the phone.

"Hello?"

This time the caller doesn't waste any time. "Katie, you've been very bad."

"Stop calling, whoever this is. It's not funny."

"You've been very bad, and you need to be punished. Feminists need to be punished. They need to learn that men are the ones in charge. We need to teach you a lesson."

"Stop calling!" I slam down the phone and brace my hands on the wall, pressing them against the white stucco to stop them from trembling.

Liv waited for the outcome of the interview. At work, she kept a cheerful, alert expression on her face at all times. She fulfilled her duties with gusto and checked her e-mail constantly. She waited. Sometimes, on the weekend, she stayed in bed for hours, unable to get out, alternating between placid contemplation and crying fits. But during the week she maintained a stoic professionalism. And then, finally, her boss called her in for a meeting.

"I'm really sorry, Liv, but we gave the position to someone else. He was more qualified for the role. A better fit." Her boss paused, letting the words sink in.

Liv's face began to twitch. First the corner of her eyes, and then her mouth. She pressed her lips together to stop them from quivering. And then the tears that were normally reserved for the weekend spilled out into the week.

"Do you want me to leave the room . . . so you can be alone?"

Liv nodded. She waited until she heard the click of the door, and then she wept openly. Her boss's words returning to her, again and again. *He was more qualified . . . A better fit.*

When the third call came so soon after the second, it gave a sense of acceleration, of urgency. In the intervening days I walked around in a suspicious fog. I studied the male students in my classes, searching each one for marks of culpability. I laughed with friends in the cafeteria as we spooned cereal into our hungry mouths, and I pretended nothing was amiss. But I maintained a steady vigilance at all times, just in case he was watching.

Close to midnight the phone rings. "Let me get it," my roommate offers, stepping toward the phone.

"No," I say, pushing past her. I pick up the receiver, but I don't say anything right away. I let the silence fester. We are dueling opponents, with pistols in our hands and a fallow field between us. After a while, he speaks. His voice more like a drawl this time, the voice synthesizer programmed to run at a slower speed. It's nonchalant yet determined.

"Katie, do you know what your punishment is?"

I remain silent.

"Since you're such a flaming feminist—"

"Stop. Calling. Me. You sick asshole—"

"We're going to have to teach the feminist a lesson. You're going to learn that men are the ones in charge. It's time to tie you up and see how you like it . . . We're going to have to tie you up, and watch you suffer."

His words enter me like a bullet. And now I'm hysterical, screaming and pleading for him to stop calling. My roommate retrieves the phone from my hand, hangs it up, and pulls me into her arms.

"They gave the role to someone else. One of my employees. A man. Younger than me. And he's only been working here for a few months. They still claim that the role is *different* from mine, that it will 'fulfill different organizational needs.'" Liv spit the words out of her mouth.

Her friend, a lawyer, began to stroke her shoulder.

"Why are they doing this? I don't understand what I did. I don't understand why this is happening. Did you know, my parents offered to fly over from Washington? I can't let them come. They don't have the money." Liv looked up desperately. "What can I do?"

"Well, you could think about suing them. I could put you in touch with someone, a good employment lawyer I used to work with. But you have to be prepared: it will get messy. And costly. They would have a whole team of lawyers prepared for just this sort of thing."

Liv nodded bitterly, looking away because she couldn't stand to see the pity on her friend's face.

Her friend lowered her voice and continued to stroke Liv's shoulder. "You don't need to decide now. Think it over."

I too was desperate. Desperate for answers. Desperate to make the phone calls stop, to feel safe again.

After the third incident, I report the calls to the dean of students, lodging a formal complaint, and he promises to investigate. In the meantime, I keep a low profile. I attend classes and chapel services but study in my room the rest of the time. My uncle offers to drive down and meet with the president of the college, but I don't want to aggravate the situation further; I want it to go away. And we both see his offer for what it is: an attempt to fulfill the paternal role left empty by his recently deceased brother, my dad.

"It's okay. I can handle this," I tell him. "Thank you though."

Our college is small—just 1,200 students—and most live on campus, so I know it is just a matter of time until I run into the caller. "I don't want to be alone right now," I tell my three roommates, as we huddle in our bedroom one evening. "So, could one of you to be with me at all times? Just in case . . ."

They nod, ready to take on the task, but I can tell they are afraid, too.

Our college might have been small, but it was beautiful. In retrospect, this exaggerated beauty made the calls all the more monstrous. The campus was like a warm Christian embrace that stretched across acres of bucolic green lawns, towering eucalyptus trees, and lilac-colored wisteria that emerged in spring and covered you like a canopy as you strolled to chapel services. That violent threats could occur in such an idyllic setting shattered my understanding of the Christian community as a safe and trusted space.

Striding up to the college mail room one day, I bump into an acquaintance from my English literature class. She is a tall woman with posture so perfect she resembles a stern algebra teacher. But on this particular afternoon, I notice, she appears slightly disheveled. We greet each other and she mentions that she'd missed class that morning because she'd stayed up too late with her boyfriend and his friend the night before.

"What did you guys get up to?" I ask absentmindedly, as I riffle through my stack of mail.

"It was stupid really," she replies. "Kris and Jon got a voice synthesizer, so we were up all night making funny recordings of ourselves using it. Definitely wasn't worth missing Dr. Davies's lecture."

I stop my riffling and peer up at her. "What'd you do with the recordings?" I ask.

"What do you mean?"

"What did you do with the recordings?" I repeated.

"Oh, we deleted them. We were just playing around."

I force a smile and gather up my mail, explaining that I am late for my next class. But instead of class, I go straight to the dean's office and tell him what I have just learned. He assures me he will handle it from there and instructs me to not do anything else.

For the rest of the afternoon, I avoid my apartment by running laps around the dirt track on campus, visiting a friend in her dorm, idling in the dining hall well past closing. If one last call comes, I want to miss it.

The next morning a call does come—from the dean. He explains that he has spoken with both boys and they confessed to making the calls. It was just a harmless prank, they said. They never meant anything serious.

"In any case," the dean continues, "we've scheduled an internal hearing for next Wednesday. I will be there, along with the vice dean, and Kris and Jon, of course."

I sigh in relief. But as soon as relief washes over me, dread also arrives, when I realize there are four more days to get through before the hearing. Four more days during which I could run into the boys and face a backlash for reporting them. A backlash to the backlash. I think about my acquaintance from class, Kris's girlfriend, and then I start to dread seeing her, too.

The day before the hearing, it happens. There, on a grassy patch outside the chapel building, concealed behind the swarm of people gathered outside, the boys sit, laughing, with a group of friends. For just a split second our eyes meet, as the joyful chapelgoers around us embrace, oblivious. I grab hold of my roommate's hand and push past the crowd, dragging her with me.

Late on Saturday morning, Liv stood in the shower, rivulets of water traveling down the length of her body. Then she crouched on the floor, drawing her knees into her chest, making herself small. Her hands reached up to her face to feel the warmth of tears as they merged with the cool shower water. Those tiny hands, so delicate and childlike, whose touch had comforted others so many times. They bear witness through touch. *I see you,* the hands conveyed, *and even though I can't take away this sad-ness, I acknowledge its presence.*

Her body rose and fell, heaving with pain. Liv committed her-self to the task at hand, the task of grieving, functional as it was instinctive. She let the bitterness inside her liquefy and drain out of her body so that, come Monday, she would be an empty res-ervoir, ready to walk into the Wellspring offices and be filled back up again.

My Christian college decided to handle the harassing phone calls in-house, as American universities commonly do in cases of sex-ual harassment and assault. When I arrive at the hearing, I find I'm the last one there. The two boys who have called and threat-ened me over the past month sit on one side of the glass table, and the two male deans of the college, who are arbitrating the case, sit on the other. Their chatter ceases and silence fills the room as I take a seat in the middle of the table.

One of the deans, a humorless-looking man with a bushy moustache, asks if I would like to press charges with the police. They are obligated to facilitate a report, he says, if I want to pur-sue criminal action.

The word *police* visibly startles the two boys, and though I take pleasure in their reaction, I shake my head no. I don't want to press charges; I just want it to stop.

The deans exchange glances and their faces relax. When it's the boys' chance to say something, they offer an apology, which, as expected, turns out to be a vacant performance. "I didn't know your dad had just died," one of them says, by way of explana-tion. "It was a joke . . . because of your feminist club," mumbles the other. And then it's my turn.

I look at these boys, bouncing my gaze from one set of light brown eyes to the other. I refuse to look away. Through the simple act of looking, I lay claim to my own agency; I reject the role of passive victim; I refuse to deny what has happened.

"It's your turn to speak, Katie," the serious-looking dean repeats. "Is there anything you'd like to say?"

There is *so much* I want to say—that's the problem. I don't lack language; I'm overflowing with it.

I want to ask these boys why feminism scares them. Why, when I created my feminist club on campus, male students were allowed to tear down the fluorescent pink signs that read "Feminism: The Radical Notion That Women Are Equal" and throw them in the bushes. I want to know why the word *equal* threatens them.

And then I want to advance beyond questions to assertions. I want to bring in the boys from my high school, including the ones who ridiculed me for supporting women in leadership, and the dean of students who punished me for wearing an ill-fitting shirt, because they also need to hear this. They need to hear everything I have to say, because I've been quiet for so long, and all the words that have never been said are starting to stick to my throat. They are welding to me, like a permanent fixture of my anatomy, and I'm starting to choke.

What I want to declare, in a bold assertive voice, one that refuses to be cowed by male authority any longer, is that this college needs a gender studies department, because I want to study feminism and I've already taken all the classes I can that have to do with gender and women and I'm still hungry for more. In fact, I'm famished. I want more women to speak at our mandatory chapel services, because right now there are only one or two women speakers a year, out of ninety chapel services. I keep writing this suggestion on the feedback forms, those little slips of yellow paper they hand me every week, but nobody seems to be reading them. I want to say that my male friend should never have cornered me in the cafeteria and demanded that I stop with my feminist club. And his friends never should have told him to get me "under control." (Also, I'd like to know what "getting me under control" would even look like.)

But in the end this excess of language leads to collapse, and only three simple sentences emerge.

"Stay away from me. And don't ever call me again." Then I turn to the deans, to drive my point home. "I just want to finish the academic year in peace."

On her last day of work, Liv arrived with gifts. Chocolates and a thank-you card for her boss, and a bouquet of flowers for her friend, the one who supported her through the past few months. She decided to take the high road, as Carys advised, to end on a positive note. But her desk was empty. No good-bye party, no parting gifts, not even a card.

In the early evening, after she said good-bye to her coworkers and her staff of forty, she gathered up her belongings and strode, alone, out the elegant oak doors of Wellspring's main office.

Let me begin again, to go back to the time before the reprisals and all the actions and counteractions that precipitated these backlashes. Let me begin back when Liv hosted a dinner party with ten other women, one Friday evening in 2015, back when a feminist uprising was nothing but a fragile seedling. A male pastor had just held another private, unofficial retreat for men, and as Liv moved back and forth from the kitchen to the dining table, delivering plates of slightly burned vegetables, she fumed.

"I've been here eight years already and never once have I been invited to any leadership training or mentorship program!" She dropped a plate of zucchini on the table. It landed with a heavy *thud.* "If I was a man, by now I'd be doing the most amazing things."

Jill, a petite redhead with freckles splattered down her face and neck spoke. "We're complaining about pastors supporting men, but where's the person who's supposed to be supporting the women? He's doing what he feels is his calling from God, so why are we downgrading him instead of asking who can step up to the plate for women?"

Silence filled the room. The other women looked at Liv expectantly. She remained standing, mulling over the question.

"You know what," she replied at last, "that's a very good point. So let's start something! We can start a women leaders' group, even with just us, and see if anyone wants to join."

Later that night, before tucking into bed, Liv and her friends had created a Facebook event called Women Rise and had invited all the Christian women they knew. By the end of the weekend, nearly one hundred women had already responded that they were going. By July of that year, Liv and her feminist collective had convinced the organizers of the church retreat to hold an event for their group, titled "Faith and Feminism." It was the first time the retreat would host an avowedly feminist event, and Liv wondered whether anyone would show up. Perhaps she'd taken too provocative an angle, she worried, in the days leading up to the panel. Perhaps she should have started with a softer approach—examining scriptural interpretations of gender equality, for example—instead of invoking the word *feminism*, a concept so long derided in Christian circles.

As Liv and Jill nervously assumed their places on the stage with a male church leader, himself a self-identified feminist, women began pouring into the large blue tent. Halfway through, as Liv scanned the audience, she saw a friend of hers, a white woman in her thirties, just like Liv, stand up and walk out. Liv clenched her jaw, willing herself to stop watching, to turn instead to the other hundred women in the audience, whose desire for feminism seeped out of them, coursed along the aisles, lapping against the stage.

The event was a huge success, according to its organizers, and afterwards women rushed forward to sign up for Women Rise, as Liv and her friends called the group, which Liv envisioned as not just a solidarity group but an *association* for women.

"You know, though," Liv told me, in a hushed voice, months after the retreat, "our panel was never put up on the church website. It was the only one not put up." She broke out in a sardonic grin, mouth tight at the edges. "Curious, right?"

"Yes, very . . . So, what's next for the association?" I asked.

"Well, we're still having our monthly events, and the association is growing. But we've also had some resistance. You know, I think I'm seen as being a bit of a problem sometimes. Recently, I asked to preach at a Sunday service and got denied. I chucked a little mini tantrum about it, so that didn't go over well!" She laughed as she tucked a few stray hairs behind her ear.

"The senior pastor and his wife have asked to have coffee with me, to talk about my views on women, but I kind of feel like it's going to be a bit of a . . ." She trailed off. "You know when you just *know* that you're seen as a bit of an issue?"

I did know. I'd been seen as an "issue" for most of my life. First as the energetic pastor's daughter who screeched up and down the church aisles, a savage little thing who couldn't be tamed. And then in high school, when I was tasked with writing a report interpreting a controversial Bible verse, 1 Timothy 2:12: "I do not permit a woman to teach or assume authority over a man; she must be quiet." To uncover the correct meaning and context of the verse, I spent hours sitting on the floor of the Christian bookshop near my house, studying what *teach* meant in the original Greek. The night before the report was due, I tossed and turned, unsure what to write in the report's conclusion. I thought of my dad, the teacher of the class, and his ardent views against women in leadership, and of my mentor, a female teacher at my Christian school, who also didn't believe women should hold any leadership roles, despite her passion for teaching about the Bible.

Around midnight, I woke up my mom. She walked me out to the living room, and we settled on the couch, wrapping a blanket around us for warmth.

"I don't know what to do. I don't know what to say. Everything I read seems to say that the verse is taken out of context, that Paul didn't mean that women can't have any leadership roles. But I don't know if I'm making a mistake. I don't want to get it wrong." I rested my head on my mom's lap and gazed up at her, this woman who had committed to female submission for decades.

She began running her fingers through my hair.

"It sounds like you do know what's right and you're just scared."

I closed my eyes, and the space between my brows, wrinkled for so long with distress, began to soften.

"Stand by what you believe. You're strong."

The reckoning came two weeks later, when, for my final exam, I faced a panel of five biblical scholars: a local pastor, my female mentor, two teachers from the school, and my dad—all of them against women in leadership. A firing squad, all at least twenty years older than me and my feeble convictions.

Over sixty minutes, I defended my interpretation of the verse, arguing that it was outdated and inapplicable today, that women should have authority equal to men, both in and out of the church.

The math teacher on the panel, known simply as "Doc," did not like my argument. A stern man, universally feared and respected by everyone, Doc had a scowl on his face the entire time I spoke. And as soon as the panel had a chance to respond, he spoke first.

"So, if you're saying that this verse is outdated and we should allow women to have leadership roles, then maybe the whole Bible is outdated. Is that what you think? That the whole Bible is outdated?"

I swallowed. "No, that's not what I'm saying. Each verse of the Bible has to be considered in context. When it was written, by whom, the setting—"

"But that would mean that some verses can just be written off as 'out of date' as suits you. That they can just be thrown out because you don't like them. Would we say the same thing for 'Thou shalt not murder'? Is that also out of date?" He chuckled as he glanced around at the other panel members.

I argued against Doc's critiques and then answered the other panelists' questions, again and again disagreeing with the Christian leaders I looked up to, contradicting my mentor and pastor, my own father. I carried words and convictions I didn't even know I had, and in that moment a feminist was born.

"When did 'feminism' become a word that spoke not just to you, but spoke you, that spoke of your existence or even spoke you into existence?" asks Sara Ahmed.[1] During that final exam, feminism, an ideology and a movement I couldn't even articulate yet, picked me out of the crowd. It spoke me into existence; it recruited me for battle.

But like most people who perform feminist acts within a patriarchal context, I would pay a price for interpreting the Bible verse the way that I did.

"Look, it's the flaming feminist!" a frizzy-haired boy shouted as I emerged from PE class the next day. Word got around that

I had stood up to the panel, had argued in support of women in leadership roles. His friends laughed. "Oh, be careful! The flaming feminist is coming!" By not taking the conventional approach to Christian women in leadership, I slid right into a problem category. I *became* the problem, by merely pointing out a problem.[2]

A few days after the defense, I came home late and found my report fastened to the garage door with pieces of Scotch tape.

My dad's messy lettering, written in red ink, covered the front page: *I may not agree with you, but I've never been prouder.* He had circled the A, my grade, repeatedly for emphasis, so that it resembled a raw wound that oozed out across the page.

The defense may have branded me a feminist, a category I would never manage to slip out of, but a year and a half later, when my dad died and all I had left of him were artifacts and objects, I would decide that every moment of taunting was worth it for those scrawled red letters.

The Christian faith and feminism have been seen as irreconcilable for decades. One historian went so far as to opine that real Christian feminist analysis was only possible after the Enlightenment, as Christian women before then could not merge their faith with their protofeminist convictions.[3] Writing in 1975, the radical feminist Leah Fritz declared that Christian women were "unloved, unrespected, unnoticed by the Heavenly Father, condescended to by the Son, and fucked by the Holy Ghost."[4] Another radical feminist, Andrea Dworkin, argued that women were "committing suicide" by aligning with the Christian right.[5] Mary Daly, a feminist theologian, declared that all religion was patriarchal, and held religion responsible for perpetuating "dynamics of delusion." She also wrote that feminist liturgy was not possible within the sexist system of Christianity.[6]

In the 1980s, as second-wave feminism roared through the United States and the United Kingdom, and the Moral Majority and the Christian Coalition gained momentum, social scientists explored the interface of Christianity and feminism. A comprehensive overview of conservative Catholic, Orthodox Jewish, and evangelical Protestant women's views on feminism reported that evangelicals were the religious group most closely connected to antifeminist attitudes.[7] Similarly, a study in 1986 reported that a higher investment in Christianity, as measured by church attendance, correlated to a higher likelihood that attendees held antifeminist beliefs.[8] These studies seemed to confirm that indeed the Christian faith and feminism were antithetical.

Other researchers took a different approach. They rushed to make sense of "right-wing women," who were portrayed as the antithesis of the liberated feminist woman, and to show that many conservative Christian women find submission empowering. Brenda Brasher's study of fundamentalist Christian women in the United States claimed that a restrictive religious environment empowered women, giving them a sense of purpose and consistency in their lives.[9] Similarly, R. Marie Griffith examined the opposition between feminism and charismatic evangelical Christian women who participated in the Women's Aglow prayer network. "Submission may help the relatively powerless recover their power and create a space within which they can feel both fulfilled and free," she reports.[10] Such scholars posit that rapid social change and the flux of late modernity increases anxiety and that some women find meaning and stability in conservative, antifeminist ideology.[11]

But this scholarship overlooks the many women who suffer under the constraints of patriarchal religion, and it also erases the rich history of Christian feminists.[12] Christian protofeminist ideology predates any of the claims that the two are irreconcilable. Hidden out of view is a rich lineage of women whose faith compelled them to fight for women's rights and for racial and class equality, both inside and outside of the church, even if they didn't invoke the word *feminism*. This includes women such as Saint Hildegard of Bingen, who lived in twelfth-century Germany and endorsed a theology that emphasized the feminine aspect of the divine, or the Italian-French writer Christine de Pizan, who in 1405 wrote *The Book of the Cities of Ladies*, in which Pizan creates an allegorical city filled with female warriors, inventors, scholars, and artists, demonstrating the importance of women's achievements and the need for women to be valued members of society. In one painting from that era, Pizan lectures men from the university about how women are made in God's image. They listen with rapt attention.

Christian feminist women also were on the front lines of the US slavery abolition movement, and later, the movement for women's suffrage. American abolitionist Sarah Moore Grimke (1792–1873) lectured on an egalitarian interpretation of the Bible. And her sister, Angelina, wrote *An Appeal to the Christian Women of the South*, a booklet against slavery and women's subordination, in 1836.

More recently, in the twentieth century, British feminist Una Kroll participated in the antiapartheid struggle in Namibia and worked as a medical doctor in housing projects in the UK. She protested when the General Synod, the Church of England's national assembly, refused to ordain women in 1978. Kroll went on to become a priest in 1992, when the church finally allowed women's ordination. Years later, living in Wales, she converted to Roman Catholicism in order to identify more closely with women who were flat-out denied entry to the priesthood. Her obituary states, "Una's life was a passionate, stormy love affair with the church," which may be the perfect way to describe Liv's or Jo's relationship with Christianity, too.[13]

The Reverend Lucy Winkett, one of the first women to be ordained in the Church of England, is a direct beneficiary of Una Kroll's efforts.[14] In 1997, as a minor canon, Winkett was the first woman appointed to St. Paul's Cathedral in central London. Her assignment was met with ire and outright resistance from some bishops and canons at the time, including Canon Halliburton, who refused to recognize her position or to take the sacrament from her. I went to see Reverend Winkett in the spring of 2016 at her church, St. James Piccadilly, in London, and I asked her how she kept going all of these years, despite such overwhelming resistance.

"I don't know if I'll be here in five years, in one year, or even next month," she said evenly. "But I know I'll be here until the end of the week, and I just focus on that."

Across the pond, another modern-day figure battling for gender equality in the church is the Reverend Dr. Amy Butler, formerly the head pastor of Riverside Church, the famously progressive Protestant church in New York City. Butler first gained media attention in 2014, when she was appointed as the first female pastor of Riverside. Four years later, in May 2018, Butler wrote an article in the Christian magazine *Patheos* about sexual harassment within the Christian church. "Of course, it matters if women are in leadership. It matters if only because it means we finally have the power to change systems that for so long had kept us silent," she wrote in the piece.

However, in July 2019, Butler faced scandal when the governing board of the church refused to renew her contract. The *New York Times* ran an article which reported that her dismissal arose from a series of sexual harassment suits, both from and against

Butler. The hashtag #WeAreAmy swept across Twitter, with other female clergy members posting their experiences of misogyny and sexual harassment. Where Butler will go next, and what really happened at Riverside, remains unclear.[15]

The evangelical feminists with whom I spoke entered feminism through the gateway of evangelicalism, just as I had. As the late Rachel Held Evans, one of the pioneers of modern-day evangelical feminism, wrote in a blog post from 2012, "I didn't learn to be a feminist from Margaret Atwood or Simone de Beauvoir. I learned to be a feminist from Jesus . . . This is my story, and I'm sticking to it. I am a follower of Jesus first and a feminist second."[16] Nearly all of the women I interviewed espoused ideas about gender equality within the church, including the importance of women in leadership. Many self-identified as feminists, and when they did, they relied on feminism not in spite of their Christian beliefs but *because* of them.

Now there is even a magazine dedicated to the alliance of Christianity and feminism. *Magnify* calls itself a magazine of "faith, feminism, and fashion." In one article, the author writes, "So I've established that Jesus leans more toward the side of the feminist."[17] *Magnify*'s editor explained that the magazine defines feminism as "equality with men" rather than as an expression of feminism associated with "sexual liberation." *Magnify* has now expanded to host training sessions and biannual Inspire networking events that promise to "spoil and surprise you with an evening of live music, canapés, drinks, and special guests."[18]

The evangelical feminists I met in both countries center their fight on having more women, especially working-class women and women of color, in leadership, and on a struggle for singlehood to be as much valued as marriage. Feminism is an ideology that supports their marginal status in their community and is a vehicle for obtaining meaningful roles within the church.[19]

But the reaction to feminism differs between American and British evangelicalism. Dr. Mimi Haddad, the president of CBE International, is an expert on gender issues in Christianity. "The word *feminism*, understood as equal access to human resources and opportunities, is better understood and accepted in the UK than the US," Dr. Haddad explains to me. Having also spent many years traversing the two countries, I agree, and I ask her why she thinks this is. "Among evangelicals in the US, the term often holds a negative connotation, possibly because of essentialism," she says. Indeed, gender essentialism, or the idea that men and women hold different innate characteristics, which determines their roles in and out of the church, is the bedrock upon which "complementarianism" is built.[20]

Kat Harris is an educator, podcaster, and author of the popular book *Sexless in the City: A Sometimes Sassy, Sometimes Painful, Always Honest Look at Dating, Desire, and Sex*. Originally from Texas but now residing in New York City, Harris challenges many taken-for-granted approaches to sex and dating in Christianity. Her approach is considered provocative in some circles, especially her view that masturbation can be a healthy part of single Christian women's sexuality. Yet this issue wasn't the one that earned Harris the biggest backlash; it was her support of feminism. "I've been called a 'man-hater' by evangelical men," Harris tells me. "By the seemingly 'open' ones, who are considered 'cool' and 'edgy' in evangelical circles." Harris's experience confirms Haddad's opinion that feminism is still unacceptable in many parts of American evangelicalism.

Fortunately, feminist women have the perfect model of a difficult and troublesome figure to reassure them. Carys explained, "If you look at the character of Jesus, he was all about disrupting hierarchies and modes of oppression." Evangelical feminists understand Jesus as a rebel, a dissident, and a feminist for the way he included women in his ministry.[21] (Liv declared, "I think Jesus was the first feminist.") Identifying Jesus as a difficult figure, a feminist, thus alleviates the sting of a word meant to harm. This rearticulation of a negative name recalls Sara Ahmed's provocative description of the feminist killjoy and her call for us to "respond to the accusation with a 'yes.'"[22] By associating Jesus with feminism, women respond affirmatively to the identity of a troublesome feminist.

Sarah Bessey promoted this rearticulation of feminism in her best-selling book *Jesus Feminist*, which put into words the feminist aspirations of millions of evangelical feminists. "Being both a Christian and a feminist can be frustrating. But it's also a gift," Bessey writes elsewhere, and she goes on to explain how she is a Christ follower first and a feminist second.[23] In addition to Bessey and the late Rachel Held Evans, Nadia Bolz-Weber, the controversial pastor who created a vagina statue out of purity rings, also identifies herself as a feminist. As part of a panel titled "Can Faith and Feminism Coexist?," Bolz-Weber was asked how she defines feminism. "Believing in the strength and power of women—that, to me, is what feminism is. It's a celebration, to me," she replied.[24] Katelyn Beaty, another key figure in evangelical feminism, founded "Her.meneutics," a section for women's issues in the popular *Christianity Today* magazine, whose website boasts 4.3 million monthly visitors. Beaty also wrote a book titled *A Woman's Place: A Christian Vision for Your Calling in the Office, the Home, and the World*, which provides a scriptural defense of women in leadership.

British and American evangelical feminists I met devoured these books and online magazines. They patiently waited for the books to arrive in the mail, giddily attended events to hear Bolz-Weber speak, and sent me articles from the Junia Project, a site promoting women in Christian leadership. *You must read this!* they'd message me, with a hyperlink attached—or sometimes it was just the link, without any accompanying text.

For four years, I joined them. Together, we read these books and articles and went to Women Rise events. We talked about feminism at Bible study gatherings. We flipped through *Magnify* magazine and laughed at Nadia Bolz-Weber's provocative Instagram posts, sending one another screenshots of our favorite quotes. We were the flaming feminists. We were on fire.

At the same time, a curious paradox arose: even as the word *feminism* gained more acceptance in this evangelical community, as it saturated evangelical material culture and events for women's equality within the church proliferated, the patriarchal gender order remained stuck. So what did "feminism," as a word to organize around and an ideological movement, give these women?

More importantly, how did feminism fail them?

At the end of my senior year of college, a local journalist called me up and asked if he could interview me. He wanted to write a story about being a feminist at a conservative evangelical college. My friend and I had run our feminist club, Par Vox (Latin for "equal voice"), for two years by this point. We held events where we examined female sexuality within the purity movement and critiqued the unreasonable beauty standards put forth by mass media. We set up a booth at the club fair on campus, fielding questions from evangelical students about abortion, the Equal Rights Amendment, and women in church leadership. The episode with the harassing phone calls had finally started to fade into the background; I rarely saw those boys anymore, and when I did, we kept our distance.

"Katie Gaddini cuts an interesting figure," the journalist wrote, in the April 13 issue of the city's local paper. He went on to say that applying to my Christian college as a young feminist "is a bit like turning up for a Student Nonviolent Coordinating Committee meeting with a Spiro Agnew button affixed to your muumuu."[25] Suddenly, my private war became public; it journeyed from the confines of a sheltered college campus out onto the inky black-and-white newspaper page, materializing into words that everyone could see. The college president's wife wrote me a letter—"just to check in"—after seeing the article in the paper. Other students wrote response pieces to the paper, defending our Christian college. Professors cornered me outside of class and in hushed voices commended me for taking a stand. "Doing the right thing will never be easy," one of them whispered on our way into class.

Liv's reprisal didn't end quite so victoriously. After Wellspring terminated her position, she quickly found a new job at a marketing firm, where she received a better salary and a more friendly work environment. But the betrayal stuck. She stopped attending services at Wellspring, even though almost all the friendships she'd cultivated in New York were there, and even though it was her place of belonging, her *family*. She tried to go back once, choosing the evening service she'd attended for more than a decade, but left within ten minutes, crying as she charged down the street. After a six-month break from church, Liv found a small Presbyterian church near her apartment, where she could be anonymous and slip in and out without anyone even knowing her name.

"I just go for the services and leave," she says. But then she fills with optimism again, like a balloon swelling with helium, rising from a shrunken state into expansion, and explains that church fills certain needs that nothing else can fill. Such as? "Well, the communal experience of worship, for one . . ."

When I ask her why she still calls herself a Christian, after everything she's gone through, Liv doesn't skip a beat.

"Because my relationship with God supersedes the church. It always has and it always will."

Even so, Liv's departure from Wellspring had a ripple effect: a few of her friends left the church soon after, and Aurelie vowed never to go back.

"Seeing how they treated Liv was too difficult; it was the last straw for me," Aurelie says as we walk through Central Park, her pace outmatching mine. "Did you know they made her sign an NDA [nondisclosure agreement]? She had to sign it to get her severance pay. But what was she supposed to do? I mean, she had to pay her rent! The church does it all the time. It happens *regularly*." Aurelie shakes her head and exhales loudly. "They just don't value women in the same way, especially in high positions."

It turns out that Christian churches and nonprofits regularly ask employees to sign such agreements, especially in cases of termination. In an interview featured in *Christianity Today*, journalist Emily Belz reported that American megachurches such as New Spring routinely use NDAs in severance packages.[26] Similarly, in the UK, a popular TV special called *Panorama* revealed that Anglican churches in England had employees who reported racist incidents sign NDAs as a condition of payment. "I'm aware of others who have complained of racism, and they too have received compensation, and that's been contingent on them signing a nondisclosure agreement. That doesn't deal with the issue of racism; that buys silence," asserted Dr. Elizabeth Henry, the former adviser on race relations in the Church of England. A few days after the show aired, the archbishop of

Canterbury, Justin Welby, who holds the most senior position in the Church of England, declared, "I have said many times that I am totally against NDAs. NDAs are unacceptable." Together with another senior archbishop, Welby reportedly wrote to church leaders instructing them to no longer use such agreements.[27]

Aurelie and I walked in silence for a few minutes. Then she stopped and turned to face me.

"You know what? My issue isn't just with Wellspring; it's white evangelicalism in general. It's the evangelicals who elected Trump. It's the racism in the church."

I ask her how she would identify herself now, what religious category encompasses her doubts and beliefs, her convictions and confusion.

"I'm somewhere between Christian and Christian*ish*. I still go to church, but I'm disillusioned. I guess I'm just working it out for myself."

There's a picture of Una Kroll standing outside the General Synod's administrative meeting in 1975, the year their demands for women's ordination were once again denied. An older man and woman flank her on either side. Contrasting shades of white, black, and gray saturate the grainy photo. A sign, off to the side, reads "PRAY FOR WOMEN IN THE CHURCH." All capital letters, written in clean, elegant handwriting. They carry lanterns, these three protesters, lanterns with candles burning inside, sending curls of smoke into golden lids. The flames struggle for visibility through the blackened glass.

All three have their eyes closed and their heads bowed. Perhaps they are praying. Or maybe they are simply gathering their thoughts. But these are not peaceful faces. Their mouths turn downward and their foreheads are riven with deep lines, like well-worn trails that develop after years of human treading.

Looking at this picture now, it's Una's expression that distresses me most. Is it despair she feels? Or is it rage? Has feminism failed her, too?

"From a real body, which was there, proceed radiations which ultimately touch me, who am here," writes Roland Barthes.[28]

Here I am as Una's defeat radiates out to me, across time and space, and pricks me, bruises me, enacts *punctum*.[29] Here I am, writing these stories of insurrection and ruin, feeling both the lightness and the heaviness that comes with defeat, both the relief and the burden, marveling at how both can be felt at the same time, in equal measure. Here I am, affected by Una's photo because I am tethered to her. My story is braided with her story, and with Liv's, and with the stories of all the evangelical feminists, past and present, who are disciplined, rejected, or dismissed. I am tied to those who fight under feminism's name, who "feel in its ups and downs, in its coming and goings, one's own ups and downs, one's own comings and goings."[30]

These Christian feminists are our foremothers; their Christian feminism is our inheritance and their victories are ours. The fact that an outright "feminist" group like the one Liv started could even exist in a large, conservative, evangelical church would have been unheard of fifty years ago. That women like Jo could even demand to see more women in leadership signifies the progress bequeathed to us by countless women (and some men), who fought for women's voices to be heard throughout church history. They, too, faced reprisals for their feminism.

Of course, it's never been "feminism," as a word or a concept, that threatens evangelical Christianity. Feminism is nothing more than an empty vessel that fills, empties, and refills over decades, across the world. It's about what feminism stands for, the ideology and the beliefs behind the concept. More specifically, it's about the *fervor* of the beliefs behind the concept that threatens patriarchal gender orders and provokes reprisals.

The various articulations of feminism espoused by Christian women throughout history reveal crucial understandings about feminism as an object of analysis. They show how feminism remains vulnerable to acquisition and rearticulation; how it remains a vital weapon for Christian women to wield; how it unites, confronts, and admonishes.[31] The philosopher Judith Butler asserts, "To deconstruct the subject of feminism is not, then, to censure its usage, but, on the contrary, to release the term into a future of multiple significations . . . For if the term permits a resignification, if its referent is not fixed, then possibilities for new configurations of the term become possible."[32]

When I first started researching evangelical women and heard about their version of feminism, I was skeptical. The Women Rise events seemed, at the time, a diluted form of feminism, lacking the requisite rage. It seemed to reside a little too comfortably within white patriarchal evangelicalism. In other words, I believed their form of feminism to be acceptable because it wasn't seen as menacing, that its approval rested on its mildness.

But now I think it's just the opposite. Now I realize that this feminism was in fact *so* threatening that women such as Liv are sidelined, disposed of, or forgotten. To preserve the gender hierarchy, some men have to threaten to tie us up and beat us, to discipline us and put us in our place, in order to make us stop.

I am certain that a new cohort of feminists will take over from where we leave off. Even though Women Rise faded away, and Liv stopped fighting, other women are already taking up the battle for women's equality within evangelical churches. Liv recently told me about a friend of hers, a single evangelical woman who preaches at Wellspring sometimes and who keeps ascending the ranks of leadership.

"It's worth it to me, that even one woman made it to a leadership position," she said resolutely. We sat inside a restaurant in Brooklyn, nearing the end of a two-hour conversation. The other customers had left, and the waiter started emptying the cash register. Liv continued anyway.

"Everything I went through, it's all worth it just to now have one woman who is making it." Liv leaned in close to me, so close that her sandalwood-scented perfume flooded my senses. "Make sure you put this in your book," she instructed. "Strong, feminist women don't get beat down by the system. We rise."

Liv's friend is not the only woman pushing forward with the conviction to make evangelicalism more equitable. Recently, I attended a leadership training event run by a Christian nonprofit organization in New York. The speaker, a popular inspirational speaker in the business world, explained how we could reach our full potential. Next to me sat a demure woman named Rose. When I told her about my research, about the real reason I was sitting in a crowded room with investment bankers and politicians at seven in the morning, she shyly admitted that she attended Wellspring. We exchanged numbers, and the following week I asked if I could interview her.

Rose, it turned out, was a feminist. The innocent, fresh-faced, I-want-to-change-the-world type of feminist. Not the outspoken kind like Jo, but a feminist, nevertheless.

"I wanted to start a group for women's leadership at the church," Rose tells me, when we meet. "And so, I went and spoke to one of the women who helped start Women Rise—I guess the group isn't running anymore? Anyway, she basically said, 'Don't even try. It's not worth it. They'll never listen to you.'"

Underneath the marble table that we share, Rose uncrosses and crosses her legs. Her gaze roams over to the street outside, where busy passersby rush to and from meetings, a blur of black and brown suits. Together, we watch them for a while, and then her eyes switch back to me. Blazing. Just like Liv's eyes had blazed, in a café not far from here, four years ago.

"But I'm not going to listen to them. I want things to change. I'm going to change things."

They hold steady, those eyes, and they won't release me from their grip. They flash with rebellion, like the initial sparks of a match as it slides across the striker, never quite catching fire.

"I'm going to change things," she says again. "Just you watch."

8

THE STRUGGLE TO STAY

Caminante, no hay puentes, se hace puentes al andar.
[Voyager, there are no bridges, one builds them as one walks.]
—Gloria Anzaldúa

Around the same time that Liv left Wellspring, Jo was leaving her church too, unbeknownst to me. Jo, who had told me about threatening to rip off men's nut sacks and being relegated to backup singer because she was "a woman of a certain ilk." Loudmouthed, wild-eyed, unrelenting Jo, who was determined to stick with her faith and make it more inclusive. Jo, who moved back to Chicago and disappeared, leaving a pool of silence in her wake.

When I call her one sticky summer day, she fills me in on the previous ten months, coloring in the blanks with bright, irreverent hues.

Soon after moving home, she says, she found a nondenominational evangelical church in downtown Chicago. And just as she'd done in New York, she began singing with the worship team. She also joined a Bible study group and a ministry to feed the homeless on Wednesday nights. She "got stuck in," as they say in evangelical circles.

And then it all went terribly wrong. It started with tiredness in the morning, that demanding tug of fatigue that urges you to stay in bed, to call in sick to work and binge-watch TV shows instead. Within a few weeks, tiredness spiraled into full-blown exhaustion. "Postviral fatigue," the doctor pronounced, upon reviewing her case. An innocuous-sounding ailment, not the kind that would require Jo to stay in bed for days on end, miss two months of work, and skip church on Sundays. An illness that would drag with it another, more familiar ailment: depression.

"And no one from church followed up or checked in on me," Jo says, her normally powerful voice starting to fray. "Not a single goddamn person."

Her doctor recommended yoga as a therapeutic remedy to counter the fatigue, and so Jo went to a Saturday morning class, rolling out her body on the mat she'd borrowed from reception. As she moved through the poses, bending her stiff body into curved shapes, the yoga teacher came up behind her. He placed a hand on her lower back, tenderly guiding the bundle of flesh and muscle into alignment.

"When he did that, a guttural, animalistic sound came out of me," Jo reports. "Because, you know what? I realized I hadn't been touched by a man in so long."

When she says this, I'm reminded of the words of philosopher Emmanuel Levinas: "Contact as sensation is part of the world of light."[1] I picture Jo, down on her knees, arms stretching forward, forehead pressing into the stickiness of the mat, breathing in and out as she scoops this light into her.

Once she started feeling better, Jo gradually went back to church. She resided in the borderlands of her new evangelical church, just as she'd done the last few years at Wellspring. But she returned with hesitation, held back by a slow-spreading resentment.

"And then—I think this was the final blow. Actually, I know it was. I was watching a program on TV about sexual misconduct and the #MeToo movement and I had this horrifying realization that this had happened to me. And a big reason my abuse happened, and I hadn't even *recognized* it as sexual abuse, was because of the fucking purity movement."

As a thirteen-year-old girl in suburban Illinois, Jo had a lot of male friends, with whom she would play soccer after school, laugh during lunchtime, hang out on the weekend. She was a "guys girl"—fun, feisty, and up for anything. The summer before eighth grade, she became close with one of her male friends, John. They spoke on the phone nearly every night for an hour, sharing whatever unimportant observations sprang from their adolescent minds. A few years later, when she turned eighteen, their friendship morphed into something romantic, and Jo had her first-ever boyfriend. As a "good Christian girl" who had never had sex, let alone kissed anyone, Jo made it clear to John what she would and would not do. Kissing was okay, as long as clothing stayed on; caressing was acceptable as long as it didn't include any genitals. John agreed to her terms and conditions, even though he wasn't a Christian. After all, he said, he loved Jo and just wanted to be with her.

But then he started softly and consistently pushing the boundaries. At first it was a hand sliding over Jo's breast as they kissed, and then pouting when she removed it. A disappointed grunt here, an exasperated sigh there. A skittish hand that has a mind of its own. Then the self-degrading comments began: "I am such a worm, and you are perfect." "I hate myself." "You know, I would feel better about myself if you would just do something sexual with me." This last one got to Jo. It played upon every Christian teaching she'd received about the importance of women being a "good help meet"² and the need to remember that "love is the highest calling; love is what we are supposed to do with our lives." She had been taught that women are responsible not only for men's sexual behavior but also for their feelings. And here was her boyfriend, feeling horrible about himself, partly because Jo kept denying him sexually.

She began to think that it must be her responsibility to assuage his bad feelings. But she also had, pulsing through her, the messages to remain pure and wholesome and to resist all forms of sexual temptation until marriage. These dueling narratives meant that Jo felt caught between John and God. John who wanted to have sex, and God who wanted her to remain pure. How could she please them both?

"Last Christmas, I bumped into John and his parents on the train platform in Chicago," Jo says, during our transatlantic phone call. "And I hugged him. I felt pressure to perform, and to save face, so I hugged him. I can't tell you how disgusted I felt afterwards . . ."

The summer after Jo finished high school, she went traveling through South America with a group of friends. When they reached Peru, John flew down to visit. Jo was staying in a ramshackle hostel in Cusco, in a room with a single bed and a lamp that flickered in and out. As soon as the door to her hostel room closed, they started making out, John's exhaustion from an international flight suddenly dissipating in the face of his sexual want. They tumbled down on the bed, shoving the pillows to the side.

"Take off your top," John instructed in a breathy, authoritative voice.

Jo ignored him and they continued kissing.

Then he started tugging at her T-shirt, the lightweight cotton one her mom had bought to keep Jo cool and dry in the Amazon.

"Come on. Take it off. I flew all this way . . . I spent all this money to see you. It's the least you could do."

The narratives in Jo's head started buzzing around like flies caught in the kitchen, flying around chaotically, diving straight into windows, desperate to get out.

Jo lifted off her T-shirt. John unhooked her bra while she lay there, still and quiet, like a corpse. He began to kiss her body, her chest, her nipples, running his tongue along the length of her abdomen, his hands and mouth roving everywhere. Jo stayed motionless, hoping for it to end soon, hoping that her God, the one who decreed no sex before marriage, would look down on what was happening and find it in his heart to forgive her.

Afterward, she felt dirty. John flew back to the United States and she continued her travels, but that feeling of numbness, of being a dead body, stayed with her. It was better, at least, than feeling overwhelming shame.

Three months later, at the end of her travels, Jo returned to Chicago and broke up with John. He protested wildly, threatening suicide, heaving all his self-loathing on her once again, but Jo was resolute. She walked away from the relationship, filled with disgust—disgust toward herself, for breaching her purity standards and letting herself become sullied and unclean; disgust, too, for being the instigator, the temptress, the responsible party.

It wasn't until thirteen years later, when Jo watched that #MeToo movement documentary, that she identified her past relationship as abusive. It was three words—"erosion of consent"—that suddenly tripped a wire, so that all of her encounters with John, sexual and otherwise, erupted like a land mine from deep in her memory.

"It just all builds up, doesn't it? All of it." It was a question posed for me but meant for herself. "I sat my parents down and told them I'm not going to church anymore and I don't know if I ever will again. I told them I don't consider myself a Christian anymore. They sobbed. They understood, and they said they still love me, but they sobbed."

I remember my mom gently weeping in a café in New England when I told her about my non-Christian boyfriend and my non-Christian friends, declaring that she didn't even know me anymore. The silence from my favorite aunt. A letter from one of my friends, imploring me to come back.

"So, what are you now, if not a Christian?" Now it's my turn to pose a question meant for myself.

"I say I'm 'Christian*ish*.' You know, like Dan Savage's idea of monogam*ish*." Then a laugh flutters forth, having made its way through a field sticky with pain.

"A relation of cruel optimism exists when something you desire is actually an obstacle to your flourishing," the late theorist Lauren Berlant writes in the opening to her book *Cruel Optimism*. She continues:

> It might involve food, or a kind of love; it might be a fantasy of the good life, or a political project. It might rest on something simpler, too, like a new habit that promises to induce in you an improved way of being. These kinds of optimistic relations are not inherently cruel. They become cruel only when the object that draws your attachment actively impedes the aim that brought you to it initially.[3]

Single evangelical women desire to be valued and treated equally within their religious communities. They want to be told that their worth lies outside of what they do or do not do with their bodies; they want more acceptance and less judgment; they want the freedom to express who they are without the pressure to conform. Some want to pursue a career, others desire to be church leaders. Most want to enjoy singlehood without being rushed into marriage. In short, they desire more acceptable ways of being.

It turns out that *all* evangelical women desire this, even the exemplars. When I first discovered the world of evangelical influencers, they dazzled me with their pictures of attractive husbands, multiple children, wealth, and good looks. But hiding beneath these images were real women with real struggles. On January 20, 2020, Alyssa Quilala uploaded a post to her Instagram account featuring three simple words: "You already knew." Without giving any details, she admitted that her marriage to worship leader Chris Quilala was over. Subsequent posts featured a new narrative: rather than focusing on her picture-perfect marriage, Alyssa, who reverted to her maiden name, shared the importance of being real and authentic. "Just remember that Jesus hung out with the outcasts," she reminded her followers recently.

Six months after Alyssa's announcement, Rachel Hollis shared on Instagram that she and her husband had also made the decision to end their marriage. Her book, *Didn't See That Coming*, describes the process leading up to her divorce.

The biggest shattering of perfection, though, came from Caressa Prescott. In early 2021, after weeks of Instagram silence, Prescott shared that she'd been in rehab, recovering from depression, anxiety, substance abuse, an eating disorder, and a suicide attempt. Although she doesn't blame the church for her struggles, she does note the unyielding pressure that pastor wives face. "If I'm not perfect and I don't have it all together then what

right to [*sic*] I have to speak into someone else's life, right? . . .
No matter what is happening, our only option is to put the brave
face on and get in the car and go to church and sit on the front
[row] and have everyone else looking at you," Prescott wrote
recently. A few months later, Prescott admitted that, like Hollis
and Quilala, she had decided to end her marriage.

Prescott's dramatic story of serious destruction and self-
harm reveals the tremendous pressure that evangelical exemplars face to uphold the ideal. The construction of the ideal,
and the pressure for perfection, doesn't just hurt those like Jo
who cannot inhabit it, who fail to meet the external and internal values of evangelical femininity—it also hurts the ideal
itself.

Of course, as Berlant notes, relations of cruel optimism arise
in various scenes of ordinary life. Relationships that we expect
to save us from our loneliness, diet plans that promise to make
us thinner and happier, political candidates who guarantee to
alleviate our suffering—all of these promises become cruel when
our attachment to them actually blocks our thriving.[4] Therefore,
the stories of single evangelical women and their cruel attachment to equality in the church is not unusual.

What these stories do, though, is provide flesh-and-blood
examples of how such cruel attachments play out over time. They
show the productive work of hope, which orients individuals
toward the future while making life more bearable in the present.
They also expose the dark side of hope, as an emotion capable of
deceit and stultification, and the harm that hopeful attachments
can inflict.[5] Hope ties women to their desired objects (or, we
might say, desired *objectives*), hope produced by Christian leaders who dangle promises of equality but keep them just out of
reach.[6] This hope keeps single women in the church until they've
had enough, and then, disillusioned, unraveled, wounded, they

leave. In this sense, women's hope might be considered cruel—not just because it doesn't deliver on its promise but also because it holds them in abeyance, leaving them expectantly waiting for a future that may never come.

One Friday evening not too long ago, Carys invited me to her house for dinner. While we waited for the pizza to arrive, Carys decanted a few weeks' worth of annoyances. She felt undervalued by the senior pastors at Wellspring and completely unnoticed by Christian men at church. She was frustrated that the leadership remained white, male, and upper middle class, despite having spoken up about the need for diversity for the past three years. She resented the fact that the only women at the top were married—usually co-pastors with their husbands. In other words, they all had validation conferred via marriage. And she'd given up on the idea of ordination—at least for now.

The doorbell chimes and Carys bounds to the front door. Alone in her living room, my eyes wander around her apartment: the muted television screen where news pundits debate, the dirty plates and bowls stacked in the sink, an array of lit candles of various heights, widening as they melt onto the table. Tiny droplets of rain splatter across the skylight above me and I watch them fall.

Carys comes back with a large cardboard box and plops it down on the coffee table. "Dig in," she says, as she rummages around her kitchen drawers looking for napkins.

"Do you remember two years ago, when you couldn't get enough church?" I say between mouthfuls. "When you were so busy with all those church activities? I even remember you saying to me how much you loved it."

Carys collapses on the armchair next to me and opens a beer, releasing a crackling sound.

"Yeah, I know the period you're talking about. I was leading a Roots course and doing that training for ordination. At that point I was really hungry for it all, you know? I was back in the fold. It was like . . . falling in love. And just like falling in love, after a while the reality settles in and you realize *Maybe I'm not that into it after all.*" She laughs and then takes a drawn-out sip of beer.

"So . . . why do you stay? You have so many issues with the church. And not just you; it's other women too. But I keep wondering why you stay."

"I *knew* you would ask me that." She smiles and tilts her head back to take another sip, holding me in suspense.

"What keeps me there is the community. I have such an amazing group of female friends. And that is where I get my spiritual community from, not from church, a Bible study group, or Roots. With those women, we are honest and vulnerable with each other and it's so powerful.

"There's a term I like, called 'muscular Christianity,' which is the pressure to act and say and do certain things in the church. To perform. So, to have the opposite of that—a group of women that you can be honest with—is very, *very* powerful. And it's specific to women, because women in the church are facing oppression, exclusion, expectation . . . You know, I miss these women when one of us is away. What I have with them, it's like a family connection."

Carys's expression is wistful now, as if she's daydreaming. Like she's far away from this cramped apartment, with the dishes piled high and the flashing TV. Not back in the throes of her love affair with the church nor careening toward exit. Maybe in her mind, at this moment, she's with that small group of women who sustain and nurture her, who form a little enclave of safety within an inhospitable environment, their intimacy all the more powerful because of it.

Religion is so much more than just a bundle of beliefs, a box to tick on a census form, or a set of rituals and practices. It is a living and breathing organism. And in this aliveness, we encounter the pleasure and pain that is bound up with religious belonging.[7] The women's stories chronicled in this book serve as a testament to the importance of religion in one's life, and they demonstrate how profoundly religion can be lived.

I have enumerated what single evangelical women gain from the evangelical community, including a deep sense of belonging.[8] Many women experience evangelical Christianity as transformative and healing; it offers them the fresh start they need. Others describe their churches as a paradoxical mix of liberating and restrictive, comforting and wounding. In writing about single women's complex relationships with Christianity, I have examined how they live out their "identity in Christ," which they told me time and again was their most important identity.

Laying claim to an identity sutures us to a category that means something, but over whose meaning we have little control. "We want suture so badly that we'll take it at any price, even with the fullest knowledge of what it entails," the theorist Kaja Silverman asserts.[9] It is exactly on this point that evangelical women face a double bind: the attachment to an identity in Christ liberates, relieves, and anchors women, but it also ensnares them in a limiting network of norms.

In white evangelicalism, the price of belonging includes embracing traditional femininity, heterosexuality, marriage, and sexual purity. It includes waging battle with an amorphous power regime whose effects are always felt but never transparent. It includes invisibility and continual marginalization, made even worse if you are not white, middle class, or straight—and if you remain single. Yet the four women central to this book have made it clear that they are acutely aware of the price they pay for staying. And they're not the only ones.

Recently, on an ordinary weekday evening, I settled into my favorite armchair, determined to finish reading my novel, whereupon I was interrupted by the insistent buzz of my phone. I begrudgingly went to retrieve it and saw a series of messages from Jo. *My friend just sent me an article and said she thought I'd like it and relate. When I opened it up I saw that you'd written it. It's so good! Well done! I hope others read this.*

After reading Jo's messages, I quickly scrolled over to the article I'd recently written for *Relevant*, a popular Christian magazine, about why Christian women are leaving the church. On *Relevant*'s Facebook page, the comments section was flooded: "This is exactly why I left the church." "I feel validated." "The article describes how I've been feeling for years." The next morning, Aurelie wrote to me from Spain, where she was hiking the Camino de Santiago, to say the article had made the rounds on Facebook and had struck a chord with her social circle. Then Maddie messaged from London to say she'd shared it with several of her friends, including a male church leader who refused to see inequality in the church. I also heard from Charlotte, another woman I interviewed several years ago, who had cried when her pastor discouraged her from pursuing ordination.

Strangers reached out to me, too. I received, and continue to receive, e-mails from other single Christian women all over the world, who share that they too have been devalued and rendered invisible for years—precisely because they are single and women.

If nothing else, the reaction this article received demonstrates that the experiences of the four women central to this book are not unique. Their stories highlight a pervasive problem within evangelical Christianity that continues to run undetected—or at least unaddressed.

At the beginning of the book, I asked why single Christian women stay in the church if they consider it oppressive. It turns out that many of them don't. Women like Maddie leave not only a church but also the religion itself. And data from both the United States and the United Kingdom indicate that this response is increasingly common, as single women in both countries are now the group most likely to leave white evangelical Christianity. If this trend continues, the very survival of evangelicalism will be put in jeopardy.

But others, like Carys, remain tethered to the church and all it provides, despite the mistreatment they face. Another woman who resided on the borderland told me that a dull antipathy had replaced the excitement she used to feel about her faith. "But I remember what it was like, and I am unwilling to let it go." Let what go? I asked. "My beliefs, my faith, Christianity, all of it," she replied in a measured voice.

Similarly, during one of our conversations after she left Wellspring, I asked Liv how she identifies her faith now.

"I'm a Christian. I'm still a Christian. Because I feel like I have a relationship with something, and I can't ignore that. I've experienced things that I just can't deny, so I would never chuck out my faith. And it might go through seasons, and it might have ups and downs, but it's a part of my identity now, it's who I am. It's kind of like breathing; you can't just shut it off, you know? It's part of your living."

By comparing her faith to breathing, Liv highlights the indispensability of her faith. Following her analogy, renouncing

Christianity would amount to collapsing her lungs—shutting off the vital and automatic mechanism that keeps her alive.

At the same time, the stories in this book show the blurriness of the categories "leaving" and "staying." "Despite all our desperate, eternal attempts to separate, contain and mend, categories always leak," Trinh T. Minh-ha states.[10] Jo calls herself "Christianish" and believes in some of the tenets of Christianity but vows to never return to church. Does she meet the criteria of leaving or of staying? And what about Naomi, the statuesque British woman who loves *Magic Mike*, believes in sex before marriage, and supports left-wing politics?

"At this particular moment in time I'm very disillusioned with evangelical Christianity. I don't really have time for it," she admitted recently. Now married with two small children, Naomi left Thames Gathering Place and found a smaller, more progressive congregation near their home in North London. They attend semiregularly, and despite her grievances, Naomi still believes many of the tenets of evangelical Christianity. Her case shows that leaving and staying are not static categories; instead, they bleed into each other, tied up with the powerful drive to belong and the complexity of religion itself.

In writing about cruel attachments, Berlant urges us to locate the "impasses in zones of intimacy that hold out the often cruel promise of reciprocity and belonging to the people who seek them."[11] An impasse is a deadlock, a stalemate, a place without movement. The situation that many single evangelical women face in evangelical churches represents an impasse. They've made their demands clear, yet they are still waiting, and hoping, for change.

In this sense, they are not so different from any of us who make concessions every day within the "impasses" in which we find ourselves—whether it's an intimate relationship laden with unequal power dynamics, a sexist boss, a racist workplace, or the larger cultural environment that favors one race, class, sexual identity, or gender over another. The charge for single evangelical women is the same charge for all of us: to evaluate the costs we bear and to bring the hidden points of compromise to light in order to see them with fresh eyes. Only then can we decide whether to stay or walk away.

My relationships with these four women continue today. I may not interview them or record what they say anymore, but we are still in each other's lives. And even if we do not meet up as much as we used to, I still think of them often.

When I do, I like to picture Liv lounging on a beach somewhere, a cocktail in her hand, enjoying the fruits of a hard year of work at her marketing firm. Feeling, with each day, each month, each year, the past receding behind her like the worries that slowly evaporate as your body descends into sleep. I think of her swiping through the latest dating app, reading a prospective match's profile aloud to friends in that exuberant way of hers.

I imagine Jo grabbing an early-morning coffee with a coworker in Chicago before they head in to the office. The coworker's head cocked back in laughter and Jo's satisfied smile, pleased that whatever irreverent quip she's made has elicited such an uproarious response. Yet there is a physical discomfort pulsing just beneath the surface of that smile, an emotional devastation that never seems to go away.

I think about Maddie arriving at her art studio in East London. Dropping her keys on the table and switching on her desktop computer. She nurses a mug of coffee and tilts her head to the side as she studies the painting she finished over the weekend, imagining little adjustments to light and color, searching for beauty.

And Carys. Maybe she's back home right now, stumbling to the breakfast table and greeting her mom with a kiss on the forehead. Or maybe she's at a café in New York, not too far from where I am at this very moment. A quick coffee break before her eleven o'clock meeting at Wellspring. Standing near the window as she waits for her order to be called. The sunlight, on this bright morning, catching in her eyes too.

Causing her to turn away.

ACKNOWLEDGMENTS

The majority of this book was written while I was a research fellow supported by departments of sociology at the University of Johannesburg and the University of Cambridge. I am thankful to both of these institutions for giving me the time and space in which to write.

Professor Manali Desai was the first person to suggest I write a book based on my research with single evangelical women. For planting that seed of possibility and for intelligent guidance over four years, I am very grateful. Thank you to Wendy Lochner at Columbia University Press for championing this story from the beginning.

I've staked this book, and in many ways my career, on the lives of four women. Carys, Maddie, Jo, and Liv—thank you for trusting me and granting me access to your world. I'm also appreciative of all the other evangelical women I interviewed, spoke with, and consulted since 2013, especially Naomi and Aurelie.

A book is as a joint endeavor in many ways, and I have had the good fortune of meeting many collaborators along the way. This includes Stefanía, Genevieve, Tim, Issy, Jeanette, Marcos, Robert, Phil, Kusha, Lea, Erin, Sam, Rob, Sonya, Linda W., Sarah, Denise—and above all, Mahvish. Her companionship and cleverness have influenced me more than she knows. The members of NYLUM, my Arvon retreat, the gender research cluster at Cambridge, and our pandemic writing group have stimulated many ideas and corrected many of my mistakes. Julia generously edited many chapters, as did Meaghan, Kelsy, Margy, and Diane. Mary and Linda K. kept me afloat.

Atefeh came along at just the right time, and was a trusted reader, colaborer, and friend.

I am indebted to Simon and Jackie for housing and feeding me during the final stages of writing.

In early 2014, Carmen and I walked the walls of Lucca and discussed the dilemmas single Christian women face. Later, she asked that I write a book to make sense of her experience in the church. This is for her, and for Hannah too.

I am grateful to my family for supporting this book, even though it comes at great personal cost. To my mother, Christine, and my sister, Natalee—thank you. Also, Pete, Addy, and Wyatt. To my father, the late Reverend Roberto Gaddini, who taught me to ask questions.

Finally, thanks to Ben, who also came along at just the right time and brought so much light.

METHODOLOGICAL NOTE

The names of all of the women mentioned in this book are pseudonyms, except for Carrie Lloyd, Mimi Haddad, Lucy Winkett, and Kat Harris, who agreed that I could use their real names, on account of being public figures.

Because of the sensitivity of the topics discussed and the personal risks that are felt to accompany disclosure, I have gone to great lengths to anonymize the four central characters, while still retaining the integrity of their stories. In some instances, I have incorporated characteristics and quotes from other women I interviewed, in order to further protect Carys, Maddie, Liv, and Jo.

The majority of the dialogue in the book is based word for word on my interview transcriptions. Where conversations occurred during participant observation, I have relied on my field notes and my memory, at times circling back to the women to verify what was said.

There will certainly be mistakes on account of the errancy of memory; however, I have endeavored, as much as possible, to capture the intentions and meanings of my generous interlocutors.

NOTES

PREFACE

1. Wellspring Community Church and Thames Gathering Place are pseudonyms. Throughout this work, identifying details of some people and locations have been changed. All of the women's names and identifying characteristics have been changed to ensure confidentiality. See "Methodological Note" at the end of the book.
2. Joan Didion, *Slouching Towards Bethlehem: Essays* (New York: Farrar, Straus and Giroux, 1978), 139.
3. Eighty-one percent of white evangelical Christians voted for Trump in the 2016 election, the highest evangelical vote in nearly twenty years. Jessica Martínez and Gregory A. Smith, "How the Faithful Voted: A Preliminary 2016 Analysis," Pew Research Center, 2016, https://www.pewresearch.org/fact-tank/2016/11/09/how-the-faithful-voted-a-preliminary-2016-analysis.
4. Susan Harding, "Representing Fundamentalism: The Problem of the Repugnant Cultural Other," *Social Research* 58, no. 2 (1991): 373–393.
5. This was also the result of R. Marie Griffith's book on women in the evangelical prayer group Aglow Ministries and Julie Ingersoll's work with female evangelical feminists. R. Marie Griffith, *God's Daughters: Evangelical Women and the Power of Submission* (Berkeley: University of California Press, 1997); Julie Ingersoll, *Evangelical Christian Women: War Stories in the Gender Battles* (New York: New York University Press, 2003).

6. Lila Abu-Lughod, "The Romance of Resistance: Tracing Transformations of Power Through Bedouin Women," *American Ethnologist* 17, no. 1 (1990): 41–55; Saba Mahmood, *The Politics of Piety: The Islamic Revival and the Feminist Subject* (Princeton, NJ: Princeton University Press, 2003); Lara Deeb, *An Enchanted Modern: Gender and Public Piety in Shi'i Lebanon* (Princeton, NJ: Princeton University Press, 2006).

7. Sally Gallagher, *Evangelical Identity and Gendered Family Life* (London: Rutgers University Press, 2003).

8. Michael Lipka, "The Most and Least Religious Diverse U.S. Religious Groups," Pew Research Center, July 17, 2015, https://www.pewresearch.org/fact-tank/2015/07/27/the-most-and-least-racially-diverse-u-s-religious-groups.

9. Nathan J. Kelly and Jana Morgan Kelly, "Religion and Latino Partisanship in the United States," *Political Research Quarterly* 58, no. 1 (2005): 93.

10. Brierley Consultancy, *Future First*, no. 44 (2016): 1.

11. Pew Research Center, "How the Faithful Voted." In their executive summary, Robert P. Jones and Daniel Cox report that one in three evangelicals today is a person of color. See Jones and Cox, *America's Changing Religious Identity: Findings from the 2016 American Values Atlas* (Washington, DC: Public Religion Research Institute, September 6, 2017), 7–9. https://www.prri.org/wp-content/uploads/2017/09/PRRI-Religion-Report.pdf.

12. Randall Balmer, "The Real Origins of the Religious Right," *Politico Magazine*, May 27, 2014; Balmer, *Bad Faith: Race and the Rise of the Religious Right* (Grand Rapids: Wm. B. Eerdmans), 2021.

13. For a thorough examination of evangelicals in the United States, see Frances Fitzgerald, *The Evangelicals: The Struggle to Shape America* (New York: Simon and Schuster, 2017); Elizabeth Bernstein and Janet Jakobsen, "Sex, Secularism, and Religious Influence in US Politics," *Third World Quarterly* 31, no. 6 (2010); Gerard Clarke, "Agents of Transformation? Donors, Faith-based Organisations and International Development," *Third World Quarterly* 28, no. 1 (2007); and Michael D. Lindsay, "Elite Power: Social Networks within American Evangelicalism," *Sociology of Religion* 67, no. 3 (2006).

14. Andy Walton, Andrea Hatcher, and Nick Spencer, *Is There a "Religious Right" Emerging in Britain?* (London: Theos, 2013).

15. For an explanation of how and why Christianity declined in Britain, see Callum Brown, *The Death of Christian Britain: Understanding Secularisation, 1800–2000* (London: Routledge, 2010).

16. Church of England, *Statistics for Mission: 2019* (London: Research and Statistics, 2020), 9. https://www.churchofengland.org/sites/default /files/2020-10/2019StatisticsForMission.pdf.

17. For the history of Christianity and evangelicalism in the UK, see Andrew Brown and Linda Woodhead, *That Was the Church That Was: How the Church of England Lost the English People* (London: Bloomsbury, 2016).

18. Academics describe the close connection between religious communities as an "imagined community" of believers who share traditions, beliefs, and values. See Meredith McGuire, *Lived Religion: Faith and Practice in Everyday Life* (Oxford: Oxford University Press, 2008).

19. All of the women I met attributed masculine pronouns to God, even when they said God was not male or female. In this book, I have decided to capitalize the word *God* and to use male pronouns, in keeping with the language of my interlocutors.

20. David McClendon, "Gender Gap in Religious Service Attendance has Narrowed in US," Pew Research Center, May 13, 2016, https://www .pewresearch.org/fact-tank/2016/05/13/gender-gap-in-religious -service-attendance-has-narrowed-in-u-s; Pew Research Center, "Women Who Are Evangelical Protestant," Religious Landscape Study, https://www.pewforum.org/religious-landscape-study/religious -tradition/evangelical-protestant/gender-composition/women /#attendance-at-religious-services-trend; Evangelical Alliance and Christian Research, *21st Century Evangelicals: A Snapshot of the Beliefs and Habits of Evangelical Christians in the UK* (London: Evangelical Alliance, 2011), https://www.eauk.org/church/resources/snapshot /upload/21st-Century-Evangelicals-Data-Report.pdf.

21. Julie Ingersoll, *Evangelical Christian Women: War Stories in the Gender Battles* (New York: New York University Press, 2003).

22. Kate Bowler, *The Preacher's Wife: The Precarious Power of Evangelical Women Celebrities* (Durham, NC: Duke University Press, 2019).

23. Interestingly, 40 percent of all white American evangelicals are single—defined as widowed, never married, or divorced/separated. According to this statistic, being single is a minority position, but

only marginally. Pew Research Center, "Women Who Are Evangelical Protestant."

24. Kristin Aune, "Evangelical Christianity and Women's Changing Lives," *European Journal of Women's Studies* 15, no. 3 (2008).

25. McClendon, "Gender Gap."

26. Linda Woodhead, "Gendering Secularization Theory," *Social Compass* 55, no. 2 (2008): 187–193; Abby Day, *The Religious Lives of Older Laywomen* (Oxford: Oxford University Press, 2017); Callum Brown, *The Death of Christian Britain: Understanding Secularisation Theory*, 2nd ed. (London: Routledge, 2009).

27. Denise Riley, *Words of Selves: Identification, Solidarity, Irony* (Palo Alto, CA: Stanford University Press, 2000), 86.

28. Clarise Lispector, *The Hour of the Star* (London: Penguin Classics, 2014), xxviii.

I. HOMECOMING

The epigraph is from Mary Jo Bang, "H Is Here Is a Song, Now Sing," from *The Bride of E* (Minneapolis: Graywolf, 2009).

1. Evangelicals understand God, Jesus, and the Holy Spirit to be three parts of a whole (the Trinity). They are one entity, while at the same time each holds its own separate function. For example, the Holy Spirit's role is associated with some of the more emotional aspects of Christianity. A common analogy given in evangelicalism is to water, which can transform into steam, ice, or liquid though it remains the same element.

2. See Joel Robbins, "Transcendence and the Anthropology of Christianity: Language, Change, and Individualism," *Suomen Antropologi: Journal of the Finnish Anthropological Society* 37, no. 2 (2012).

3. As I mentioned in the preface, the organization I'm calling Roots International is a global evangelizing program operating in churches, universities, prisons, and homes. Several of the women in this study joined Wellspring and Thames Gathering through Roots, and many went on to run Roots sessions for years afterwards.

4. For a similar analysis, see Simon Coleman, *The Globalisation of Charismatic Christianity: Spreading the Gospel of Prosperity* (Cambridge: Cambridge University Press, 2000).

5. Sallie McFague, "Conversion: Life on the Edge of the Raft," *Union Seminary Review* 32, no. 3 (1978): 255.

6. For more accounts of evangelical conversions, see Susan Harding, *The Book of Jerry Falwell: Fundamentalist Language and Politics* (Princeton, NJ: Princeton University Press, 1987); Harding, "Convicted by the Holy Spirit: The Rhetoric of Fundamental Baptist Conversion," *American Ethnologist* 14, no. 1 (1987); Tanya Luhrmann, *When God Talks Back: Understanding the American Evangelical Relationship with God* (New York: Alfred E. Knopf, 2004); Robert Hefner, *Conversion to Christianity: Historical and Anthropological Perspectives on a Great Transformation* (Berkeley: University of California Press, 1993); and R. Marie Griffith, *God's Daughters: Evangelical Women and the Power of Submission* (Berkeley: University of California Press, 1997). For writings about conversion within Orthodox Judaism, see Lynn Davidman, *Tradition in a Rootless World: Women Turn to Orthodox Judaism* (Oakland: University of California Press, 1991).

7. Robbins states, "Christianity is a religion that focuses a good deal on the need for radical change and, I will argue, grounds the possibility for change in ideas about the ways the transcendent realm can sometimes influence the mundane." Robbins, "Transcendence and the Anthropology of Christianity," 8.

8. All biblical references draw from the New International Version, unless otherwise noted.

9. Harding, *Book of Jerry Falwell*, 57.

10. Elliot Aronson and Judson Mills, "The Effect of Severity of Initiation on Liking for a Group," *Journal of Abnormal and Social Psychology* 59, no. 2 (1993): 177–181.

11. Zygmunt Bauman, *Identity: Conversations with Benedetto Vecchi* (Cambridge: Polity Press, 2004). See also Matt Dawson, "Bauman, Beck, Giddens, and Our Understanding of Politics in Late Modernity," *Journal of Power* 3, no. 2 (2010); Anthony Giddens, *Modernity and Self-identity: Self and Society in the Late Modern Age* (Palo Alto, CA: Stanford University Press, 1991); Francis Fukuyama, *Trust: The Social Virtues and the Creation of Prosperity* (New York: Free Press, 1996); Robert Putnam, *Bowling Alone: The Collapse and Revival of American Community* (New York: Simon and Schuster, 2000); and David

Campbell and Robert Putnam, *American Grace: How Religion Divides and Unites Us* (New York: Simon and Schuster, 2010).

12. George Orwell, "Inside the Whale," in *A Collection of Essays* (New York: Houghton Mifflin Harcourt, 1947/1970), 244.

13. About world religions, Hefner writes, "Their genius lies in their curious ability to renounce this world and announce another, more compelling and true." Hefner, *Conversion to Christianity*, 34.

14. Benjamin Beit-Hallahmi and Michael Argyle, *The Psychology of Religious Behaviour, Belief and Experience* (London: Routledge, 1997), 118.

15. Indeed, this concept can be traced back to Saint Augustine, who in the late fourth century wrote, "Our hearts are restless until they can find rest in you." Augustine, *Confessions*, trans. Henry Chadwick (Oxford: Oxford University Press, 2008), 3. Likewise, the seventeenth-century philosopher and Christian Blaise Pascal wrote, "What is it then that this desire and this inability proclaim to us, but that there was once in man a true happiness of which there now remain to him only the mark and empty trace, which he in vain tries to fill from all his surroundings, seeking from things absent the help he does not obtain in things present? But these are all inadequate, because the infinite abyss can only be filled by an infinite and immutable object, that is to say, only by God Himself." Pascal, *Pensées*, trans. W. F. Trotter (New York: Dover, 2003), 113.

16. See Adrienne Rich, "Compulsory Heterosexuality and Lesbian Existence," *Signs* 5, no. 4 (1980): 631–660.

17. McFague, "Conversion," 259.

18. See Rebecca Lester, *Jesus in Our Wombs: Embodying Modernity in a Mexican Convent* (London: University of California Press, 2005); Luhrmann, *When God Talks Back*.

19. Harding, "Convicted by the Holy Spirit," 167–181. Lauren Berlant writes, "But intimacy also involves an aspiration for a narrative about something shared, a story about both oneself and others that will turn out in a particular way." Berlant, *The Queen of America Goes to Washington City: Essays on Sex and Citizenship* (Durham, NC: Duke University Press, 1997), 281. See also Sertaç Sehlikoglu, "Intimate Publics, Public Intimacies," *Cambridge Journal of Anthropology* 33, no 2 (2015).

20. Émile Durkheim claims that the search for God is also the search for a shared identity with a community of believers. He writes, "But God is also a source of a shared identity, and as society enlarges, we all

become His children." N. J. Allen, W. S. F. Pickering, and William Watts Miller, *On Durkheim's Elementary Forms of Religious Life* (London: Routledge, 1912/1998), 75–76.

21. Themes in this chapter originally appeared in Katie Gaddini, "Apostate Women: The Sacrifices Doubt Demands," *Marginalia Review of Books*, October 8, 2021.

2. WITHOUT YOU, I AM NOTHING

The epigraph is from Emmanuel Levinas, *Humanism of the Other*, trans. N. Poller (Champaign: University of Illinois Press, 2006), 56–57.

1. Youth With a Mission, an evangelical missionary organization with a headquarters in the United States.

2. See Katherine P. Erwig, "Dreams from a Saint: Anthropological Atheism and the Temptation to Believe," *American Anthropologist* 96, no. 3 (1994): 571–583.

3. I consider clasping hands during prayer, as well as frequent embraces and the laying of hands on one another during intercession for miracles—all of which took place within the evangelical community I studied—to be embodied religious practices. See Meredith McGuire, *Everyday Religion: Observing Modern Religious Lives* (Oxford: Oxford University Press, 2007), 189.

4. See Amanda Coffey, *The Ethnographic Self* (London: Sage, 1999), 21; Erving Goffman, "On Fieldwork," *Journal of Contemporary Ethnography* 18, no. 2 (1989).

5. Mirabai Starr, *Saint John of the Cross: Devotion Prayers and Living Wisdom* (Louisville, CO: Sounds True, 2008), 90. "Dark Night of the Soul" begins with a set of eight "Stanzas of the Soul." The saint describes the dark journey that the believer will travel, full of tribulations and straits. Rather than being a burden, according to the saint, this journey is rendered a joy, as it draws the believer in closer communion with God.

6. Emmanuel Levinas, *The Levinas Reader*, ed. Sean Hand (Oxford: Blackwell, 1993), 51.

7. See Joan Didion, *Slouching Towards Bethlehem: Essays* (New York: Farrar, Straus and Giroux, 1978), 40.

8. See Jennifer Butler, *Born Again: The Christian Right Globalized* (London: Pluto Press, 2006); Simon Coleman, *The Globalisation of*

Charismatic Christianity: Spreading the Gospel of Prosperity (Cambridge: Cambridge University Press, 2000); Donald Miller and Tetsunao Yamamori, *Global Pentecostalism: The New Face of Christian Social Engagement* (Berkeley: University of California Press, 2007); Joel Robbins, "The Globalization of Pentecostal and Charismatic Christianity," *Annual Review of Anthropology* 33 (2004); and Heather Shipley, *Globalized Religion and Sexual Identity* (Leiden: Brill, 2004). Another, related body of literature interrogates the spread of Christianity through missions and colonialism. See Dana Robert, *Christian Mission: How Christianity Became a World Religion* (Hoboken: John Wiley and Sons, 2009); and Webb Keane, *Christian Moderns: Freedom and Fetish in the Mission Encounter* (Berkeley: University of California Press, 2007).

9. Zygmunt Bauman, *Liquid Times: Living in an Age of Uncertainty* (Cambridge: Polity Press, 2007), 68.

10. Sonya Sharma and Matthew Guest, "Navigating Religion Between University and Home: Christian Students' Experiences in English Universities," *Social and Cultural Geography* 14, no. 1 (2013): 59–79.

11. Michael Hogg, Janice Adelman, and Robert Blagg, "Religion in the Face of Uncertainty: An Uncertainty-Identity Theory Account of Religiousness," *Personality and Social Psychology Review* 14, no. 1 (2009).

12. Lynn Davidman, *Tradition in a Rootless World: Women Turn to Orthodox Judaism* (Berkeley: University of California Press, 1991).

13. Anna Strhan, *Aliens and Strangers? The Coherence in the Everyday Lives of Evangelicals* (Oxford: Oxford University Press, 2015).

14. Zygmunt Bauman, *Identity: Conversations with Benedetto Vecchi* (Cambridge: Polity Press, 2004), 72. Also see Bauman, *Liquid Times*.

15. Dimitris Ballas, "What Makes a 'Happy City'?," *Cities* 32, no. 1 (2013); Adam Okulicz-Kozaryn, "Unhappy Metropolis (When an American City Is Too Big)," *Cities* 61 (2017); Putnam, *Bowling Alone*; Richard Sennett, *Corrosion of Character: The Personal Consequences of Work in the New Capitalism* (New York: Norton, 1998).

16. Bauman affirms, "We need relationships, and we need relationships in which we count for something, relationships to which we can refer in order to define ourselves . . . for the sake of the cohesion and logic of our own being." Bauman, *Identity*, 68.

17. The literature on identity politics and politicized identity is vast. I have drawn mostly from Wendy Brown, *States of Injury: Power and Freedom in*

Late Modernity (Princeton, NJ: Princeton University Press, 1995); Rogers Brubaker, *Trans: Gender and Race in an Age of Unsettled Identities* (Princeton, NJ: Princeton University Press, 2017); Judith Butler, *Gender Trouble: Feminism and the Subversion of Identity* (New York: Routledge, 1990); Nancy Fraser, "Mapping the Feminist Imagination: From Redistribution to Recognition to Representation," *Constellations* 12, no. 3 (2005); Chris Weedon, *Identity and Culture* (London: Open University Press, 2004); and William Connolly, *Identity/Difference: Democratic Negotiations of Political Paradox* (Ithaca, NY: Cornell University Press, 1991).

18. See Suzanna Danuta Walters, "In Defense of Identity Politics," *Signs: Journal of Women in Culture and Society* 43, no. 2 (2018): 473–488; Adam Gopnik "The Democrats and the Seesaw of Identity Politics," *New Yorker*, December 2, 2016; and Rebecca Traister, "Blaming Clinton's Base for Her Loss Is the Ultimate Insult," *The Cut*, November 23, 2016, https://www.thecut.com/2016/11/blaming-clintons-base-for-her-loss -is-the-ultimate-insult.html.

19. Lynn Davidman describes how "the well-known sense of rootlessness, alienation, and anomie of modern life" contribute to young Jewish women's conversion to Orthodoxy." Davidman, *Tradition*, 107.

20. Judith Butler, *Giving an Account of Oneself* (New York: Fordham University Press, 2005), 82.

21. Tanya Luhrmann, *When God Talks Back: Understanding the American Evangelical Relationship with God* (New York: Alfred E. Knopf, 2004).

22. Other scholars have documented evangelicals' intimate relationship with God. See, for example, Luhrmann, *When God Talks Back*; Joel Robbins, *Becoming Sinners: Christianity and Moral Torment in a Papua New Guinea Society* (Berkeley: University of California Press, 2004); and Strhan, *Aliens and Strangers*.

23. In evangelical lingo, "quiet time" consists of prayer and Bible reading.

3. IN THE WORLD

The epigraph is from Lauren Berlant's blog *Supervalent Thought*, 2008, https://supervalentthought.com/about.

1. Some biblical scholars assert that "seven days" is symbolic of a different measurement of time. Days, as understood in Genesis, could mean years or even decades. Some maintain that evolution exists within

creationism, that God created and orchestrated evolution. Other biblical scholars, however, do ascribe to the literal interpretation.

2. Another verse often used to support the idea of being "in the world
but not of the world" is 1 John 2:15, "Do not love the world or anything
in the world. If anyone loves the world, love for the Father is not in
them."

3. Meredith McGuire, along with other scholars, argues that such categories as "religious," "secular," and "sacred" are themselves social
constructs and need to be interrogated. I agree, yet I also maintain
that these categories are salient and material to the evangelicals I
studied. Thus, in this chapter I am not deconstructing them or inter-
rogating their social fabrication but rather taking them as a priori
reality, in order to reach a more relevant question of how evangelical
women navigate these spheres. Meredith B. McGuire, *Lived Religion:
Faith and Practice in Everyday Life* (Oxford: Oxford University Press,
2008); Talal Asad, *Formations of the Secular: Christianity, Islam,
Modernity* (Palo Alto, CA: Stanford University Press, 2003); José
Casanova, "The Secular and Secularisms," *Social Research: An International Quarterly* 76, no. 4 (2009); Courtney Bender and Ann Taves,
What Matters? Ethnographies of Value in a Not So Secular Age (New
York: Columbia University Press, 2012).

4. This follows a "lived religion" approach to the study of religion,
which focuses on the social realities of everyday religious life. Nancy
Ammerman, "Finding Religion in Everyday Life," *Sociology of Reli-
gion* 75, no. 2 (2014): 6. See also Ammerman, *Sacred Stories, Spiritual
Tribes: Finding Religion in Everyday Life* (Oxford: Oxford University
Press, 2013); Courtney Bender, "Practicing Religions," in *The Cam-
bridge Companion to Religious Studies*, ed. Robert A. Orsi (Cambridge:
Cambridge University Press, 2008), 273–295; Robert Orsi, *Between
Heaven and Earth: The Religious Worlds People Make and the Scholars
Who Study Them* (Princeton, NJ: Princeton University Press, 2005);
Bender and Taves, *What Matters?*; and McGuire, *Lived Religion*.

5. Courtney Bender, *Heaven's Kitchen: Living Religion at God's Love We
Deliver* (Chicago: University of Chicago Press, 2003), 8. See also Talal
Asad, "Thinking About the Secular Body, Pain, and Liberal Politics,"
Cultural Anthropology 26, no. 4 (2011).

6. Anna Strhan, *Aliens and Strangers? The Coherence in the Everyday Lives of Evangelicals* (Oxford: Oxford University Press, 2015), 204.

7. Olivier Roy, *Secularism Confronts Islam* (New York: Columbia University Press, 2009), 11.

8. Tanya Luhrmann, *When God Talks Back: Understanding the American Evangelical Relationship with God* (New York: Alfred E. Knopf, 2004), 107, 110. See also Nancy Ammerman, *Bible Believers: Fundamentalists in the Modern World* (New Brunswick, NJ: Rutgers University Press, 1987).

9. I am here drawing on Ayala Fader, *Mitzvah Girls: Bringing Up the Next Generation of Hasidic Jews in Brooklyn* (Princeton, NJ: Princeton University Press, 2009); Jonathan Boyarin, *Jewish Families* (New Brunswick, NJ: Rutgers University Press, 2013); Samuel C. Heilman, *Defenders of the Faith: Inside Ultra-Orthodox Jewry* (Palo Alto, CA: University of California Press, 2000); and Nurit Stadler and Lea Taragin-Zeller, "Like a Snake in Paradise: Fundamentalism, Gender, and Taboos in the Haredi Community," *Archives de Sciences Sociales des Religions* 117 (2017).

10. Samuel C. Heilman and Menachem Friedman, "Religious Fundamentalism and Religious Jews: The Case of the Haredim," in *Fundamentalisms Observed*, ed. M. E. Marty and R. S. Appleby (Chicago: Chicago University Press, 1991), 198.

11. Heilman, *Defenders of the Faith*, 31.

12. Michele Lamont's work on boundaries provides excellent empirical examples of how identities are crafted through difference. See Lamont, "Culture and Identity," in *Handbook of Sociological Theory*, ed. Jonathan Turner (Boston: Springer, 2001); and Michele Lamont and Virag Molnar, "The Study of Boundaries Across the Social Sciences," *Annual Review of Sociology* 28 (2002).

13. Worship Hymns, "Set Apart by the Spirit, John Piper Sermon, Christian Revival, Bible Teaching," YouTube video, 11:34, November 8, 2017, https://www.youtube.com/watch?v=FcHvGCbnv1Q.

14. Leslie Ludy, *The Set-Apart Woman* (Colorado Springs, CO: NavPress, 2015); Ludy, *Set-Apart Femininity* (Eugene, OR: Harvest House, 2008); Ludy, *Set-Apart Motherhood* (Colorado Springs, CO: NavPress, 2014).

15. In her study of a conservative evangelical church in central London, Anna Strhan emphasizes how her respondents saw themselves as

"aliens and strangers" in a secular metropolis, and instead of battling with it, sought to live in within it. Strhan, *Aliens and Strangers*.

16. For theoretical approaches to understanding collective identity as constructed through difference, see Stuart Hall, "Who Needs 'Identity'?," in *Identity*, ed. L. Grossberg and C. Nelson (London: Sage, 2000); and William Connolly, *Identity/Difference: Democratic Negotiations of Political Paradox* (Ithaca, NY: Cornell University Press, 1991). For examples of religious groups establishing identities through difference, see John Bartkowski and Jen'nan Read, "Veiled Submission: Gender, Power, and Identity Among Evangelical and Muslim Women in the United States," *Qualitative Sociology* 26, no. 1 (2003): 71–92; Abby Day, *Believing in Belonging: Belief and Social Identity in the Modern World* (Oxford: Oxford University Press, 2011); Matthew Guest, *Evangelical Identity and Contemporary Culture: A Congregational Study in Innovation* (Milton Keyes: Paternoster, 2007); and Oonagh Reitman, "On Exit," in *Minorities Within Minorities: Equality, Rights, and Diversity*, ed. Avigail Eisenberg and Jeff Spinner-Halev (Cambridge: Cambridge University Press, 2005).

17. See Orit Avishai, "'Doing Religion' in a Secular World: Women in Conservative Religions and the Question of Agency," *Gender and Society* 22, no. 4 (2008); Lynn Davidman, *Tradition in a Rootless World: Women Turn to Orthodox Judaism* (Berkeley: University of California Press, 1991); Fader, *Mitzvah Girls*; Debra Kaufman, *Rachel's Daughters: Newly Orthodox Jewish Women* (New Brunswick, NJ: Rutgers University Press, 1991); and Lea Taragin-Zeller, "Modesty for Heaven's Sake: Authority and Creativity Among Female Ultra-Orthodox Teenagers in Israel," *Nashim: A Journal of Jewish Women's Studies and Gender Issues* 26, no. 5774 (2014).

18. Roy, *Secularism Confronts Islam*, 67.

19. Both Lisa Tillmann-Healy and Ann Oakley provide illuminating meditations on the role of friendship in qualitative research methods and its utility in enacting a feminist praxis of nonhierarchical research relationships. Tillmann-Healy, "Friendship as Method," *Qualitative Inquiry* 8, no. 5 (2003); Oakley, "Interviewing Women Again: Power, Time, and the Gift," *Sociology* 50, no. 1 (2016).

20. See Loic Wacquant, "Following Pierre Bourdieu into the Field," *Ethnography* 5, no. 4 (2004): 398.

21. See Rebecca Lester, *Jesus in Our Wombs: Embodying Modernity in a Mexican Convent* (Palo Alto: University of California Press, 2005).

22. Fader, *Mitzvah Girls*, 85.

23. Saba Mahmood, "Feminist Theory, Embodiment, and the Docile Agent: Some Reflections on the Egyptian Islamic Revival," *Cultural Anthropology* 16, no. 2 (2001): 208. See also Mahmood, *Politics of Piety.*

24. In writing this, I nod to Talal Asad's provocative questions: "Why does it seem so important to us to insist that the converted are 'agents'? Why do we discount the convert's claim that he or she has been 'made into' a Christian?" Asad, "Comments on Conversion," in *Conversion to Modernities: The Globalization of Christianity*, ed. Peter van der Veer (New York: Routledge, 1996), 271.

25. The dancer Martha Graham wrote, "I don't work from counts. I have a very physical memory. I work from body phrase." Graham, *Blood Memory: An Autobiography* (New York: Doubleday Press, 1991), 231.

26. Thomas Tweed, *Crossing and Dwelling: A Theory of Religion* (Boston: Harvard University Press, 2006): 96.

27. McGuire, *Lived Religion.*

4. PURITY CULTURE

1. Evangelicals are not a uniform group, of course, and as Monique Moultrie points out in her study of Black evangelical women's sexuality within Black-majority churches, "Sexual purity is generally defined as avoiding sexual intimacy outside of heterosexual marriage, but the meaning behind sexual purity varies based on race." As the four women central to this book are white, and all the women in my study attended majority-white churches, the sexual ethics they contended with corresponds with white racial imaginings. Moultrie, *Passionate and Pious: Religious Media and Black Women's Sexuality* (Durham, NC: Duke University Press, 2017), 27.

2. Comprehensive research on abstinence-only education found a conflation of evangelical doctrine with scientifically derived information. A. Lord, *Condom Nation: The U.S. Government's Sex Education Campaign from World War I to the Internet* (Baltimore, MD: Johns Hopkins University Press, 2010); Randall Patterson, "Students of Virginity," *New York Times*, March 30, 2008.

3. A poll carried out by the Public Religion Research Institute reports that only 17 percent of Americans identify as white evangelical these days, down from 23 percent in 2006. Daniel Cox and Robert P. Jones, "Additional Evidence for White Evangelical Decline," Public Religion Research Institute, September 11, 2017, https://www.prri.org/spotlight /additional-evidence-white-evangelical-protestant-decline. Similarly, a Pew Research Center poll reports the figure of white "born again" evangelical Protestants as 16 percent, down from 19 percent a decade ago. "In U.S., Decline of Christianity Continues at Rapid Pace," Pew Research Center, October 17, 2019, https://www.pewforum.org/2019 /10/17/in-u-s-decline-of-christianity-continues-at-rapid-pace.

4. Donna Freitas, *Sex and the Soul: Juggling Sexuality, Spirituality, Romance, and Religion on America's College Campuses* (Oxford: Oxford University Press, 2008); Kristin Aune, "Evangelical Christianity and Women's Changing Lives," *European Journal of Women's Studies* 15, no. 3 (2008); Sonya Sharma, "Young Women, Sexuality and Protestant Church Community: Oppression or Empowerment?," *European Journal of Women's Studies* 15, no. 4 (2008).

5. Linda Kay Klein, *Pure: Inside the Evangelical Movement That Shamed a Generation of Young Women and How I Broke Free* (New York: Touchstone, 2018); Jamie Lee Finch, *You Are Your Own: A Reckoning with the Religious Trauma of Evangelical Christianity* (self-published, 2019); Amy Deneson, "True Love Waits: The Story of My Purity Ring and Feeling Like I Didn't Have a Choice," *Guardian*, February 18, 2017, https:// www.theguardian.com/lifeandstyle/2017/feb/18/purity-ring-virginity -abstinence-sexual-education.

6. Kris Valloton, "6 Ways to Catch the Man of God You've Been Waiting For," November 29, 2018, https://www.krisvallotton.com/6-ways -to-catch-the-man-of-god-youve-been-waiting-for.

7. Diarmaid MacCulloch, *Sex and the Church*, episode 1, "From Pleasure to Sin," video, 59:00, BBC, May 1, 2015.

8. Holly Furneaux, "Victorian Sexualities," *Literature Compass* 8, no. 10 (2011): 767–775.

9. Michel Foucault, *The History of Sexuality*, vol. 1, *An Introduction*, trans. Robert Hurley (New York: Pantheon, 1978), 77.

10. Christine Gardner, *Making Chastity Sexy: The Rhetoric of Evangelical Abstinence Campaigns* (Berkeley: University of California Press, 2011), 30.

11. Moral Revolution, "Masturbation and Intimacy, Day 11, Caitlin Zick," YouTube video, 3:30, July 26, 2021, https://www.youtube.com/watch?v=noCNf_NHj4k.

12. In 2010, Joshua Harris apologized for the harm his book had caused a generation of evangelical young people. In 2018, he released a freely available documentary explaining his revised opinions around dating and sex.

13. The Defining the Moment campaign aimed to "evangelize and disciple" people. This included Bible translation, church development, and the implementation of True Love Waits.

14. I use the term *religious right* to refer to "Christian-identified conservative political groups" in the United States. This includes Catholics, mainline Protestants, and evangelicals. Rosemary Radford Ruether, "Church, Feminism, and Family," in *God Forbid: Religion and Sex in American Public Life*, ed. Kathleen M. Sands (Oxford: Oxford University Press, 2014), 110. See also Elizabeth Bernstein and Janet Jakobsen, "Sex, Secularism and Religious Influence on US Politics," *Third World Quarterly* 31, no. 6 (2000); Jean Calterone Williams, "Battling a 'Sex-Saturated Society': The Abstinence Movement and the Politics of Sex Education," *Sexualities* 14, no. 4 (2011); and Fitzgerald, *Evangelicals*.

15. Bernstein and Jakobsen, "Sex, Secularism."

16. *The Content of Federally Funded Abstinence-Only Education Programs*, prepared for Rep. Henry A. Waxman, US House of Representatives, Committee on Government Reform—Minority Staff, Special Investigations Division, December 2004. https://spot.colorado.edu/~tooley/HenryWaxman.pdf.

17. Dagmar Herzog, *Sex in Crisis: The New Sexual Revolution and the Future of American Politics* (New York: Basic Books, 2008); Jennifer Butler, *Born Again*.

18. Kathrin Stanger-Hall and David Hall, "Abstinence-Only Education and Teen Pregnancy Rates: Why We Need Comprehensive Sex Education in the US," *PloS One* 6, no. 10 (October 14, 2011).

19. The phrase "sanctity of marriage" is from the Romance Academy website (2016). As of 2019, Romance Academy closed its doors to take time to update their messaging for youth.

20. Nigel Genders, "Relationships and Education," Church of England, March 12, 2018, https://www.churchofengland.org/more/media-centre/stories-and-features/relationships-and-education.

21. James Dobson, *Preparing for Adolescence* (Ventura: Gospel Light, 1974), 65.

22. Carrie Lloyd, *Prude: Misconceptions of a Neo-Virgin* (Milton Keyes: Authentic Media, 2016): 183.

23. Amy DeRogatis, *Saving Sex: Sexuality and Salvation in American Evangelicalism* (Oxford: Oxford University Press, 2014).

24. Anjani Chandra et al., "Sexual Behavior, Sexual Attraction, and Sexual Identity in the United States: Data from the 2006–2008 National Survey of Family Growth," *National Health Statistics Report*, March 3, 2011, https://www.cdc.gov/nchs/data/nhsr/nhsr036.pdf.

25. Lamont and Molnar, "Study of Boundaries"; Christian Smith, *American Evangelicalism: Embattled and Thriving* (Chicago: University of Chicago Press, 1998).

26. Other scholars have examined how evangelical leaders entice rather than repress sexuality. See Gardner, *Making Chastity Sexy*; and Kelsy Burke, *Christians Under Covers: Evangelicals and Sexual Pleasure on the Internet* (Berkeley: University of California Press, 2016).

27. Jessica Valenti, *The Purity Myth: How America's Obsession with Virginity Is Hurting Young Women* (Berkeley, CA: Seal Press, 2010), 30, 50.

28. DeRogatis, *Saving Sex*; Burke, *Christians Under Covers*; Gardner, *Making Chastity Sexy*.

29. Jessica Johnson, *Biblical Porn: Affect, Labor, and Pastor Mark Driscoll's Evangelical Empire* (Durham, NC: Duke University Press, 2018).

30. Klein, *Pure*, 12.

31. Foucault, *History of Sexuality*, 157–158.

32. Sara Ahmed, "Snap!," *Feminist Killjoys*, May 21, 2017, https://feminist killjoys.com/2017/05/21/snap.

5. THE IDEAL WOMAN

The epigraph is from Judith Butler, "Bodies and Power, Revisited," *Radical Philosophy* 114 (July/August 2002).

1. Pew Research Center, "Evangelical Protestant," *Religious Landscape Study* (2014).

2. Evangelical Alliance, "21st Century Evangelicals," 8; Clive D. Field, "21st Century Evangelicals," *British Religion in Numbers*, January 12, 2011, http://www.brin.ac.uk/21st-century-evangelicals.

3. Katie Gaddini, "Between Pain and Hope: Examining Women's Marginality in Evangelical Christianity," *European Journal of Women's Studies* 26, no. 4 (2018). See also Kristin Aune, *Single Women: Challenge to the Church?* (Milton Keyes: Paternoster, 2002).

4. Stuart Hall, "The Spectacle of the 'Other,'" in *Representation: Cultural Representations and Signifying Practices* (London: Sage, 1997), 259.

5. However, this theorization of power and representation was prevalent in the 1990s, propagated by Foucauldian feminist theorists such as Susan Bordo and Sandra Bartky.

6. Dannah Gresh, *And the Bride Wore White: Seven Secrets to Sexual Purity* (Chicago: Moody, 2012), 135.

7. Feminist Jessica Valenti also critiques a racist narrative in purity discourse that purports that "'innocent' white girls [are] being lured into an oversexualized culture, while young Black women are already part of it." Jessica Valenti, *The Purity Myth: How America's Obsession with Virginity Is Hurting Young Women* (Berkeley: Seal Press, 2010), 94. See also Monique Moultrie, *Passionate and Pious: Religious Media and Black Women's Sexuality.* (Durham, NC: Duke University Press, 2017), 7.

8. Pauline Hope Cheong, Shirlena Huang, and Jessie P. H. Poon, "Religious Communication and Epistemic Authority of Leaders in Wired Faith Organizations," *Journal of Communication* 61, no. 5 (2011): 938–958; Pauline Hope Cheong, "Religious Leaders, Mediated Authority, and Social Change," *Journal of Applied Communication Research* 39 (2011): 452–454; Cheong, "Tweet the Message? Religious Authority and Social Media Innovation," *Journal of Religion, Media and Digital Culture* 3, no. 3 (2014): 1–19; Morgan Clarke, "Neo-Calligraphy: Religious Authority and Media Technology in Contemporary Shiite Islam," *Comparative Studies in Society and History* 52, no. 2, (2010): 351–383; Reina Lewis, "Uncovering Modesty: Dejabis and Dewigies Expanding the Parameters of the Modest Fashion Blogosphere," *Fashion Theory* 19, no. 2 (2017); Katie Gaddini, "'Wife, Mommy, Pastor and Friend': The Rise of Female Evangelical Microcelebrities," *Religions* 12, no. 9 (2021): 758, https://doi.org/10.3390/rel12090758.

9. All of the information presented in this chapter was accurate at the time it was originally written. Since then, Alyssa has written on her social media account (January 20, 2020) that she and her husband, Chris, are divorced. See chapter 8 for more on this.

10. Ana Elias, Rosalind Gill, and Christina Scharff, "Aesthetic Labour: Beauty Politics in Neoliberalism," in *Aesthetic Labour: Rethinking Beauty Politics in Neoliberalism*, ed. Elias, Gill, and Scharff (London: Palgrave Macmillan, 2017), 30.

11. Caressa Prescott, "Valentines [*sic*] Gift Guide for Him," February 3, 2019, https://www.leoandluca.com/blog.

12. See Kelsy Burke, *Christians Under Covers: Evangelicals and Sexual Pleasure on the Internet* (Berkeley: University of California Press, 2016); Christine Gardner, *Making Chastity Sexy: The Rhetoric of Evangelical Abstinence Campaigns* (Berkeley: University of California Press, 2011), and Jessica Johnson, *Biblical Porn: Affect, Labor, and Pastor Mark Driscoll's Evangelical Empire* (Durham, NC: Duke University Press, 2018).

13. Amanda Winters, "Bethel Burgeons Under Pastor's Visions of Prosperity," *Record Searchlight*, January 16, 2010; Joe Carter, "9 Things You Should Know About the Bethel Church Movement," *Gospel Coalition*, September 29, 2018, https://www.thegospelcoalition.org/article/9 -things-you-should-know-about-the-bethel-church-movement.

14. David Benda, "Bethel Church Was Key in Securing Redding's Flights to Los Angeles," *Record Searchlight*, December 13, 2019.

15. Sean Longoria, "Redding Planning Commission OK's Bethel's New Campus," *Record Searchlight*, December 12, 2019.

16. K. J. Ramsey, "There's No Shame When a Miracle Doesn't Come," *Christianity Today*, December 27, 2019, https://www.christianitytoday .com/ct/2019/december-web-only/wakeupolive-heiligenthal-bethel -church-miracle-doesnt-come.html; Martyn Wendell Jones, "Inside the Popular, Controversial Bethel Church," *Christianity Today*, April 24, 2016, https://www.christianitytoday.com/ct/2016/may/cover -story-inside-popular-controversial-bethel-church.html.

17. Carey Lodge, "Bethel Church's Bill Johnson: Why I Voted for Trump," *Christian Today*, November 10, 2016, https://www.christiantoday.com /article/bethel-churchs-bill-johnson-why-i-voted-for-trump/100306 .htm.

18. None of the churches featured in this chapter are considered "prosperity churches" under Kate Bowler's classification system. Nevertheless, Bowler writes, "The prosperity gospel thrives in diverse forms on the American religious terrain." Bowler, *Blessed: A History of the American Prosperity Gospel* (Oxford: Oxford University Press, 2013), 5.

19. Elizabeth Bernstein, "Militarized Humanitarianism Meets Carceral Feminism: The Politics of Sex, Rights, and Freedom in Contemporary Antitrafficking Campaigns," *Signs* 31, no. 1 (2010): 45–72.

20. Tara McKelvey, "The Evangelical Women Who Reject Trump," *BBC News*, October 23, 2018, https://www.bbc.co.uk/news/world-us-canada-45956033.

21. Faye Ginsburg, *Contested Lives: The Abortion Debate in an American Community*, updated ed. (Berkeley: University of California Press, 1998); Gardner, *Making Chastity Sexy*; Bernstein, "Militarized Humanitarianism."

22. Monique Moultrie, "#BlackBabiesMatter: Analyzing Black Religious Media in Conservative and Progressive Evangelical Communities," *Religions* 8, no. 11 (2017), 255.

23. Stuart Hall, "The Work of Representation," in *Representation: Cultural Representations and Signifying Practices*, 2nd ed., ed. Stuart Hall, Jessica Evans, and Sean Nixon (London: Sage, 2013). See also Hall, "A Toad in the Garden: Thatcherism Among the Theorists," in *Marxism and the Interpretation of Culture*, ed. Cary Nelson and Lawrence Grossberg (Urbana: University of Illinois Press, 1988).

24. Judith Butler states, "For photographs to communicate in this way, they must have a transitive function. They do not merely portray or represent, but they relay affect." Butler, "Photography, War, Outrage," *PMLA* 120, no. 3 (2005): 823.

25. Griselda Pollock, "Feminism/Foucault— Surveillance/Sexuality," in *Visual Culture: Images and Interpretations*, ed. Norman Bryson, Michael Ann Holly, and Keith Moxey (Middletown, CT: Wesleyan University Press, 1994), 14. See also Monica Moreno Figueroa, "Looking Emotionally: Photography, Racism and Intimacy in Research," *History of the Human Sciences* 21, no. 4 (2008); and Stuart Hall, Jessica Evans, and Sean Nixon, eds., *Representation: Cultural Representations and Signifying Practices*, 2nd ed. (London: Sage, 2013).

6. WOUNDS THAT NEVER HEAL

The epigraph is from Cristina Rivera Garza, *Grieving: Dispatches from a Wounded Country*, trans. Sarah Booker (New York: First Feminist Press, 2020).

1. This material first appeared in the Winter 2021 issue of CBE International's *Mutuality* magazine (www.cbeinternational.org).

2. Shani Orgad and Rosalind Gil write that neoliberal feminism posits "women's lack of confidence as the fundamental obstacle to women's success, achievement and happiness." Shani Orgad and Rosalind Gill, "The Confidence Cult(ure)," *Australian Feminist Studies* 30, no. 86 (2016): 326.

3. See Julie Ingersoll, *Evangelical Christian Women: War Stories in the Gender Battles* (New York: New York University Press, 2003) for another account of women battling sexism within evangelical churches.

4. Michel Foucault, *The History of Sexuality*, vol. 1, *An Introduction*, trans. Robert Hurley (New York: Pantheon, 1978), 86.

5. Gloria Anzaldúa, *Borderlands/La Frontera*, 4th ed. (San Francisco: Aunt Lute Books, 2012).

6. Denise Riley, *Words of Selves: Identification, Solidarity, Irony* (Palo Alto, CA: Stanford University Press, 2000), 46.

7. In reference to race, Nirmal Puwar calls this the "racialized somatic norm." Similarly, Beverley Skeggs describes how class norms pervade the embodied gestures, language, and habitus of her participants. Puwar, "The Racialised Somatic Norm and the Senior Civil Service," *Sociology* 35, no. 3 (2011); Skeggs, *Formations of Class and Gender: Becoming Respectable* (London: Sage, 1997). See also Ruth Frankenberg, *White Women, Race Matters: The Social Construction of Whiteness* (London: Routledge, 1993).

8. Sianne Ngai, *Ugly Feelings* (Cambridge, MA: Harvard University Press, 2005).

9. In this passage, Cathy Park Hong is drawing from Claudia Rankine's work on racism. Park Hong, *Minor Feelings: An Asian American Reckoning* (New York: Penguin Random House, 2020), 55; Rankine, *Citizen: An American Lyric* (London: Penguin Random House UK, 2015).

10. Mark Chaves, "National Congregations Study, Cumulative Dataset (1998, 2006–2007, 2012, and 2018–2019)," Association of Religion Data Archive, 2021.

11. Madeleine Davics, "Women in Leadership: Is 2017 the Year that HTB Will Practise What It Preaches?," *Christian Today*, December 23, 2016, https://www.christiantoday.com/article/women.in.leadership.is.2017 .the.year.htb.will.practise.what.it.preaches/103265.htm; Davies, "Why Women Clergy Lead so Few Large Churches," *Church Times*, April 13,

2017, https://www.churchtimes.co.uk/articles/2017/13-april/news/uk/why-women-clergy-lead-so-few-large-churches.

12. Suzanne Calulu, "The 'Feminisation' of the Church," *Patheos*, January 9, 2015.

13. Greg Smith, *21st Century Evangelicals: Reflections on Research by the Evangelical Alliance* (Watford: Instant Apostle, 2015); Sonya Sharma, "Young Women, Sexuality and Protestant Church Community: Oppression or Empowerment?," *European Journal of Women's Studies* 15, no. 4 (2008): 345–359.

14. Kristin Aune, "Evangelical Christianity and Women's Changing Lives," *European Journal of Women's Studies* 15, no. 3 (2008): 283.

15. Linda Woodhead, "Gendering Secularization Theory," *Social Compass* 55, no. 2 (2008): 187–193.

16. Smith, *21st Century Evangelicals.*

17. Barna Group, "What Americans Think About Women in Power," *Research Releases,* March 8, 2017, https://www.barna.com/research/americans-think-women-power.

18. Andrew Yip and Sarah-Jane Page, *Religious and Sexual Identities: A Multi-Faith Exploration of Young Adults* (Farnham: Ashgate, 2013); Sharma, "Young Women."

19. Kimberle Crenshaw, "Demarginalizing the Intersection of Race and Sex: A Black Feminist Critique of Antidiscrimination Doctrine, Feminist Theory, and Antiracist Politics," *University of Chicago Legal Forum* 1989, no. 1, article 8: 139–167.

20. Sara Ahmed, *The Cultural Politics of Emotion*, 2nd ed. (Edinburgh: Edinburgh University Press, 2014).

21. In their study on "fundamentalist" Christian women, Miriam Winter, Adair Lummis, and Allison Stokes report that many women "defect in place," meaning they employ strategies such as emphasizing their relationships, in order to make life livable. At the same time, these women find it hard to stay, and "impossible to live with a divided heart." Winter, Lummis, and Stokes, *Defecting in Place: Women Claiming Responsibility for Their Own Spiritual Lives* (New York: Wellspring, 1994), 197. For examples of strategies other Christian women employ, see Kelly Chong, "Negotiating Patriarchy: South Korean Evangelical Women and the Politics of Gender," *Gender and Society* 20, no. 6 (2006): 711; and Ingersoll, *Evangelical Christian Women.*

22. In her poem "Laibach Lyrik," Denise Riley writes, "The settling scar agrees to voice / what seems to speak its earliest cut. / A rage to be some wholeness gropes / past damage that it half recalls— / where it was, I will found my name." Riley, "Laibach Lyrik: Slovenia, 1991," in *Penguin Modern Poets 10* (London: Penguin, 1996), 60.

23. Winter, Lummis, and Stokes, *Defecting*, 201. See also Ingersoll, *Evangelical Christian Women*, 138.

7. REPRISALS

The epigraph is from Ocean Vuong, "Seventh Circle of Earth," in *Night Sky with Exit Wounds* (Port Townsend, WA: Copper Canyon Press, 2016).

1. Sara Ahmed, *Living a Feminist Life* (Durham, NC: Duke University Press, 2010), 4.

2. See Sara Ahmed, "The Problem of Perception," *Feminist Killjoys*, February 17, 2014, https://feministkilljoys.com/2014/02/17/the-problem-of-perception.

3. Stephen Davies, "Libertarian Feminism in Britain, 1860–1910," Libertarian Alliance pamphlet 7 (1987): 2.

4. Leah Fritz, *Thinking Like a Woman* (Rifton, NY: Win Books, 1975), 130.

5. Andrea Dworkin, *Right-Wing Women* (New York: Perigee Books, 1983), 35.

6. Mary Daly, *Beyond God the Father: Toward a Philosophy of Women's Liberation* (Boston: Beacon Press, 1973), 2, 145–146.

7. Christel Manning, *God Gave Us the Right: Conservative Catholic, Evangelical Protestant, and Orthodox Jewish Women Grapple with Feminism* (New Brunswick, NJ: Rutgers University Press, 1999), 29.

8. Jerome Himmelstein, "The Social Basis of Antifeminism: Religious Networks and Culture," *Journal for the Scientific Study of Religion* 25, no. 1 (1986): 1–15. In her study of American Christianity, Sally Gallagher found that feminism remained suspect, with some Christian women seeing feminism as a secular import, out of sync with Christian values. Gallagher, "The Marginalization of Evangelical Feminism," *Sociology of Religion* 65, no. 3 (2004).

9. Brenda Brasher, *Godly Women: Fundamentalism and Female Power* (New Brunswick, NJ: Rutgers University Press, 1998).

10. R. Marie Griffith, *God's Daughters: Evangelical Women and the Power of Submission* (Berkeley: University of California Press, 1997), 186. See also Christel Manning, *God Gave Us the Right.*

11. Himmelstein, "Social Basis of Antifeminism."

12. Julie Ingersoll, "Against Univocality: Re-reading Ethnographies of Conservative Protestant Women," in *Personal Knowledge and Beyond: Reshaping Ethnography of Religion*, ed. J. Spickard, S. Landres, and M. McGuire (New York: New York University Press, 2002), 163–164.

13. Paul Oestreicher, "The Rev. Dr. Una Kroll Obituary," *Guardian*, January 8, 2017. https://www.theguardian.com/world/2017/jan/08/the-rev -dr-una-kroll-obituary.

14. Clare Garner, "Woman Priest Tells of Her Vision on Road to St. Paul's," *Independent*, October 23, 2011, https://www.independent.co .uk/news/woman-priest-tells-of-her-vision-on-road-to-st-pauls -1279542.html.

15. As of June 2020, Dr. Butler was appointed interim pastor at National City Christian Church in Washington, DC, for a two-year period.

16. Rachel Held Evans, "Confessions of an Accidental Feminist," August 29, 2012, https://rachelheldevans.com/blog/accidental-feminist.

17. Yosola Olorunshola, "She Doesn't Look Like Jesus," *Magnify* 1 (2014): 30.

18. MAGLondon, "If MAGNIFY Magazine is an experience of life-changing words, 'inspiring, energising, surprising,' then #MAGLondon is an experience of those words in action." Facebook, May 23, 2016, https://www.facebook.com/events/ace-hotel-london-shoreditch /maglondon/1052439194827706.

19. Judith Stacey and Susan Elizabeth Gerard address the fusion of Christian faith and feminism and identify "the simultaneous incorporation, revision and depoliticization of some of the central goals of Second Wave feminism" within their study of American evangelical women. More recently, Kristin Aune reported that feminism is associated with church disaffiliation, but "only slightly" with rejection of Christian beliefs and practices. Stacey and Gerard, "'We Are Not Doormats': The Influence of Feminism on Contemporary Evangelicals in the United States," in *Uncertain Terms: Negotiating Gender in American Culture*, ed. Faye Ginsburg and Anna Lowenhaupt Tsing (Boston: Beacon Press, 1990), 99; Kristin Aune, "Feminist Spirituality as Lived

Religion: How UK Feminists Forge Religio-Spiritual Lives," *Gender and Society* 29, no. 1 (2015): 139. See also Dawn Llewellyn and Marta Trzebiatowska, "Secular and Religious Feminisms: A Future of Disconnection?," *Feminist Theology* 21, no. 3 (2013): 244–258.

20. For more on evangelical complementarianism, see Mimi Haddad and Sean Callagan, *Is Women's Equality a Biblical Ideal?* (Minneapolis, Minnesota: Christians for Biblical Equality, 2021); Beth Allison Barr, *The Making of Biblical Womanhood: How the Subjugation of Women Became Gospel Truth* (Ada, MN: Brazos Press, 2021).

21. David Joel Hamilton and Loren Cunningham, *Why Not Women? A Fresh Look at Scripture on Women in Missions, Ministry and Leadership* (Edmonds, WA: YWAM Publishing, 2001); Rosemary Radford Ruether, *Sexism and God-Talk: Toward a Feminist Theology* (Boston: Beacon Press, 1983).

22. Sara Ahmed writes, "Whilst hearing feminists as killjoys might be a form of dismissal, there is an agency that this dismissal rather ironically reveals. We can respond to the accusation with a 'yes.'" Ahmed, "Feminist Killjoys (and Other Willful Subjects)," *Polyphonic Feminisms: Acting in Concert* 8, no. 3 (2010): 2. See also Ahmed, *Differences That Matter: Feminist Theory and Postmodernism* (Cambridge: Cambridge University Press, 1998), 117.

23. Sarah Bessey, "On Being a Christian and Being a Feminist . . . and Belonging Nowhere," January 24, 2017, https://sarahbessey.com /christian-feminist.

24. Makers, "FaithMAKERS: Can Faith and Feminism Coexist?," Facebook, May 23, 2018, https://www.facebook.com/events/20389341700 3898.

25. Stephen Murdoch, "Support Feminism? At Westmont, You're Politically Incorrect," *Santa Barbara News-Press*, April 13, 2006.

26. Morgan Lee, "When Christian Ministries Ask Their Ex-Employees Not to Talk," *Christianity Today*, November 6, 2019, https://www .christianitytoday.com/ct/podcasts/quick-to-listen/christian-ministries -non-disclosure-agreements-non-competes.html.

27. Jane Clinton, "Church of England in New 'Racism' Row as Staff Speak Out," *inews*, April 19, 2021, https://inews.co.uk/news/church -of-england-racism-staff-speak-out-panorama-non-disclosure-agree ment-963947; "Justin Welby Tells Church of England to Stop Using

NDAs Amid Racism Claims," *BBC News*, April 20, 2021, https://www.bbc.com/news/uk-56817048.

28. Roland Barthes, *Camera Lucida: Reflections on Photography* (New York: Hill and Wang, 1981), 80–81.

29. Barthes, *Camera Lucida*, 27.

30. Ahmed, "Feminist Killjoys," 1.

31. See Rosalind Gill, "Post-postfeminism? New Feminist Visibilities in Postfeminist Times," *Feminist Media Studies* 16, no. 4 (2016): 610–630; Angela McRobbie, "Notes on the Perfect," *Australian Feminist Studies* 38, no. 83 (2015): 3–20; and Rebecca Stringer, *Knowing Victims: Feminism, Agency, and Victim Politics in Neoliberal Times* (Hove: Routledge, 2014).

32. Judith Butler, "Contingent Foundations: Feminism and the Question of 'Postmodernism,'" in *The Postmodern Turn: New Perspectives on Social Theory*, ed. Steven Seidman (Cambridge: Cambridge University Press, 1994), 16.

8. THE STRUGGLE TO STAY

The epigraph is from Gloria Anzaldúa, "Forward to the Second Edition, 1983," in *This Bridge Called My Back: Writings by Radical Women of Color*, 4th ed., ed. Cherrie Moraga and Gloria Anzaldúa (New York: State University of New York Press, 2015), 254.

1. Sean Hand, ed., *The Levinas Reader* (Oxford: Blackwell, 1993), 51.

2. This phrase comes from Genesis 2:18 in the King James Version, where God created Eve as a companion for Adam: "And the Lord God said, It is not good that the man should be alone; I will make him an help meet for him."

3. Lauren Berlant, *Cruel Optimism* (Durham, NC: Duke University Press, 2011), ix.

4. Berlant, *Cruel Optimism*, 21.

5. For more on the productive work of hope, see Gaddini, "Between Pain and Hope"; Anna Potamianou, *Hope: A Shield in the Economy of Borderline States* (New York: Routledge, 1996); José Esteban Muñoz, *Cruising Utopia: The Then and There of Queer Futurity* (New York: New York University Press, 2009); Sianne Ngai, *Ugly Feelings* (Cambridge, MA: Harvard University Press, 2005); Sara Ahmed, *The Promise of Happiness*, (Durham, NC: Duke University Press, 2010); and Ernest

Bloch, *The Principle of Hope*, vol. 1, trans. Neville Plaice, Stephen Plaice, and Paul Knight (Cambridge, MA: MIT Press, 1995).

6. Writing about the Asian American "condition," Cathy Park Hong states, "*Belonging* is always promised yet just out of reach" (emphasis in the original). Park Hong, *Minor Feelings: An Asian American Reckoning* (New York: Penguin Random House, 2020), 202.

7. See Robert Orsi, *The Cambridge Companion to Religious Studies* (Cambridge: Cambridge University Press, 2012).

8. Early in her career, the radical feminist Mary Daly considered herself a Catholic reformist. She sought to reform the misogyny in the Catholic Church and make it more equitable toward women, though she was rightly criticized for her emphasis on white women's emancipation. Later, Daly discarded religion altogether, declaring it too entrenched in sexism. Even while remaining ambivalent, however, she acknowledged the benefits that some women gain from faith, including an enduring sense of peace. "I have pointed out that these qualities, and particularly this peace, have been attained at too high a price," she wrote, speaking about the Catholic context. Mary Daly, *Beyond God the Father: Toward a Philosophy of Women's Liberation* (Boston: Beacon Press, 1973), 53.

9. Kaja Silverman, *The Subject of Semiotics* (Oxford: Oxford University Press, 1984), 85.

10. Trinh T. Minh-ha, *Woman, Native, Other: Writing Postcoloniality and Feminism* (Indianapolis: Indiana University Press, 1989), 94.

11. Berlant, *Cruel Optimism*, 21.

BIBLIOGRAPHY

Abu-Lughod, Lila. "The Romance of Resistance: Tracing Transformations of Power Through Bedouin Women." *American Ethnologist* 17, no. 1 (1990): 41–55.

Augustine. *Confessions*. 4th ed. Trans. Henry Chadwick. Oxford: Oxford University Press, 2008.

Ahmed, Sara. *The Cultural Politics of Emotion*. 2nd ed. Edinburgh: Edinburgh University Press, 2014.

——. *Differences That Matter: Feminist Theory and Postmodernism*. Cambridge: Cambridge University Press, 1998.

——. "Feminist Killjoys (and Other Willful Subjects)." *Polyphonic Feminisms: Acting in Concert* 8, no. 3 (2010).

——. *Living a Feminist Life*. Durham, NC: Duke University Press, 2010.

——. *The Promise of Happiness*. Durham, NC: Duke University Press, 2010.

——. "The Problem of Perception." *Feminist Killjoys*, February 17, 2014, https://feministkilljoys.com/2014/02/17/the-problem-of-perception.

——. "Snap!" *Feminist Killjoys*, May 21, 2017, https://feministkilljoys.com/2017/05/21/snap.

Allen, N. J., W. S. F. Pickering, and William Watts Miller. *On Durkheim's Elementary Forms of Religious Life*. 1912. London: Routledge, 1998.

Ammerman, Nancy. *Bible Believers: Fundamentalists in the Modern World*. New Brunswick, NJ: Rutgers University Press, 1987.

——, ed. *Everyday Religion: Observing Modern Religious Lives*. Oxford: Oxford University Press, 2007.

——. "Finding Religion in Everyday Life." *Sociology of Religion* 75, no. 2 (2014).

——. *Sacred Stories, Spiritual Tribes: Finding Religion in Everyday Life.* Oxford: Oxford University Press, 2013.

Anzaldúa, Gloria. *Borderlands/La Frontera.* 4th ed. San Francisco: Aunt Lute Books, 2012.

——. "Forward to the Second Edition, 1983," in *This Bridge Called My Back: Writings by Radical Women of Color*, 4th ed., ed. Cherrie Moraga and Gloria Anzaldua, 253–254. New York: State University of New York Press, 2015.

Aronson, Elliot, and Judson Mills. "The Effect of Severity of Initiation on Liking for a Group." *Journal of Abnormal and Social Psychology* 59, no. 2 (1993): 177–181.

Asad, Talal. "Comments on Conversion." In *Conversion to Modernities: The Globalization of Christianity*, ed. Peter van der Veer, 263–274. New York: Routledge, 1996.

——. *Formations of the Secular: Christianity, Islam, Modernity.* Palo Alto, CA: Stanford University Press, 2003.

——. "Thinking About the Secular Body, Pain, and Liberal Politics." *Cultural Anthropology* 26, no. 4 (2011).

Aune, Kristin. "Evangelical Christianity and Women's Changing Lives." *European Journal of Women's Studies* 15, no. 3 (2008).

——. "Feminist Spirituality as Lived Religion: How UK Feminists Forge Religio-Spiritual Lives." *Gender and Society* 29, no. 1 (2015).

——. *Single Women: Challenge to the Church?* Milton Keyes: Paternoster, 2002.

Avishai, Orit. "'Doing Religion' in a Secular World: Women in Conservative Religions and the Question of Agency." *Gender and Society* 22, no. 4 (2008).

Ballas, Dimitris. "What Makes a 'Happy City'?" *Cities* 32, no. 1 (2013).

Balmer, Randall. *Bad Faith: Race and the Rise of the Religious Right.* Grand Rapids: Wm. B. Eerdmans, 2021.

——. "The Real Origins of the Religious Right." *Politico*, May 27, 2014.

Bang, Mary Jo. *The Bride of E.* Minneapolis: Graywolf Press, 2009.

Barna Group. "What Americans Think About Women in Power." *Research Releases*, March 8, 2017, https://www.barna.com/research/americans-think-women-power.

Barr, Beth Allison. *The Making of Biblical Womanhood: How the Subjugation of Women Became Gospel Truth.* Ada, MN: Brazos Press, 2021.

Barthes, Roland. *Camera Lucida: Reflections on Photography*. New York: Hill and Wang, 1981.

Bartkowski, John, and Jen'nan Read. "Veiled Submission: Gender, Power, and Identity Among Evangelical and Muslim Women in the United States." *Qualitative Sociology* 26, no. 1 (2003).

Bauman, Zygmunt. *Identity: Conversations with Benedetto Vecchi*. Cambridge: Polity Press, 2004.

——. *Liquid Times: Living in an Age of Uncertainty*. Cambridge: Polity Press, 2007.

Beit-Hallahmi, Benjamin, and Michael Argyle. *The Psychology of Religious Behaviour, Belief and Experience*. London: Routledge, 1997.

Benda, David. "Bethel Church Was Key in Securing Redding's Flights to Los Angeles." *Record Searchlight*, December 13, 2019.

Bender, Courtney. *Heaven's Kitchen: Living Religion at God's Love We Deliver*. Chicago: Chicago University Press, 2003.

——. "Practicing Religions." In *The Cambridge Companion to Religious Studies*, ed. Robert A. Orsi, 273–295. Cambridge: Cambridge University Press, 2012.

Bender, Courtney, and Ann Taves. *What Matters? Ethnographies of Value in a Not So Secular Age*. New York: Columbia University Press, 2012.

Berlant, Lauren. *Cruel Optimism*. Durham, NC: Duke University Press, 2011.

——. *The Queen of America Goes to Washington City: Essays on Sex and Citizenship*. Durham, NC: Duke University Press, 1997.

Bernstein, Elizabeth. "Militarized Humanitarianism Meets Carceral Feminism: The Politics of Sex, Rights, and Freedom in Contemporary Anti-trafficking Campaigns." *Signs* 31, no. 1 (2010): 45–72.

Bernstein, Elizabeth R., and Janet R. Jakobsen. "Sex, Secularism and Religious Influence in US Politics." *Third World Quarterly* 31, no. 6 (2010).

Bessey, Sarah. "On Being a Christian and Being a Feminist . . . and Belonging Nowhere," January 24, 2017, https://www.sarahbessey.com/essays/christian-feminist.

Bloch, Ernest. *The Principle of Hope*. Vol. 1. Trans. Neville Plaice, Stephen Plaice, and Paul Knight. Cambridge, MA: MIT Press, 1995.

Bolz-Weber, Nadia. *Shameless: A Sexual Reformation*. London: Canterbury Press, 2019.

Bowler, Kate. *Blessed: A History of the American Prosperity Gospel*. Oxford: Oxford University Press, 2013.

Boyarin, Jonathan. *Jewish Families*. New Brunswick, NJ: Rutgers University Press, 2013.

Brasher, Brenda. *Godly Women: Fundamentalism and Female Power*. New Brunswick, NJ: Rutgers University Press, 1998.

Brierley Consultancy. *FutureFirst* no. 44 (2016): 1.

Brown, Andrew, and Linda Woodhead. *That Was the Church That Was: How the Church of England Lost the English People*. London: Bloomsbury, 2017.

Brown, Callum. *The Death of Christian Britain: Understanding Secularisation Theory*. 2nd ed. London: Routledge, 2009.

Brown, Wendy. *States of Injury: Power and Freedom in Late Modernity*. Princeton, NJ: Princeton University Press, 1995.

Brubaker, Rogers. *Trans: Gender and Race in an Age of Unsettled Identities*. Princeton, NJ: Princeton University Press, 2017.

Burke, Kelsy. *Christians Under Covers: Evangelicals and Sexual Pleasure on the Internet*. Berkeley: University of California Press, 2016.

Butler, Jennifer. *Born Again: The Christian Right Globalized*. London: Pluto Press, 2006.

Butler, Judith. "Bodies and Power, Revisited." *Radical Philosophy* 114 (July/August 2002).

——. "Contingent Foundations: Feminism and the Question of 'Postmodernism.'" In *The Postmodern Turn: New Perspectives on Social Theory*, ed. Steven Seidman, 153–170. Cambridge: Cambridge University Press, 1994.

——. *Gender Trouble: Feminism and the Subversion of Identity*. New York: Routledge, 1990.

——. *Giving an Account of Oneself*. New York: Fordham University Press, 2005.

——. "Photography, War, Outrage." *PMLA* 120, no. 3 (2005).

Calulu, Suzanne. "The 'Feminisation' of the Church." *Patheos*, January 9, 2015.

Campbell, David, and Robert Putnam. *American Grace: How Religion Divides and Unites Us*. New York: Simon and Schuster, 2010.

Carter, Joe. "9 Things You Should Know About the Bethel Church Movement." *Gospel Coalition*, September 29, 2018, https://www.thegospel coalition.org/article/9-things-you-should-know-about-the-bethel-church -movement.

Casanova, José. "The Secular and Secularisms." *Social Research: An International Quarterly* 76, no. 4 (2009).

Chandra, Anjani, William Mosher, Casey Copen, and Catlainn Sionean. "Sexual Behavior, Sexual Attraction, and Sexual Identity in the United States: Data from the 2006–2008 National Survey of Family Growth." *National Health Statistics Report* 36 (March 3, 2011):1–36.

Chaves, Mark. "National Congregations Study, Cumulative Dataset (1998, 2006–2007, 2012, and 2018–2019)." Association of Religion Data Archive, January 2021.

Cheong, Pauline Hope. "Religious Leaders, Mediated Authority, and Social Change." *Journal of Applied Communication Research* 39 (2011).

——. "Tweet the Message? Religious Authority and Social Media Innovation." *Journal of Religion, Media and Digital Culture* 3, no. 3 (2014).

Cheong, Pauline Hope, Shirlena Huang, and Jessie P. H. Poon. "Religious Communication and Epistemic Authority of Leaders in Wired Faith Organizations." *Journal of Communication* 61, no. 5 (2011).

Chong, Kelly. "Negotiating Patriarchy: South Korean Evangelical Women and the Politics of Gender." *Gender and Society* 20, no. 6 (2006): 711.

Church of England. *Statistics for Mission: 2019*. London: Research and Statistics, 2020. https://www.churchofengland.org/sites/default/files/2020 -10/2019StatisticsForMission.pdf.

Clarke, Gerard. "Agents of Transformation? Donors, Faith-Based Organisations and International Development." *Third World Quarterly* 28, no. 1 (2007).

Clarke, Morgan. "Neo-Calligraphy: Religious Authority and Media Technology in Contemporary Shiite Islam." *Comparative Studies in Society and History* 52, no. 2 (2010).

Clinton, Jane. "Church of England in New 'Racism' Row as Staff Speak Out," *inews*, April 19, 2021, https://inews.co.uk/news/church-of-england -racism-staff-speak-out-panorama-non-disclosure-agreement-963947.

Coffey, Amanda. *The Ethnographic Self*. London: Sage Press, 1999.

Coleman, Simon. *The Globalisation of Charismatic Christianity: Spreading the Gospel of Prosperity*. Cambridge: Cambridge University Press, 2000.

Connolly, William. *Identity/Difference: Democratic Negotiations of Political Paradox*. Ithaca, NY: Cornell University Press, 1991.

The Content of Federally Funded Abstinence-Only Education Programs. Prepared for Rep. Henry A. Waxman, US House of Representatives, Committee on Government Reform—Minority Staff, Special Investigations Division, December 2004, https://spot.colorado.edu/~tooley/HenryWaxman.pdf.

Cox, Daniel, and Robert P. Jones. "Additional Evidence of White Evangelical Decline." Public Religion Research Institute, September 11, 2017, https://www.prri.org/spotlight/additional-evidence-white-evangelical-protestant-decline.

Crenshaw, Kimberle. "Demarginalizing the Intersection of Race and Sex: A Black Feminist Critique of Antidiscrimination Doctrine, Feminist Theory, and Antiracist Politics." *University of Chicago Legal Forum* 1989, no. 1, article 8.

Daly, Mary. *Beyond God the Father: Toward a Philosophy of Women's Liberation*. Boston: Beacon Press, 1973.

Davidman, Lynn. *Tradition in a Rootless World: Women Turn to Orthodox Judaism*. Berkeley: University of California Press, 1991.

Davies, Madeleine. "Why Women Clergy Lead So Few Large Churches." *Church Times*, April 13, 2017, https://www.churchtimes.co.uk/articles/2017/13-april/news/uk/why-women-clergy-lead-so-few-large-churches.

——. "Women in Leadership: Is 2017 the Year That HTB Will Practise What It Preaches?" *Christian Today*, December 23, 2016, https://www.christiantoday.com/article/women.in.leadership.is.2017.the.year.htb.will.practise.what.it.preaches/103265.htm.

Davies, Stephen. "Libertarian Feminism in Britain, 1860–1910." Libertarian Alliance pamphlet 7 (1987).

Dawson, Matt. "Bauman, Beck, Giddens and Our Understanding of Politics in Late Modernity." *Journal of Power* 3, no. 2 (2010)

Day, Abby. *Believing in Belonging: Belief and Social Identity in the Modern World*. Oxford: Oxford University Press, 2011.

——. *The Religious Lives of Older Laywomen*. Oxford: Oxford University Press, 2017.

Deeb, Lara. *An Enchanted Modern: Gender and Public Piety in Shi'i Lebanon*. Princeton, NJ: Princeton University Press, 2006.

Deneson, Amy. "True Love Waits: The Story of My Purity Ring and Feeling Like I Didn't Have a Choice." *Guardian*, February 18, 2017, https://www.theguardian.com/lifeandstyle/2017/feb/18/purity-ring-virginity-abstinence-sexual-education.

DeRogatis, Amy. *Saving Sex: Sexuality and Salvation in American Evangelicalism*. Oxford: Oxford University Press, 2014.

Didion, Joan. *Slouching Towards Bethlehem: Essays*. New York: Farrar, Straus and Giroux, 1978.

Dobson, James. *Preparing for Adolescence*. Ventura, CA: Gospel Light, 1974.

Donnelly, Mark. "*The Death of Christian Britain: Understanding Secularisation 1800–2000* by Callum G. Brown." *Gender & History* 22, no. 2 (2010).

Dworkin, Andrea. *Right-Wing Women*. New York: Perigee Books, 1983.

Elias, Ana, Rosalind Gill, and Christina Scharff, eds. "Aesthetic Labour: Beauty Politics in Neoliberalism." In *Aesthetic Labour: Rethinking Beauty Politics in Neoliberalism*, 3–50. London: Palgrave Macmillan, 2017.

Ensler, Eve. *The Vagina Monologues*. New York: Ballantine, 1998.

Erwig, Katherine P. "Dreams from a Saint: Anthropological Atheism and the Temptation to Believe." *American Anthropologist* 96, no. 3 (1994).

Evangelical Alliance and Christian Research. *21st Century Evangelicals: A Snapshot of the Beliefs and Habits of Evangelical Christians in the UK*. London: Evangelical Alliance, 2011. https://www.eauk.org/church/resources/snapshot/upload/21st-Century-Evangelicals-Data-Report.pdf.

Evans, Rachel Held. "Confessions of an Accidental Feminist," August 29, 2012, https://rachelheldevans.com/blog/accidental-feminist.

Fader, Ayala. *Mitzvah Girls: Bringing Up the Next Generation of Hasidic Jews in Brooklyn*. Princeton, NJ: Princeton University Press, 2009.

Field, Clive D. "21st Century Evangelicals." *British Religion in Numbers*, January 12, 2011, http://www.brin.ac.uk/21st-century-evangelicals.

Figueroa, Monica Moreno. "Looking Emotionally: Photography, Racism, and Intimacy in Research." *History of the Human Sciences* 21, no. 4 (2008).

Finch, Jamie Lee. *You Are Your Own: A Reckoning with the Religious Trauma of Evangelical Christianity*. Self-published, 2019.

FitzGerald, Frances. *The Evangelicals: The Struggle to Shape America*. New York: Simon and Schuster, 2017.

Foucault, Michel. *The History of Sexuality*. Vol. 1: *An Introduction*. Trans. Robert Hurley. New York: Pantheon, 1978.

Frankenberg, Ruth. *White Women, Race Matters: The Social Construction of Whiteness*. London: Routledge, 1993.

Fraser, Nancy. "Mapping the Feminist Imagination: From Redistribution to Recognition to Representation." *Constellations* 12, no. 3 (2005).

Freitas, Donna. *Sex and the Soul: Juggling Sexuality, Spirituality, Romance, and Religion on America's College Campuses*. Oxford: Oxford University Press, 2008.

Fritz, Leah. *Thinking Like a Woman*. Rifton, NY: Win Books, 1975.

Fukuyama, Francis. *Trust: The Social Virtues and the Creation of Prosperity.* New York: Free Press, 1996.

Furneaux, Holly. "Victorian Sexualities." *Literature Compass* 8, no. 10 (2011).

Gaddini, Katie. "Apostate Women: The Sacrifices Doubt Demands." *Marginalia Review of Books*, October 8, 2021.

——. "Between Pain and Hope: Examining Women's Marginality in Evangelical Christianity." *European Journal of Women's Studies* 26, no. 4 (2018).

——. "'Wife, Mommy, Pastor and Friend': The Rise of Female Evangelical Microcelebrities." *Religions* 12, no. 9 (2021): 758. https://doi.org/10.3390/rel12090758.

Gallagher, Sally. *Evangelical Identity and Gendered Family Life.* London: Rutgers University Press, 2003.

——. "The Marginalization of Evangelical Feminism." *Sociology of Religion* 65, no. 3 (2004).

Gardner, Christine. *Making Chastity Sexy: The Rhetoric of Evangelical Abstinence Campaigns.* Berkeley: University of California Press, 2011.

Garner, Clare. "Woman Priest Tells of Her Vision on Road to St. Paul's." *Independent*, October 23, 2011, https://www.independent.co.uk/news/woman-priest-tells-of-her-vision-on-road-to-st-pauls-1279542.html.

Garza, Cristina Rivera. *Grieving: Dispatches from a Wounded Country.* Trans. Sarah Booker. New York: First Feminist Press, 2020.

Genders, Nigel. "Relationships and Education." Church of England, March 12, 2018, https://www.churchofengland.org/more/media-centre/stories-and-features/relationships-and-education.

Giddens, Anthony. *Modernity and Self-identity: Self and Society in the Late Modern Age.* Palo Alto, CA: Stanford University Press, 1991.

Gill, Rosalind. "Post-postfeminism? New Feminist Visibilities in Postfeminist Times." *Feminist Media Studies* 16, no. 4 (2016).

Ginsburg, Faye. *Contested Lives: The Abortion Debate in an American Community.* Updated ed. Berkeley: University of California Press, 1998.

Goffman, Erving. "On Fieldwork." *Journal of Contemporary Ethnography* 18, no. 2 (1989).

Gopnik, Adam. "The Democrats and the Seesaw of Identity Politics." *New Yorker*, December 2, 2016.

Graham, Martha. *Blood Memory: An Autobiography.* New York: Doubleday, 1991.

Gresh, Dannah. *And the Bride Wore White: Seven Secrets to Sexual Purity.* Chicago: Moody Publishers, 2012.

Griffith, R. Marie. *God's Daughters: Evangelical Women and the Power of Submission.* Berkeley: University of California Press, 1997.

Guest, Matthew. *Evangelical Identity and Contemporary Culture: A Congregational Study in Innovation.* Milton Keyes: Paternoster, 2007.

Haddad, Mimi, and Sean Callagan. *Is Women's Equality a Biblical Ideal?* Minneapolis: Christians for Biblical Equality, 2021.

Hall, Stuart, ed. "The Spectacle of the 'Other.'" In *Representation: Cultural Representations and Signifying Practices,* 223–290. London: Sage, 1997.

——. "A Toad in the Garden: Thatcherism Among the Theorists." In *Marxism and the Interpretation of Culture,* ed. C. Nelson and L. Grossberg, 35–57. Urbana: University of Illinois Press, 1988.

——. "Who Needs 'Identity'?" In *Identity: A Reader,* ed. Paul du Gay, Jessica Evans, and Peter Redman, 15–30. London: Sage, 2000.

——. "The Work of Representation." In *Representation: Cultural Representations and Signifying Practices,* ed. Stuart Hall, Jessica Evans, and Sean Nixon, 13–74. London: Sage, 1997.

Hall, Stuart, Jessica Evans, and Sean Nixon, eds. *Representation: Cultural Representations and Signifying Practices.* 2nd ed. London: Sage, 2013.

Hamilton, David Joel, and Loren Cunningham. *Why Not Women? A Fresh Look at Scripture on Women in Missions, Ministry, and Leadership.* Edmonds, WA: YWAM Publishing, 2001.

Hand, Sean, ed. *The Levinas Reader.* Oxford: Blackwell, 1993.

Harding, Susan. *The Book of Jerry Falwell: Fundamentalist Language and Politics.* Princeton, NJ: Princeton University Press, 1987.

——. "Convicted by the Holy Spirit: The Rhetoric of Fundamental Baptist Conversion." *American Ethnologist* 14, no. 1 (1987).

——. "Representing Fundamentalism: The Problem of the Repugnant Cultural Other." *Social Research* 58, no. 2 (1991).

Harris, Kat. *Sexless in the City: A Sometimes Sassy, Sometimes Painful, Always Honest Look at Dating, Desire and Sex.* Grand Rapids: Zondervan, 2021.

Hefner, Robert. *Conversion to Christianity: Historical and Anthropological Perspectives on a Great Transformation.* Berkeley: University of California Press, 1993.

Heilman, Samuel C. *Defenders of the Faith: Inside Ultra-Orthodox Jewry.* Palo Alto: University of California Press, 2000.

Heilman, Samuel C., and Menachem Friedman. "Religious Fundamentalism and Religious Jews: The Case of the Haredim." In *Fundamentalisms Observed*, ed. M. E. Marty and R. S. Appleby, 197–264. Chicago: University of Chicago Press, 1991.

Herzog, Dagmar. *Sex in Crisis: The New Sexual Revolution and the Future of American Politics*. New York: Basic Books, 2008.

Himmelstein, Jerome. "The Social Basis of Antifeminism: Religious Networks and Culture." *Journal for the Scientific Study of Religion* 25, no. 1 (1986): 1–15.

Hogg, Michael, Janice Adelman, and Robert Blagg. "Religion in the Face of Uncertainty: An Uncertainty-Identity Theory Account of Religiousness." *Personality and Social Psychology Review* 14, no. 1 (2009).

Ingersoll, Julie. "Against Univocality: Re-reading Ethnographies of Conservative Protestant Women." In *Personal Knowledge and Beyond: Reshaping Ethnography of Religion*, ed. James V. Spickard, J. Shawn Landres, and Meredith B. McGuire, 162–174. New York: New York University Press, 2002.

——. *Evangelical Christian Women: War Stories in the Gender Battles*. New York: New York University Press, 2003.

"In U.S., Decline of Christianity Continues at Rapid Pace." Pew Research Center, October 17, 2019, https://www.pewforum.org/2019/10/17/in-u-s-decline-of-christianity-continues-at-rapid-pace.

Johnson, Jessica. *Biblical Porn: Affect, Labor, and Pastor Mark Driscoll's Evangelical Empire*. Durham, NC: Duke University Press, 2018.

Jones, Robert P., and Daniel Cox. *America's Changing Religious Identity: Findings from the 2016 American Values Atlas*. Washington, DC: Public Religion Research Institute, September 6, 2017. https://www.prri.org/wp-content/uploads/2017/09/PRRI-Religion-Report.pdf.

Kaufman, Debra. *Rachel's Daughters: Newly Orthodox Jewish Women*. New Brunswick, NJ: Rutgers University Press, 1991.

Keane, Webb. *Christian Moderns: Freedom and Fetish in the Mission Encounter*. Berkeley: University of California Press, 2007.

Kelly, Nathan J., and Jana Morgan Kelly. "Religion and Latino Partisanship in the United States." *Political Research Quarterly* 58, no. 1 (2005): 93.

Klein, Linda Kay. *Pure: Inside the Evangelical Movement That Shamed a Generation of Young Women and How I Broke Free*. New York: Atria Paperback, 2018.

Lamont, Michele. "Culture and Identity." In *Handbook of Sociological Theory*, ed. Jonathan Turner, 171–186. Boston: Springer, 2001.

Lamont, Michele, and Virag Molnar. "The Study of Boundaries Across the Social Sciences." *Annual Review of Sociology* 28 (2002).

Lee, Morgan. "When Christian Ministries Ask Their Ex-Employees Not to Talk." *Christianity Today*, November 6, 2019, https://www.christianity today.com/ct/podcasts/quick-to-listen/christian-ministries-non-disclosure -agreements-non-competes.html.

Lester, Rebecca. *Jesus in Our Wombs: Embodying Modernity in a Mexican Convent*. Palo Alto: University of California Press, 2005.

Levinas, Emmanuel. *Humanism of the Other*. Trans. Nancy Poller. Champaign: University of Illinois Press, 2006.

Lewis, Reina. "Uncovering Modesty: Dejabis and Dewigies Expanding the Parameters of the Modest Fashion Blogosphere." *Fashion Theory* 19, no. 2 (2015).

Lindsay, D. M. "Elite Power: Social Networks Within American Evangelicalism (Winner of the Robert J. McNamara Student Paper Award 2005)." *Sociology of Religion* 67, no. 3 (Fall 2006): 207–227.

Lipka, Michael. "The Most and Least Religious Diverse U.S. Religious Groups." Pew Research Center, July 17, 2015, https://www.pewresearch.org /fact-tank/2015/07/27/the-most-and-least-racially-diverse-u-s-religious -groups.

Lispector, Clarice. *The Hour of the Star*. London: Penguin Classics, 2014.

Llewellyn, Dawn, and Marta Trzebiatowska. "Secular and Religious Feminisms: A Future of Disconnection?" *Feminist Theology* 21, no. 3 (2013).

Lloyd, Carrie. *Prude: Misconceptions of a Neo-Virgin*. Milton Keyes: Authentic Media, 2016.

——. *The Virgin Monologues: Confessions of a Christian Girl in a Twenty-First-Century World*. Milton Keyes: Authentic Media, 2015.

Lodge, Carey. "Bethel Church's Bill Johnson: Why I Voted for Trump." *Christian Today*, November 10, 2016, https://www.christiantoday.com /article/bethel-churchs-bill-johnson-why-i-voted-for-trump/100306.htm.

Longoria, Sean. "Redding Planning Commission OK's Bethel's New Campus." *Redding Record Searchlight*, September 26, 2017.

Lord, A. *Condom Nation: The US Government's Sex Education Campaign from World War I to the Internet*. Baltimore, MD: Johns Hopkins University Press, 2010.

Ludy, Leslie. *Set-Apart Femininity*. Eugene, OR: Harvest House, 2008.

——. *Set-Apart Motherhood*. Colorado Springs, CO: NavPress, 2014.

——. *The Set-Apart Woman*. Colorado Springs, CO: NavPress, 2015.

Luhrmann, Tanya. *When God Talks Back: Understanding the American Evangelical Relationship with God*. New York: Alfred E. Knopf, 2004.

MacCullouch, Diarmaid. *Sex and the Church*. Episode 1: "From Pleasure to Sin." Video. BBC, May 1, 2015.

Mahmood, Saba. "Feminist Theory, Embodiment, and the Docile Agent: Some Reflections on the Egyptian Islamic Revival." *Cultural Anthropology* 16, no. 2 (2001).

——. *The Politics of Piety: The Islamic Revival and the Feminist Subject*. Princeton, NJ: Princeton University Press, 2003.

Manning, Christel. *God Gave Us the Right: Conservative Catholic, Evangelical Protestant, and Orthodox Jewish Women Grapple with Feminism*. New Brunswick, NJ: Rutgers University Press, 1999.

Martínez, Jessica, and Gregory A. Smith. "How the Faithful Voted: A Preliminary 2016 Analysis." Pew Research Center, November 9, 2016, https://www.pewresearch.org/fact-tank/2016/11/09/how-the-faithful-voted-a-preliminary-2016-analysis.

McClendon, David. "Gender Gap in Religious Service Attendance Has Narrowed in U.S." Pew Research Center, May 13, 2016, https://www.pewresearch.org/fact-tank/2016/05/13/gender-gap-in-religious-service-attendance-has-narrowed-in-u-s.

McFague, Sallie. "Conversion: Life on the Edge of the Raft." *Union Seminary Review* 32, no. 3 (1978): 255–268.

McGuire, Meredith B. *Lived Religion: Faith and Practice in Everyday Life*. Oxford: Oxford University Press, 2008.

McKelvey, Tara. "The Evangelical Women Who Reject Trump." *BBC News*, October 23, 2018, https://www.bbc.co.uk/news/world-us-canada-45956033.

McRobbie, Angela. "Notes on the Perfect." *Australian Feminist Studies* 83 (2015): 3–20.

Miller, Donald, and Tetsunao Yamamori. *Global Pentecostalism: The New Face of Christian Social Engagement*. Berkeley: University of California Press, 2007.

Minh-ha, Trinh T. *Woman, Native, Other: Writing Postcoloniality and Feminism*. Indianapolis: Indiana University Press, 1989.

Moultrie, Monique. "#BlackBabiesMatter: Analyzing Black Religious Media in Conservative and Progressive Evangelical Communities." *Religions* 8, no. 11 (2017).

——. *Passionate and Pious: Religious Media and Black Women's Sexuality.* Durham, NC: Duke University Press, 2017.

Muñoz, José Esteban. *Cruising Utopia: The Then and There of Queer Futurity.* New York: New York University Press, 2009.

Murdoch, Stephen. "Support Feminism? At Westmont, You're Politically Incorrect." *Santa Barbara News-Press*, April 13, 2006.

Nelson, Cary, and Lawrence Grossberg. *Marxism and the Interpretation of Culture.* Urbana: University of Illinois Press, 1988.

Ngai, Sianne. *Ugly Feelings.* Cambridge, MA: Harvard University Press, 2005.

Oakley, Ann. "Interviewing Women Again: Power, Time, and the Gift." *Sociology* 50, no. 1 (2016).

Oestreicher, Paul. "The Rev. Dr. Una Kroll Obituary." *Guardian*, January 8, 2017, https://www.theguardian.com/world/2017/jan/08/the-rev-dr-una -kroll-obituary.

Okulicz-Kozaryn, Adam. "Unhappy Metropolis (When an American City Is Too Big)." *Cities* 61 (2017).

Olorunshola, Yosola. "She Doesn't Look Like Jesus." *Magnify* 1 (2014).

Orgad, Shani, and Rosalind Gill. "The Confidence Cult(ure)." *Australian Feminist Studies* 30, no. 86 (2016): 326.

Orsi, Robert. *Between Heaven and Earth: The Religious Worlds People Make and the Scholars Who Study Them.* Princeton, NJ: Princeton University Press, 2005.

——. *The Cambridge Companion to Religious Studies.* Cambridge: Cambridge University Press, 2012.

Orwell, George, ed. "Inside the Whale." In *A Collection of Essays.* New York: Houghton Mifflin Harcourt, 1947/1970.

Park Hong, Cathy. *Minor Feelings: An Asian American Reckoning.* New York: Penguin Random House, 2020.

Pascal, Blaise. *Pensées.* Trans. W. F. Trotter. New York: Dover, 2003.

Patterson, Randall. "Students of Virginity." *New York Times*, March 30, 2008.

Pew Research Center. "Evangelical Protestant." *Religious Landscape Study* (2014).

——. "Women Who Are Evangelical Protestant." *Religious Landscape Study* (May 11, 2015).

Pollock, Griselda. "Feminism/Foucault—Surveillance/Sexuality." In *Visual Culture: Images and Interpretations*, ed. Norman Bryson, Michael Ann Holly, and Keith Moxey, 1–43. Middletown, CT: Wesleyan University Press, 1994.

Potamianou, Anna. *Hope: A Shield in the Economy of Borderline States.* New York: Routledge, 1996.

Prescott, Caressa. "Valentines [*sic*] Gift Guide for Him," February 3, 2019, https://www.leoandluca.com/blog.

Putnam, Robert. *Bowling Alone: The Collapse and the Revival of American Community.* New York: Simon and Schuster, 2001.

Puwar, Nirmal. "The Racialised Somatic Norm and the Senior Civil Service." *Sociology* 35, no. 3 (2011).

Ramsey, K. J. "There's No Shame When a Miracle Doesn't Come." *Christianity Today*, December 27, 2019, https://www.christianitytoday.com/ct /2019/december-web-only/wakeupolive-heiligenthal-bethel-church -miracle-doesnt-come.html.

Rankine, Claudia. *Citizen: An American Lyric.* London: Penguin Random House UK, 2015.

Reitman, Oonagh. "On Exit." In *Minorities Within Minorities: Equality, Rights, and Diversity*, ed. Avigail Eisenberg and Jeff Spinner-Halev, 189–208. Cambridge: Cambridge University Press, 2005.

Rich, Adrienne. "Compulsory Heterosexuality and Lesbian Existence." *Signs* 5, no. 4 (1980): 631–660.

——. *On Lies, Secrets, and Silence: Selected Prose.* New York: Norton, 1995.

Riley, Denise. "Laibach Lyrik: Slovenia, 1991." In *Penguin Modern Poets 10*, 60–63. London: Penguin, 1996.

——. *Words of Selves: Identification, Solidarity, Irony.* Palo Alto, CA: Stanford University Press, 2000.

Robbins, Joel. *Becoming Sinners: Christianity and Moral Torment in a Papua New Guinea Society.* Berkeley: University of California Press, 2004.

——. "The Globalization of Pentecostal and Charismatic Christianity." *Annual Review of Anthropology* 33 (2004).

——. "Transcendence and the Anthropology of Christianity: Language, Change, and Individualism." *Suomen Antropologi: Journal of the Finnish Anthropological Society* 37, no. 2 (2012).

Robert, Dana. *Christian Mission: How Christianity Became a World Religion.* Hoboken, NJ: John Wiley and Sons, 2009.

Roy, Olivier. *Secularism Confronts Islam.* New York: Columbia University Press, 2009.

Ruether, Rosemary Radford. "Church, Feminism, and Family." In *God Forbid: Religion and Sex in American Public Life*, ed. Kathleen M. Sands, 93–103. Oxford: Oxford University Press, 2014.

——. *Sexism and God-Talk: Toward a Feminist Theology.* Boston: Beacon Press, 1983.

Sehlikoglu, Sertac. "Intimate Publics, Public Intimacies." *Cambridge Journal of Anthropology* 33, no 2 (2015).

Sennett, Richard. *The Corrosion of Character: The Personal Consequences of Work in the New Capitalism.* New York: Norton, 1998.

Sharma, Sonya. "Young Women, Sexuality and Protestant Church Community: Oppression or Empowerment?" *European Journal of Women's Studies* 15, no. 4 (2008): 345–359.

Sharma, Sonya, and Matthew Guest. "Navigating Religion Between University and Home: Christian Students' Experiences in English Universities." *Social and Cultural Geography* 14, no. 1 (2013).

Shipley, Heather. *Globalized Religion and Sexual Identity.* Leiden: Brill, 2004.

Silverman, Kaja. *The Subject of Semiotics.* Oxford: Oxford University Press, 1984.

Skeggs, Beverley. *Formations of Class and Gender: Becoming Respectable.* London: Sage, 1997.

Smith, Christian. *American Evangelicalism: Embattled and Thriving.* Chicago: University of Chicago Press, 1998.

Smith, Greg. *21st Century Evangelicals: Reflections on Research by the Evangelical Alliance.* Watford: Instant Apostle, 2015.

Stacey, Judith, and Susan Elizabeth Gerard. "'We Are Not Doormats': The Influence of Feminism on Contemporary Evangelicals in the United States." In *Uncertain Terms: Negotiating Gender in American Culture*, ed. Faye Ginsburg and Anna Lowenhaupt Tsing, 98–117. Boston: Beacon, 1990.

Stadler, Nurit, and Lea Taragin-Zeller. "Like a Snake in Paradise: Fundamentalism, Gender, and Taboos in the Haredi Community." *Archives de Sciences Sociales des Religions* 117 (2017).

Stanger-Hall, Kathrin, and David Hall. "Abstinence-Only Education and Teen Pregnancy Rates: Why We Need Comprehensive Sex Education in the US." *PLoS One* 6, no. 10 (October 14, 2011).

Starr, Mirabai. *Saint John of the Cross: Devotion Prayers and Living Wisdom.* Louisville, CO: Sounds True, 2008.

Strhan, Anna. *Aliens and Strangers? The Coherence in the Everyday Lives of Evangelicals.* Oxford: Oxford University Press, 2015.

Stringer, Rebecca. *Knowing Victims: Feminism, Agency, and Victim Politics in Neoliberal Times.* Hove: Routledge, 2014.

Taragin-Zeller, Lea. "Modesty for Heaven's Sake: Authority and Creativity Among Female Ultra-Orthodox Teenagers in Israel." *Nashim: A Journal of Jewish Women's Studies and Gender Issues* 26, no. 5774 (2014).

Tillmann-Healy, Lisa. "Friendship as Method." *Qualitative Inquiry* 8, no. 5 (2003).

Traister, Rebecca. "Blaming Clinton's Base for Her Loss Is the Ultimate Insult." *The Cut,* November 23, 2016, https://www.thecut.com/2016/11/blaming-clintons-base-for-her-loss-is-the-ultimate-insult.html.

Tweed, Thomas. *Crossing and Dwelling: A Theory of Religion.* Boston: Harvard University Press, 2006.

Valenti, Jessica. *The Purity Myth: How America's Obsession with Virginity Is Hurting Young Women.* Berkeley: Seal Press, 2010.

Valloton, Kris. "6 Ways to Catch the Man of God You've Been Waiting For," November 29, 2018, https://www.krisvallotton.com/6-ways-to-catch-the-man-of-god-youve-been-waiting-for.

Vuong, Ocean. "Seventh Circle of Earth." In *Night Sky with Exit Wounds.* Port Townsend, WA: Copper Canyon Press, 2016.

Wacquant, Loic. "Following Pierre Bourdieu into the Field." *Ethnography* 5, no. 4 (2004).

Walters, Suzanna Danuta. "In Defense of Identity Politics." *Signs: Journal of Women in Culture and Society* 43, no. 2 (2018).

Walton, Andy, Andrea Hatcher, and Nick Spencer. *Is There a "Religious Right" Emerging in Britain?* London: Theos, 2013.

Weedon, Chris. *Identity and Culture.* London: Open University Press, 2004.

Wendell Jones, Martyn. "Inside the Popular, Controversial Bethel Church." *Christianity Today,* April 24, 2016, https://www.christianitytoday.com/ct/2016/may/cover-story-inside-popular-controversial-bethel-church.html.

Williams, Jean Calterone. "Battling a 'Sex-Saturated Society': The Abstinence Movement and the Politics of Sex Education." *Sexualities* 14, no. 4 (2011).

Winter, Miriam, Adair Lummis, and Allison Stokes. *Defecting in Place: Women Claiming Responsibility for Their Own Spiritual Lives*. New York: Wellspring, 1994.

Winters, Amanda. "Bethel Burgeons Under Pastor's Visions of Prosperity." *Record Searchlight*, January 16, 2010, http://archive.redding.com/news /bethel-burgeons-under-pastors-visions-of-prosperity-ep-377155239–3553 98251.html.

Woodhead, Linda. "Gendering Secularization Theory." *Social Compass* 55, no. 2 (2008): 187–193.

Yip, Andrew, and Sarah-Jane Page. *Religious and Sexual Identities: A Multi-Faith Exploration of Young Adults*. Farnham: Ashgate, 2013.

INDEX